TERRORIZING GENDER

Expanding Frontiers:
Interdisciplinary
Approaches to Studies
of Women, Gender,
and Sexuality

SERIES EDITORS:

Karen J. Leong

Andrea Smith

TERRORIZING GENDER

TRANSGENDER VISIBILITY AND
THE SURVEILLANCE PRACTICES
OF THE U.S. SECURITY STATE

MIA FISCHER

UNIVERSITY OF NEBRASKA PRESS | LINCOLN

Parts of the introduction originally appeared in "Queer and Feminist Approaches to Transgender Media Studies" in *Feminist Approaches to Media Theory and Research*, edited by Dustin Harp, Jaime Loke, and Ingrid Bachmann (London: Palgrave Macmillan, 2018), and are reproduced with permission of Palgrave Macmillan. An earlier version of chapter 2 appeared as "Contingent Belonging: Chelsea Manning, Transpatriotism, and Iterations of Empire" in *Sexualities: Studies in Culture and Society* 19, nos. 5–6 (2016): 567–86. An earlier version of chapter 4 was previously published as "#Free_CeCe: The Material Convergence of Social Media Activism" in *Feminist Media Studies* 15, no. 5 (2016): 755–71.

Library of Congress Control Number: 2019005291

Set in Lyon Text by E. Cuddy.

To CeCe and all the "nobodies"
speaking truth to power.

CONTENTS

ILLUSTRATIONS

ACKNOWLEDGMENTS

This project has been more than five years in the making. Thank you to my editor at the University of Nebraska Press, Alicia Christensen, for "chasing" me while I was still in graduate school and believing in this project from day one. I appreciate her attentive care throughout various stages of the review process and her editorial guidance in helping me to finalize this manuscript. Thank you also to Abby Stryker, Natalie O'Neal, Haley Mendlik, and Ann Baker, as well as Nebraska's marketing department for an incredibly smooth production process. I would also like to thank the Expanding Frontiers editors, Karen Leong and Andrea Smith, for supporting this project and bringing this important series to life. Thank you to both anonymous reviewers for their thoughtful and constructive comments, which helped me to think through critical parts of my argument. Much gratitude to Sarah C. Smith from Arbuckle Editorial and Cathy Hannabach from Ideas on Fire for carefully copy editing and indexing this book. Thank you also to Dawn Durante at the University of Illinois Press for her interest in this project. A huge shout-out especially to Cassils for the badass cover art and Annie Shahan for the thoughtful design.

At the University of Minnesota, I was blessed with a stellar dissertation committee comprised of Aren Aizura, Laurie Ouellette, Catherine Squires, and my co-advisers, Jigna Desai and Mary Douglas Vavrus. This book is mostly a product of their sharp engagement, analytical insight, and constructive criticism. Conversations with Aren about transgender studies, specifically trans of color critiques, were crucial for this project. Catherine provided key advice for navigating criticism about the project's disciplinary legibility within communication studies. Laurie models what it means to be an incredibly productive and excellent scholar who is also deeply invested in teaching. She has taught me a deep appreciation for Foucault and helped me to think through the connections between media and surveillance studies. Early in my graduate studies, Jigna showed me that there is a place for my work and encouraged me to take several gender, women, and sexuality studies courses "upstairs." Nothing has probably benefited this project more than this training in feminist and critical sexuality studies. Jigna also continues to push me to take into account my own subject positionality and the hierarchies of (academic) knowledge production. Her professional and personal advice on navigating the neoliberal academy's superficial obsession with "diversity and inclusion" has been indispensable. Mary has been my biggest cheerleader and helped me to navigate numerous academic and personal crises. She has also consistently pushed me to write with better clarity—thank you for all the hours spent line editing to make my prose comprehensible. I can't thank you all enough for your ongoing mentorship and support of my work.

Several scholars at the University of Minnesota and beyond have contributed to and shaped my thinking over the years. I would like to thank Amanda Ruth-McSwain, Ron Greene, Gil Rodman, Art Walzer, Karlyn Kohrs Campbell, Kevin Murphy, David Valentine, Elliott Powell, Stef Wilenchek Jarvi, Charles Morris III, Michael Butterworth, Jen Jack Gieseking, Laura Portwood-Stacer, Rachel Hall, Rachel Dubrofsky, Torin Monahan, and Shoshana Magnet for their support. A big thank you also to Carol Stabile for her ongoing mentorship. I admire the work of Dean Spade, C. Riley Snorton, Jin Haritaworn, Michelle Alexander, Eric A. Stanley, Tourmaline, and the Against Equality collective—their thinking has significantly shaped this manuscript. I'm also indebted to my conference and writing partner in crime Jennifer McClearen for being my favorite travel buddy and supportive friend over the years.

In particular two writing groups at the University of Minnesota—the Graduate Interdisciplinary Group in Sexuality Studies and the Critical Gender and Sexuality Studies Dissertation Writing Group—helped me to think through key areas of the book. Thank you to Angela Carter, Diane Cormany, Lars Mackenzie, Jayne Swift, and Elizabeth Williams for reading early versions of my chapters and commenting on drafts.

The late Jesús Estrada-Pérez constantly pushed me to take into account the intersections of oppressive systems. As a working-class, brown queer boi in academia, Jesús walked the talk as an activist-scholar. We miss you dearly.

The research on CeCe McDonald's case would not have been possible without the following organizations and individuals generously donating their time and expertise. Thank you to the Legal Rights Center in Minneapolis, which specializes in pro-bono representation of low-income and poor people of color. I am indebted to Abigail Cerra, Hersch Izek, and Norma Gaona-Gonzalez for granting me access to legal files and for clarifying numerous legal questions. I am incredibly thankful for the CeCe Support Committee, especially for Lex Horan's willingness to provide me with an in-depth account of the workings of the committee and sharing his experiences. Lex was a generous interlocutor who patiently answered my questions and took great care in reading various draft chapters. Micah Bazant kindly granted permission to reprint their powerful portrait of CeCe. Of course, I also need to thank CeCe herself—it has been such a privilege meeting her and participating in ongoing collaborations. CeCe frequently reminds me that by checking our own privileges we can become better coconspirators and less self-serving allies.

My colleagues at the University of Colorado Denver and the larger Auraria campus have been very welcoming and generous, including Lisa Keränen, Stephen J. Hartnett, Hamilton Bean, Larry Erbert, Sarah Fields, Patrick Shaou-Whea Dodge, and the irreplaceable Michelle Médal. Much gratitude to Amy Hasinoff for providing critical feedback in the final stages. I also need to give a big thank you to Alfred L. Martin Jr. for navigating the first two years on the tenure track together. I miss you, officemate. I'm glad I have been able to forge friendships and connections with folks across numerous programs, including Margaret Wood, Chad Shomura, Sarah Hagelin, Joanna Luloff, Gillian Silverman, Edelina Burciaga, Margaret Woodhull, as well as Steven Willich, Jacob McWilliams, Netty Rodriguez Arauz, and Xajés Martinez. I would also like to thank the students whom I have the privilege of teaching at CU Denver and from whom I continue to learn: a big shout-out to Patrycja Humienik and the Dances for Solidarity prison pen pal project, Aimee

Andrews, Reydesel Salvidrez Rodriguez, Selim Ready, Anya Dickson, and Miranda Johnson just to name a few. Your commitment to various social justice causes is truly inspiring and shows what engaged learning can look like. A special thank you to Sarah Slater, who invited me to collaborate with her on bringing the #BlackExcellenceTour to campus in the spring of 2018.

The research for this project was generously supported by a Steven J. Schochet Interdisciplinary Dissertation Fellowship at the University of Minnesota, a dissemination grant from CU Denver's College of Liberal Arts and Sciences, and publication and research grants from CU Denver's Office of Research Services. Much gratitude especially to Bob Damrauer, Marjorie Levine-Clark, and Brenda J. Allen for their institutional commitment to and support of interdisciplinary research at CU Denver.

I am incredibly lucky that some of my cohort members at the University of Minnesota have become my closest friends over the years. Thank you especially to Jackie Arcy, Cohen Gamboa, David Tucker, Kate Ranachan, and little Maddie. We've been through a lot together, and I couldn't have done it without your friendship. I miss the barbecues, cabrewing, and *Game of Thrones* viewing sessions. Thanks especially for indulging my love for a last round of shots at the CC Club and for putting up with my German crankiness during the job search. Thank you also to Megan Jones, Evelyn Volz, and Chala Mohr for being part of our Denver adventures.

Pursuing my academic endeavors in the United States would not have been possible without the unconditional support from my family back home in Germany. Thanks and love especially to Mäm, who always encouraged me to be creative and queer—far before I knew what that really meant. If I have any talent for teaching it undoubtedly comes from seeing her as a passionate elementary school teacher growing up. I am very grateful that I still get to experience the sharp wit and everyday wisdom of my ninety-five-year-old grandma, Alice. I promise I will come home again to visit soon. Thanks also to my sister, Kim, who has been there through the ups and downs and made sure I stayed on track when things were falling apart. To my dad, Ralph, thank you for always encouraging me to follow my dreams even if I was chasing them some three thousand miles across the ocean. Thank you also to Friso for sharing your love of sports, especially skiing, with me. To all my nephews and nieces, Matteo, Fabio, Allegra, Julius, Jona, Magnus, and Malia—I miss you and can't wait to spend more time with you. To my Minneapolis ersatz family, the Kasellas—thank you for giving me a home away from home during my five years in Minneapolis. For all the dog sitting and laundry loads. I miss the laughter at your house and the Sunday dinners that always provided me with a much-needed break from academics. Similarly, the Mohrmans graciously welcomed me into their home and have become family. Thank you for all your professional and home-buying advice, as well as delicious holiday meals throughout the years.

Finally, I need to thank Katy. In the acknowledgments to her book, A. Naomi Paik notes that the only thing worse than living with your own project is living with your partner's. I am sure Katy has felt that way numerous times. Thank you for sacrificing your own time by tirelessly reading and editing every single page of this manuscript. Thank you for insisting I take a break when I was hitting my head against the wall, for "toning down" my language when dealing with various immigration or tenure bureaucracies, and for building me up in moments of self-doubt and rejection. There are not enough words to express my gratitude, appreciation, and love. As the late José Esteban Muñoz writes: "Queerness is that thing that lets us feel that this world is not enough, that indeed something is missing." Thank you for dealing with my obstinate, pessimist self and investing in a queer futurity with me. While pets probably don't make the acknowledgments very often, I do owe most of my mental sanity during the writing process to my two loyal dog pals, Landing and Zadie. I couldn't have done it without your unlimited paw snuggles and love. 🐾

TERRORIZING GENDER

America's Transition: Almost one year after the Supreme Court ruled that Americans were free to marry the person they loved, no matter their sex, another civil rights movement is poised to challenge long-held cultural norms and beliefs. Transgender people . . . are emerging from the margins to fight for an equal place in society.

Katy Steinmetz on "The Transgender Tipping Point," *Time*

After decades of erasure, transgender people have gained unprecedented visibility within mainstream media and national discourse.[1] *Rolling Stone* magazine proclaimed 2014 as the "Biggest Year in Transgender History" and the media's fascination with transgender people reached an initial high in June 2014 when actress and transgender rights activist Laverne Cox became the first openly trans person to grace the cover of *Time* magazine under the headline "The Transgender Tipping Point."[2] Wearing black heels and an elegant navy blue dress, Cox was depicted in a full-body portrait, standing serenely in front of a cream-colored background as she gazes directly at the camera and the reader. Her posture and gaze thereby evoked a sense of calm defiance and confidence, mirroring the cover story's subtitle, "America's Next Civil Rights Frontier." In the article, author Katy Steinmetz credited the Internet as a "revolutionary tool for the trans community, providing answers to questions that previous generations had no one to ask, as well as robust communities of support," which helped to generate a "radical increase in trans consciousness" in the larger public.[3] After the now-iconic *Time* cover, media and pop culture content featuring transgender issues and characters has been high demand: from Netflix's hit show *Orange Is the New Black* (2013–19), to Amazon's *Trans-*

parent (2014–), to Caitlyn Jenner's much-publicized transition and her reality TV show *I Am Cait* (2015–2016), and to trans YouTube stars Gigi Gorgeous and Kat Blaque attracting millions of followers.

Yet despite the public's increased interest in trans people and a broader consciousness about their existence, media portrayals often continue to stereotype or fetishize them rather than providing in-depth or critical coverage of issues trans people face in society. For example, in February 2014 trans activist and writer Janet Mock was invited to appear on Piers Morgan's show on CNN to promote her acclaimed memoir *Redefining Realness: My Path to Womanhood, Identity, Love and So Much More*. During the interview, Morgan repeatedly asserted that Mock was "a boy until age eighteen" and praised her flawless ability to pass: "So this is the amazing thing about you—had I not known anything about your story, I would have had absolutely not a clue that you had ever been a boy, a male, which makes me absolutely believe you should have always been a woman."[4] The show's Twitter account further sensationalized Mock's personal life by posing the question, "How would you feel if you found out the woman you were dating was formerly a man?"[5] Instead of focusing on Mock's extensive advocacy for transgender rights or her accomplished career as a writer, she was reduced to and fetishized for her transition. After the show, a public feud between Mock and Morgan ensued as Mock took to Twitter, calling Morgan out for his comments.

Another such fetishizing moment of mediated trans visibility occurred on Katie Couric's daytime talk show just five months before Laverne Cox appeared on the cover of *Time*. When Cox joined transgender model Carmen Carrera for an interview with Couric to discuss their careers and experiences as prominent trans women, Couric repeatedly questioned Carrera about her transition and genitals: "Your private parts are different now, aren't they?" Couric later justified her invasive questions as an attempt to "educate" others who may not be "familiar with transgenders [*sic*]."[6] Cox, however, provided Couric and her viewers with an education of her own: "The preoccupation with transition and surgery objectifies trans people. And then we don't get to really deal with the real lived experiences. The reality of trans people's lives is that so often we are targets of violence. We experi-

Fig. 1. "The Transgender Tipping Point," *Time* 183, no. 22 (June 9, 2014).
© 2014 Time Inc. Used under license. *Time* and Time Inc. are not affiliated with, and do not endorse products or services of, Licensee.

ence discrimination disproportionately to the rest of the community. Our unemployment rate is twice the national average; if you are a trans person of color, that rate is four times the national average. The homicide rate is highest among trans women. If we focus on transition, we don't actually get to talk about those things."[7] Cox's response reflects a seemingly paradoxical aspect of the increase in transgender visibility that points to the disturbing truths of the lived realities of the vast majority of trans people: namely, that despite an exponential increase in media attention, trans communities, particularly those of color, remain disproportionately affected by poverty, discrimination, violence, and harassment.

The release of the U.S. Transgender Survey in 2015, the largest study to date examining the experiences of trans people in the United States with almost twenty-eight thousand respondents, confirms Cox's statement that trans people are subject to pervasive patterns of violence and discrimination: 29 percent of the survey's respondents were living in poverty, compared to 14 percent of the general population; 15 percent of respondents were unemployed, three times higher than the overall unemployment rate in the United States; and 30 percent of respondents who had a job reported being fired, denied promotion, or experiencing harassment in the workplace due to their gender identity. Nearly one-third or 30 percent of respondents also experienced homelessness at some point. The survey further revealed that a staggering 40 percent of respondents had attempted suicide in their lifetime, and almost half, 47 percent, had experienced sexual assault. Respondents reported particularly high levels of mistreatment and harassment by law enforcement agencies: of those who were incarcerated, nearly one-quarter, 23 percent, were physically assaulted by staff or other inmates, and one in five, 20 percent, were sexually assaulted. Additionally, the survey confirmed that trans people of color experienced higher rates and more pervasive patterns of discrimination than white respondents.[8] The year 2017 also marked one of the deadliest years on record for trans people in the United States; at least twenty-six trans people, predominantly trans women of color, were murdered.[9] These statistics illustrate the stark contrast between the increased media visibility of transgender people and their everyday lived experiences.[10]

How does the exponential increase in trans visibility coexist with an increase in documented violence against trans communities? *Terrorizing Gender: Transgender Visibility and the Surveillance Practices of the U.S. Security State* challenges the popular assumption that the increased visibility of trans individuals in public discourse automatically translates into improvement in transgender people's daily lives. More specifically, I argue that this alleged "transgender tipping point" has actually resulted in a conservative backlash, with increased surveillance and regulation of trans people by the security state and media organizations. Most recently, this backlash can be seen in the surge of "bathroom" laws that criminalize trans people's use of public restrooms based on their gender identity and the Trump administration's rescindment of federal protections for transgender students and workers. *Terrorizing Gender* thus contends that the popularity of *transgender* in the current moment is a contingent cultural and national belonging, given the gendered and racialized violence that the state continues to enact against gender-nonconforming people, particularly those of color.[11] As trans people's rights continue to be attacked, revoked, and limited across the United States, this book sheds light on the relationship between the increase in trans visibility and the numerous political and legal efforts to discriminate against trans communities.

Historically, many national LGBT advocacy organizations, such as the HRC (Human Rights Campaign) and GLAAD (formerly known as the Gay and Lesbian Alliance Against Defamation), have relied on visibility politics as a productive means to promote (predominantly) gay acceptance and inclusion into national belonging and assimilation into normative frameworks of citizenship. Similarly, some media studies scholarship evaluating the "progress" of LGBT visibility often contents itself by using LGBT or *queer* as broad umbrella terms that end up referring solely to depictions of cisgender gays and lesbians or by making universal value judgments about "good" and "bad" representations.[12] Yet only assessing the numerical increase of LGBT people and characters on-screen or the types of representation present—for example, whether harmful stereotypes are perpetuated or not—does not address what these representations actually *do* and how they impact the lives of queer, trans, and gender-nonconforming communities. In an effort to account for the multifaceted dispersal of state power and violence, *Terrorizing Gender* uses an interdisciplinary framework drawing on transgender, queer, critical race, ethnic, legal, and surveillance studies to center trans people and their experiences in media studies to move beyond an exclusive focus on visibility politics and to scrutinize the relationship between cultural representations and their material consequences. Fusing critical discourse analysis with ethnography, the book explores how media representations of transgender people connect to and (re)produce their surveillance and management by state institutions such as federal and state governments, the military, and the legal system. By highlighting the material realities of trans people's lives, this book challenges popular narratives of progress that claim equality and civil rights victories for LGBT people over the last decade. Rather, dominant representations of trans people as deceptive, deviant, and threatening continue to permeate mass-mediated discourses and are used to justify and frequently normalize state-sanctioned violence against gender-nonconforming populations.

It is particularly the circulation of the popular discourse of color-blindness—a pervasive belief that race should not and no longer does matter—that becomes central to the state's management, easy dismissal, and devaluation of transgender lives. Drawing on women of color feminisms, the case studies in this book illustrate that the dismissal and disposability of trans lives by society and the state is inevitably connected to the intersection of oppressive systems, including racism, sexism, classism, homophobia, and transphobia.[13] Relatedly, the book contributes to surveillance studies, specifically work on the racialized surveillance practices of the state, by highlighting its gendered aspects, an often ignored dimension of such practices. Frameworks of intersectionality bring together and make possible cross-disciplinary conversations about this alleged tipping point.

To illustrate the book's key arguments and interventions, *Terrorizing Gender* is composed of three case studies that highlight the connection between media coverage and the state's regulation of trans people. The first takes as its subject Chelsea Manning, a former U.S. Army intelligence analyst who was sentenced to thirty-five years in prison in 2013 for violating the Espionage Act and leaking more than seven hundred thousand sensitive military and diplomatic documents to the whistleblowing website WikiLeaks. After her trial, Manning's public coming out as transgender generated an unprecedented degree of media coverage which cast trans people as threats to the state. The second case study follows CeCe McDonald, a black trans woman who was charged with murder for killing her attacker during a transphobic and racist assault in 2011 in Minneapolis, Minnesota. McDonald's case elucidates the connections between the media and the state's violent disciplining of trans people of color, as well as social justice activists' response to that disciplining. Finally, Monica Jones, a trans woman of color and sex work activist from Phoenix, Arizona, made international headlines when she was deported from Australia in 2014 because she was deemed a "possible threat" to Australian national security. Jones's encounter with Australian customs agents was also filmed by an Australian reality TV crew eager to profit from her story. Her case, therefore, represents the most explicit example of how corporate media and state agencies directly collude in criminalizing and surveilling trans and gender-nonconforming people.

Chapter 1, "Pathologizing and Prosecuting a (Gender) Traitor," examines the intersections between the news media's and military's treatment of Manning. Together these institutions systematically ostracized and disparaged her to promote imperialist U.S. foreign policy. The news media's pathologizing portrayal of Manning provided a rationale for the state's extralegal—if not illegal—treatment of Manning by equating her alleged sexual orientation and gender nonconformity with mental instabilities that threatened state interests. While previous scholarship on Manning has addressed how media discourses consistently psychopathologized her to explain her decision to leak classified materials, I explicitly connect the pathologizing of Manning to a process of racialization that ascribes her the status of a domestic alien enemy and allows her treatment to mirror that of a foreign terrorist other.[14] Chapter 2, "Transpatriotism and Iterations of Empire," analyzes mediated responses from other transgender veterans and national LGBT groups to Manning's revelations and introduces the concept of *transpatriotism*. As a corollary concept to Jasbir Puar's influential theorizing on homonationalism, in which certain queers are contingently incorporated into the nation for the purpose of justifying and forwarding U.S. imperial interests, I conceptualize *transpatriotism* as a form of jingoism characterized by both an unwavering devotion to the state and a strict adherence to the gender binary to illuminate the conditional inclusion and recognition of certain, privileged trans people into the national imaginary.[15] The chapter concludes with a critique of the recent push for trans inclusion in the military as an extension of transpatriotic discourse.

Chapter 3, "Blind(ing) (In)justice and the Disposability of Black Life," scrutinizes local news and legal discourses about CeCe McDonald, specifically the racialization of her gender nonconformity to present her as a threatening subject whose actions did not qualify as self-defense. Her attacker was frequently idealized as a loving father figure in the news, and the judge refused to admit his swastika tattoo as evidence of his belief in white supremacy—the collusion of these discourses reinforced the justice system's ostensible colorblindness and sought to condone and recuperate the violence of a white perpetrator. McDonald's experiences are thereby not an exception but reflect that certain racialized others are always already criminal. Chapter 4, "Materializing Hashtag Activism and the #FreeCeCe Campaign," uses ethnography to examine how the CeCe Support Committee inspired national support for McDonald by using social media platforms to circumvent traditional media gatekeepers and challenge the legal system's alleged colorblindness by creating alternative epistemologies about the violent experiences of trans women of color. This chapter also illustrates that intersecting oppressions do not simply disappear in online spaces; instead, those oppressions continue to constrain social media's ability to achieve transformative social justice objectives.

In chapter 5, "Sex Work, Securitainment, and the Transgender Terrorist," I first trace how Monica Jones's criminalization in Phoenix for a manifesting prostitution charge not only reflects the routine harassment and profiling of trans women for "walking while trans" but extends long histories of criminalizing sex work in the United States and is inextricably tied to the state's management and regulation of certain "at-risk" populations. Jones's encounters with U.S. law enforcement and Australian custom officials attest to the precarity and constant surveillance trans people face, particularly in moments of border crossing and travel post-9/11. Furthermore, Jones's story highlights that dominant media and state agencies deliberately collude in framing trans people as a terrorist threat in order to both economically and ideologically capitalize on promoting the ongoing War on Terror.

The cases of Manning, McDonald, and Jones illustrate that despite the purported "transgender tipping point"—in which the increased visibility of gender-nonconforming people is sought to eventually lead to a civil rights breakthrough—trans people continue to be discursively constructed and treated as fraudulent, deviant, and threatening both by dominant media and state institutions. Moreover, the portrayals of Manning, McDonald, and Jones exemplify how media coverage is integral to the state's efforts to surveil, harass, and ultimately criminalize trans communities, both through the circulation of derogatory and sensational images of gender-nonconforming people and through the general lack of coverage of issues trans people face. For the security state, these constructions further demarcate who belongs to the nation and who does not, who is granted access to citizenship rights and legal protections and who is placed firmly outside of the state's care and protection, to be left for disposal.

The Normative Strivings of LGB(T) Politics

To understand the origins and the political as well as cultural implications of transgender visibility, it is necessary to contextualize the current moment within larger sociopolitical discourses about securing citizenship rights for certain members of the LGBT community. Before doing so, my use of the terms *transgender, trans, queer,* and *LGBT* requires explanation. Defining an identity category such as transgender is inherently difficult because there is always a risk of "assigning a normative telos to an identity category that is often employed to oppose ... modernist, binary logic."[16] Conscious of this problem, for the purposes of this book, *transgender* and *trans* are conceptualized to include a wide range of gender-variant practices, embodiments, and identities that challenge the assumed stability of and relationality between biological sex, the gender binary, and sexuality.[17] I employ a broad definition of *trans* not only to acknowledge the social construction of sex, gender, and sexuality but also to remain inclusive of nonbinary people who do not necessarily identify as transgender.

It can be theoretically and methodologically difficult to draw a clear line between transgender and queer, not least because these terms circulate with different meanings and uses—sometimes even contradictory ones—in multiple spaces.[18] Although the term *transgender* emerged in activist and academic circles and was quickly institutionalized, its universal application is resisted by some who fall under its domain because it (re)produces class and racial hierarchies that lead to erasures and the absorption of more nuanced subjectivities (e.g., that of "drag queens," "girls," "fem queens," and "male-bodied women who also identify as gay") into a monolithic category.[19] Similarly, *queer* emerged simultaneously in both activist and academic contexts with varying meanings. Originally used as an epithet in the early twentieth century, *queer* reemerged as a radical political term among activists during the HIV/AIDS crisis in the 1980s and 1990s. Concurrently, academics began to use queer to refer to a new poststructuralist academic theory that sought to challenge the naturalizing assumptions of heteronormativity and the stability of gender and sexual identities. Despite its anti-identarian meanings in queer theory and in some queer politics, colloquially, *queer* has come to be used as an umbrella term chiefly associated with nonnormative sexual practices and desires, but it is also sometimes used to refer to gender nonnormativity.[20] Reflective of the multiple meanings that adhere to *queer*, I use the term in two key ways. First, I use *queer* in its popular sense: as an identificatory umbrella term that includes not only sexual but gender identities. I do this simply to acknowledge the term's widespread and, more important, productive usage among vast groups of people. Second, and quite differently, I use *queer* as advocated by Cathy Cohen, who argues for a politics that targets "the link between the ideological, social, political, and economic marginalization of punks, bulldaggers, and welfare queens."[21] This kind of queer politics is committed to intersectional analyses of power that move beyond individual or group identities to coalitional work that focuses on improving the living conditions of those at the intersections of economic, racial, gendered, and sexual oppression.

Finally, I employ the acronym LGB(T) when referring to the collective organizing efforts and activism of mainstream gay, lesbian, bisexual, and transgender rights organizations. Sometimes I utilize parentheses around the T to signal the contingent and mostly nominal inclusion of transgender issues and people in these organizations and their political agendas.[22] As Mary L. Gray points out, references to an allegedly coherent and tangible "LGBT community" signify "the power of nationally mass-mediated conversations to manifest an 'imagined community' of lesbian, gay, bisexual, and transgender people, whether L, G, B, and T-identifying people are present or not."[23] During the past three decades, queer and trans studies scholars have critiqued mainstream LGB(T) organizing for, as Lisa Duggan explains, its homonormative, assimilationist single-issue politics "that does not contest dominant heteronormative assumptions and institutions, but upholds and sustains them, while promising the possibility of a demobilized gay constituency and a privatized, depoliticized gay culture anchored in domesticity and consumption."[24] While LGB(T) political organizing has come under scrutiny for its narrow and normative agenda, the prevalence of *queer*'s usage in mainstream culture and politics also opens it up to the same critiques that queer studies scholars have leveled against this imagined LGBT community.[25]

These homonormative, assimilationist politics have secured citizenship rights only for *some* members of the LGBTQ community. This is evident in unprecedented legal victories, including the passage of federal hate crime legislation, the repeal of the military's Don't Ask, Don't Tell policy (DADT), and, most prominently, the legalization of gay marriage in the U.S. Supreme Court's 2015 *Obergefell v. Hodges* decision. These victories have systematically excluded and ignored the contributions and needs of people of color, poor and gender-nonconforming people, and those who engage in nonnormative sexual and kinship practices.[26] These exclusions are also evident in the very mythology surrounding the origins of LGBT/queer politics and community. Despite the fact that the activism of drag queens and trans women of color was a fundamental part of the riots at Compton's Cafeteria in San Francisco's Tenderloin district in 1966 and at the Stonewall Inn in 1969—the latter commonly hailed as a foundational moment for the modern LGBT movement—

the contributions of transgender, gender-nonconforming, and queer people of color have been all too frequently dismissed, ignored, and erased from official and popular histories of LGBT rights. Subsequent decades have illustrated that activism surrounding issues of sexuality and gender identity do not necessarily always align themselves with one another and have, at times, been very contentious, as, for example, the battle over passage of the Employment Non-Discrimination Act (ENDA) in the United States shows.[27]

Similarly, persistent transphobic discourses within radical feminist spaces, which posit trans women as "unwanted penetrators" into (cis) women's space, continue to cause rifts in feminist and LGB(T) communities. In 1973 the West Coast Lesbian Conference in Los Angeles heatedly split over a scheduled performance by transgender folk singer Beth Elliott.[28] In 1979 Janice G. Raymond's publication *The Transsexual Empire: The Making of the She-Male* cemented anti-transgender sentiment in certain feminist communities with her transphobic contention that "all transsexuals rape women's bodies by reducing the real female form to an artifact, appropriating this body for themselves."[29] Raymond argued that male-to-female transsexuals were agents of the patriarchal oppression and that their presence in (cis) women's spaces violated (cis) women's sexuality and spirit. Some of these trans-exclusionary radical feminism debates have recently been revived with the 2014 publication of *Gender Hurts: A Feminist Analysis of the Politics of Transgenderism*, in which Sheila Jeffreys reinforces transphobic tropes of "male-bodied transgenders," that is, trans women, infiltrating, dividing, and obliterating feminist spaces, while "female-bodied transgenders," that is, trans men, allegedly escape misogyny by masquerading as men.[30] Similarly, while the national Women's March in January 2017 drew record crowds in numerous U.S. cities—significantly with many participants wearing pink pussy hats that equated gender identity not only with genitals but genitals of a particular color—the organizers faced criticism for continuing to sideline trans women and their concerns despite nominally inclusionary principles in their mission statement. As transgender studies has also become an increasingly vibrant field of interdisciplinary inquiry in academia, its increased institutionalization has fueled similar debates about trans studies' place within women's and gender studies programs because it continues to "problematize the political efficacy of the category 'woman.'"[31]

While it may be easy to assume that quarrels over identity politics and who is part of the feminist and LGBT movements are in the past, the difficult and at times contested relationship in and between gay, lesbian, feminist, and trans communities is still a major source of conflict. Detailed in chapter 2, Chelsea Manning's retraction as a grand marshal for San Francisco's Pride march in 2013 serves as an example of these kinds of conflicts in contemporary mainstream LGB(T) politics; these conflicts, I argue, illustrate how the mainstream LGBT political movement has become aligned with neoliberal economic and imperial interests. None of the major national LGBT organizations, many of whom were involved in SF Pride, such as the HRC or the National LGBTQ Task Force (not incidentally known exclusively as the National Gay and Lesbian Task Force until 2014), issued a statement in support of Manning during her lengthy pretrial confinement. Similarly, chapter 4 highlights how local Minneapolis and Saint Paul organizers used grassroots efforts to garner national attention about the violence that trans women of color such as CeCe McDonald face, while mainstream LGBT organizations ignored this issue and instead continued to invest in the state's right to regulate monogamous marriage.

Despite the nominal changes to officially include the T in organizations' titles and policies since the mid-2010s, *Terrorizing Gender* scrutinizes whether the T is really a constituency substantively included in mainstream LGB(T) politics. If trans issues are not being consistently and centrally addressed in political organizing, is trans visibility erroneously heralded as a "transgender tipping point"? Or does the framework of transgender visibility allow mainstream LGB(T) organizations to allege the inclusion of the T without actually addressing the urgent needs and issues of transgender people? *Terrorizing Gender* thus promotes a critical queer politics that fully acknowledges and engages with trans experiences and the material realities of transgender lives.

Visibility and Its Traps

As Michel Foucault succinctly put it in *Discipline and Punish*, "visibility is a trap."[32] While greater media visibility and recognition are often seen as a measure of cultural justice and social equality, they can also produce a pathway to biopolitical management, promoting techniques of surveillance, self-monitoring, and self-responsibility for marginalized communities. Stuart Hall, for example, remarks about black popular culture that "what replaces invisibility is a kind of carefully regulated, segregated visibility."[33] Similarly, Herman Gray argues that the propagation of visibility and access to cultural representation often engender new forms of subjection, marginalization, and regulation.[34] In other words, being visible also means that one is being counted and administered according to the state's normative and normalizing imperatives. Within the security state and its capitalist modes of production, being recognizable always comes with an extraction of value. As Aren Aizura asserts, "being a somebody means visibility: becoming a population, becoming a demographic, becoming (part of) a class, becoming clockable."[35] The recent surge in anti-trans bathroom legislation, for example, illustrates that being readable as trans is often accompanied with harm and abjection: particularly those facing intersecting oppressions "are socially denied interiority and forms of reserve, privacy, and respect enjoyed by nontrans people."[36] Being recognized as a trans subject therefore creates a double bind—where visibility does not necessarily lead to more protection and safety but may even generate increased harm and surveillance.

While Larry Gross contends that the increasingly visible presence of gay and lesbian people in the media is illustrative of how media can positively serve as "both . . . carriers and reflections of transformations that the forces of cultural reaction have been powerless to reverse," the politics of representation are inherently more complex.[37] Questions of *who* gets to be seen (in the media) and what it *means* to be seen varies greatly for different constituencies within queer and trans communities. Recognizing the political utility of visibility discourses, mainstream LGBT organizations have focused much of their energy and money on campaigns that aim to increase queer media visibility in the interest of assimilationist practices and goals, most prominently exemplified by GLAAD. This focus, according to Douglas Crimp, has generated a "visibility predicated on homogeneity and on excluding everyone who does not conform to norms."[38] This quest for media recognition also tends to unduly place the burden of representation on a few token figures, as exemplified by Caitlyn Jenner or Laverne Cox. Queer visibility often includes an inherent trade-off whether it is promoting tolerance through harmful stereotyping, lessening isolation at the expense of activism, trading assimilation into dominant institutions for equality, or transforming a radical politics into a commoditized market niche.[39] The increase of LGBT visibility in the media, therefore, does not automatically equate to sociopolitical and cultural progress for queer and trans people and in fact may eschew, if not deny, the legitimacy of more critical and complex engagements with sexual and gender-nonconforming politics and activism.

An initial wave of scholarship on mediated trans visibility in the early 2000s focused on the murder of Brandon Teena and its subsequent filmic adaptions *The Brandon Teena Story* (1998) and *Boys Don't Cry* (1999).[40] This scholarship points to a prevalence of pathologizing and disciplining discourses surrounding Teena's trans identity, which sought to reinforce the gender binary and commonly portrayed him as a trickster and deceiver.[41] In *Disciplining Gender*, a foundational text for communication and rhetorical studies, John M. Sloop uses Teena's case to illustrate how the increased visibility of gender ambiguity in the 1990s did not always subversively work to denaturalize and undo gender but rather reinforced prevailing cultural expectations of heteronormativity by positioning these cases as "aberrations in nature's plan."[42] C. Jacob Hale notes that the visibility of transgender and gay political activism around Teena's case also worked to harden the borders between butch and trans masculine identities through essentialist constructions between the vagina and womanhood. For Hale, such constructions negate self-chosen identifications for others who craft different relationships between gender presentation, biological characteristics, embodiment, and subjectivity: "Border zones need not be battle zones, but they must be demilitarized."[43]

Much media and communication studies scholarship on queer visibility tends to focus on representations of white, middle-class gay and lesbian subjectivities, but it often does not address how race figures into representations of gender identity and sexuality.[44] In his recent book, C. Riley Snorton, for example, illustrates how the erasure from the "Brandon archive" of Phillip DeVine, a black man and amputee who was also killed by Teena's murderers, raises questions about the intersections between black and trans lives and deaths. DeVine's name is rarely acknowledged in broader public memory, and the erasure of his race and disability speaks to the influence of antiblackness and able-bodiedness on which LGBT subjects become digestible and legible for mass-mediated consumption and which ones do not.[45]

While intersectionality has been incorporated widely into feminist, ethnic, and sexuality studies and has emerged as an important analytic in queer of color critique, its uptake in communication and media studies has been less prominent.[46] *Terrorizing Gender* takes intersectionality as a key framework for understanding how mediated representations of trans people are linked to their daily interactions and experiences with systems of state power and violence. Because gender is always already produced in and through other social formations, including but not limited to race, ethnicity, sexuality, and class, the case studies I present illustrate that media and state institutions conceptualize trans people as deceptive, deviant, and threatening precisely because they fail to account for these lives at the intersections of multiple identity categories. In McDonald's case, for example, it is impossible to separate her trans identity from her identity as a poor woman of color. She and her friends were viciously attacked because of not just homophobia and transphobia but racism as well. Yet local news media and state prosecutors denied these intersecting oppressions, considering McDonald undeserving of legal protection. Similarly, Manning's leaking of classified information and her inability to "properly" embody and perform hetero- and homonormativity rendered her as the alien enemy who both betrayed and failed to "duly" enact whiteness. The gendered and sexualized othering of Manning as a threat to national security is, therefore, inextricably tied to processes of racialization. Drawing on black and women of color feminisms highlights the importance of intersectional analyses for critical media and legal studies to address the means by which oppressive systems interlock and expose the limitations of visibility politics and law reform, which alone do not suffice to produce truly liberating, intersectional social justice efforts.

With the increase in transgender visibility there has been a corresponding surge in scholarship that scrutinizes news coverage and fictionalized representations of trans people. Particularly, the publication of the anthology *Transgender Communication Studies: Histories, Trends, and Trajectories* (2015), edited by Leland Spencer and Jamie C. Capuzza, has made important contributions to understanding trans identities in the broader context of health, interpersonal, and organizational communication as well as media-framing analyses. Looking especially at news media, scholars have noted some positive recent trends when discussing trans people and issues, including a decrease in misgendering, focus on genitals, and deadnaming.[47] However, there generally remains little coverage to begin with, and this coverage disproportionally revolves around trans women, while trans men and nonbinary folks remain notably absent.[48] Sourcing practices also reveal that journalists continue to rely on nontransgender "experts" as proxies rather than letting trans people tell their own stories, which often individualizes struggles and failures but does not address the systemic nature of intersecting oppressions. Particularly notable is the prominence of "wrong body discourse," which is frequently deployed as a "fixing strategy" to explain and acknowledge trans identities, yet as Bernadette Barker-Plummer notes, this discourse reasserts the gender binary, ignoring more fluid understandings of gender. Elaborating on the "wrong body" trope, Michael Lovelock argues that trans has become "fashionable" in recent years precisely because of a larger cultural imperative that encourages women to express their "true" femininity via bodily transformation and makeovers, as exemplified by trans celebrity figures such as Caitlyn Jenner and Jazz Jennings. However, as Lovelock acknowledges, this visibility is fraught with exclusions around race and gender normativity as it problematically works "to demarcate ideals of 'acceptable' transgender subjectivity."[49]

Similarly, scripted and fictional content engaging trans characters often reasserts heteronormativity rather than challenging or subverting gender binaries in efforts to appeal to dominant cisgender audiences.[50] Andre Cavalcante, therefore, scrutinizes the "double work" of paratexts (e.g., film reviews, movie posters, and director commentary on DVDs) accompanying "break-out" movies such as *Transamerica* (2005) because they create important spaces for trans people themselves to explore, validate, and celebrate transgender subjectivity.[51] Furthermore, crime shows in particular continue to rely problematically on storylines that solely depict trans people as deceptive villains, prostitutes, and murderers.[52] Comparable to news coverage, scripted and fictional shows thus have yet to fully acknowledge a variety of trans experiences, including nonbinary ones, as a political constituency and social movement.[53] More recently, media scholars have also begun to explore the importance of social media spaces for counterhegemonic trans cultural production. Specifically, tagging practices as well as new modes of self-representation and self-definition on Tumblr and Twitter constitute modes of resistance to mainstream media's coopting and fetishizing of trans identities and the ongoing violence trans communities face.[54]

Building and expanding on this scholarship, I use intersectional analyses and queer of color critique to make sense of this current sociocultural moment in which heightened trans visibility also coincides with trans surveillance and death. Treating trans identities as a central analytical category, *Terrorizing Gender* refocuses our attention on the relationship between cultural representations and the material conditions of trans people by asking what the connections are between mediated trans visibilities and the increased exposure of trans people to state surveillance practices. Moreover, what types of trans visibilities and identities are constituted as normative subjectivities deserving of national belonging and access to U.S. citizenship rights? Whose bodies and identities are rendered as deviant and thus undeserving and abject by media and state institutions?

The Surveillance Practices of the U.S. Security State

While the explosion of media content around trans visibilities insinuates that trans is "hot shit," to quote filmmaker and trans rights activist Tourmaline (formerly known as Reina Gossett), mainstream media rarely depict or reference the policing, discrimination, and violence—in short, what I refer to as state surveillance practices—that disproportionately harm trans communities.[55] Such surveillance practices manifest themselves in the criminalization of trans communities (particularly those of color), for example, through frequent stop-and-frisk searches, tightened ID laws, full-body scanners at airports, the denial of access to public restrooms, and placement in gender-inappropriate facilities within the prison-industrial complex. I examine the media's and the state's treatment of trans individuals as an entry point through which to analyze visibility politics within the contemporary United States because it affords the ability to interrogate the security state's racialized and gendered surveillance practices after 9/11.

I conceptualize the security state as an amalgam of governmental, corporate, and civil entities that are invested in advancing the expansion of national security and surveillance under the mantle of protecting its citizenry at the expense of civil liberties. According to Inderpal Grewal, the United States has entered a phase of advanced neoliberalism, which is marked by the waning of U.S. global empire, endless war, and increased surveillance. Securitization thereby has become a dominant mode of power that the U.S. security state uses to exert control over its populations. Security always carries a duplicitous promise. It may connote protection and safety for *some* citizens, yet it also evokes insecurities, threats, and violence for others: "It can refer to individual and biological processes of welfare and biopolitics that in the US context are based on biometrics, pathologization of new racial formations, old and new Orientalisms, and widespread surveillance."[56] In response to these insecurities, "exceptional citizens"—typically white, Christian males—take it upon themselves to "defend" and "save" the security state, while black and brown others are criminalized in old and new ways.[57] The logics of this process are especially evident with the criminalization of CeCe McDonald in chapter 3 and her perpetrator's concurrent elevation to grievable victim through mediated and legal discourses. Yet such exceptionalism does not only pertain to traditionally heteronormative subjects: the emergence of transpatriotism, which I trace in detail in chapter 2, illustrates how certain transnormative people—in this case particularly transgender veterans—become contingently accepted into the nation because of their patriotic investments in and nationalist support of the security state. These "exceptional citizens" simultaneously demarcate new lines of abjection as systematic state violence and discriminatory laws continue to target gender-nonconforming and trans of color communities.

Media corporations themselves are also increasingly embroiled in the security state. Driven by neoliberal ideologies and free-market logics, the state increasingly outsources security duties and national security onto the populace and private agencies, including media corporations and technology companies. For example, citizens increasingly use media products such as parental control software, which monitors children's Internet access, to securitize themselves as well as the security state. Laurie Ouellette and James Hay have argued that especially television, as a cultural technology, becomes a key instrument to educate, regulate, shape, and improve the idealized citizen-subject.[58] News media and popular culture actively (re)produce the state's risk framing of who and what represents a threat to national security. Expanding the work of Mark Andrejevic on securitainment, I illustrate in chapter 5 how the reality TV show *Border Security: Australia's Front Line* explicitly cooperated with Australian customs officials to capitalize on Monica Jones's detention at the Sidney airport as her racialized gender nonconformity was seen as a national security threat.[59] *Terrorizing Gender* thus explores how the mediated visibility of trans people is linked to their bio- and necropolitical management by state agencies.

I interrogate in particular the prison-industrial complex—characterized by the synthesis of private, political, and financial interests in promoting prison expansionism and mass incarceration—as well as attendant criminal justice, military, and immigration (detention) systems as sites of queer necropolitics, where the containment of certain racialized and a priori criminalized populations is legitimated by state agents in order to protect the lives of others. Under biopolitical governance, Foucault argues that racism becomes the key means and premise upon which the state claims the legitimate right to kill—"the right to 'make' live and 'let' die"—to maintain and improve the health and value of the population as a whole.[60] Extending Foucault's concept of biopolitics, Achille Mbembe uses the notion of necropolitics to account for the various ways in which technologies of power are deployed to create death worlds, "new and unique forms of social exis-

tence in which vast populations are subjected to conditions of life con-
ferring upon them," not necessarily the status of literal physical death
but social, political, and civil death—"the status of *living dead*."[61] Thus,
while biopolitics is primarily concerned with the project of managing,
investing in, and fostering the lives of those deemed worthy of care and
protection, necropolitics seeks to account for the ways in which that
process simultaneously depends on the disposal and deaths of others.
Manning's, McDonald's, and Jones's experiences with various systems
of detention exemplify the death worlds that many racialized, trans,
and gender-nonconforming people are forced to endure: from being
criminalized for "walking while trans" to placement in sex-segregated
facilities based on birth-assigned sex to prolonged periods of solitary
confinement out of "safety concerns" and to the denial of hormone
treatments and other medical care. These tactics of administrative
violence are part and parcel in the security state's ever-expanding
arsenal of necropolitical detention practices to further surveil, discipline, silence, and slowly break detainees, and they reveal its ongoing
investment in and enforcement of the gender binary.

While a critical queer and trans politics is committed to challenging
the institutionalization and normalization of queer and trans people
into the conservative and repressive workings of the security state,
mainstream LGBT activism now often actively supports expanding
forms of state violence and punishment, for example, through federal hate crime legislation. Jasbir Puar, Jin Haritaworn, and C. Riley
Snorton aptly describe how such phenomena are specifically reflective
of a queer and trans necropolitics where the folding of certain queer
and trans subjects "(back) into life" is predicated on the simultaneous
abandonment and death of queer and trans people of color.[62] I question these dubious queer investments in the penal system in chapter 3
by examining how hate crime legislation isolates specific instances of
violence against LGBT people as acts of individual prejudice without
considering how exposure to systemic violence impacts oppressed
communities. Engaging women of color feminisms reveals that the
legislative logic of hate crime statutes, which explicitly attempts to
account for race, gender, and sexuality among other categories, is
unable to address structural and institutionalized violence because

it is solely premised on the mobilization of discrete identity categories. However, the violence that trans people experience can only be accounted for through intersectional analyses that acknowledge the interpellation of subjects by multiple identity categories. Hate crime statutes, therefore, present another political and legal mechanism by which the security state and its politics of colorblindness masks an ongoing investment in white supremacy.

The renewed emphasis on national security after the events of 9/11 and the expansion of neoliberal policies has resulted in an increased interest and surge in scholarship on surveillance studies across numerous disciplines. Such scholarship has frequently addressed how surveillance technologies, for example, automated facial recognition software and closed-circuit television cameras, (re)produce fears and stereotypes of a racialized terrorist other.[63] Similarly, gender-nonconforming people have not been invisible to contemporary systems of surveillance, which David Lyon defines as "the focused, systematic and routine attention to personal details for purpose of influence, management, protection or direction."[64] More recently, a growing body of explicitly critical feminist surveillance studies scholarship has extended Foucauldian analyses on the long-standing pathologizing of nonnormative sexual and gendered practices and embodiments in the West.[65] Because much of queer media scholarship usually remains focused on questions of representation and their role in meaning-making processes, surveillance studies can offer a better understanding of the political, legal, and technical infrastructures interpellating LGBTQ identities and their socio-material consequences.

Terrorizing Gender asks how and why certain trans people come under the scrutiny of state surveillance practices as it analyzes the power relations underlying those practices. Monica Jones's encounters with U.S. law enforcement and Australian custom officials, for example, illustrate how the imperial security state operates not only nationally but transnationally in its framing of risk and safety, especially in evoking the specter of the "transgender terrorist." Expanding Foucauldian thinking about governmentality and security, the case studies in this book contribute to an understanding that state surveillance practices of gendered, classed, and racialized bodies are central to the state's constructions of national security—of who is granted access to national belonging and citizenship and who is considered a threat in need of immediate containment and neutralization.

Queer(ing) Methods

By following Mary L. Gray's call to consciously decenter media as the sole object of analysis and instead paying "greater ethnographic attention to the uptake and meaning of media in our everyday lives," the queer "scavenger methodology" that I employ in this book is informed by both ethnographic "on-the-ground" observations and critical discourse analysis to understand how media representations and visibility politics impact and reflect the everyday experiences of trans people.[66] Thus, *Terrorizing Gender*'s methodology is fundamentally interdisciplinary, moving beyond media and communication studies' focus on textual analysis. Despite the increased valorization of interdisciplinary scholarship across the humanities in recent years, efforts to substantively engage interdisciplinary perspectives tend to fall short because, as anthropologist Tom Boellstorff argues, "the citation networks and the methodologies remain largely unchanged, the metaphorical construal of objects of study as 'texts' sufficing as theoretical mandate." Avoiding these pitfalls, the objects of this study have guided me toward varied and at times unruly methodological and theoretical engagements that comprise this queer inquiry. In fact, *Terrorizing Gender* came to cohere precisely by refuting the "tidy vessel" of disciplinary boundaries.[67] Queering disciplinary boundaries and methodologies allow this book to challenge and disrupt the prevalence of white heteronormative knowledge production around gender and sexuality, particularly in media studies, and to complicate and resist the popularity of linear progress narratives circulating about the LGBT movement's victories toward "equality."

Therefore, *Terrorizing Gender* assembles an array of primary sources—composed of international, national, and local newspapers, news broadcasts and websites, social media, television shows, policy documents, court and legal records, and organizational press releases and manifestos, as well as interviews with reporters and activists—to critically account for the current moment of transgender visibility.

Drawing on these varied and, at times, seemingly unrelated sources provides an alternative understanding of trans visibility—one that explicitly contextualizes and connects it to the histories of racialized and gendered violence that the state continues to enact against marginalized communities. Through Foucauldian discourse analysis and a fusion of cultural studies' conceptions of the media's (re)production of dominant ideologies with frameworks of intersectionality, *Terrorizing Gender* links how the discursive production of "deviant" versus "acceptable" trans identity is connected to the state's violent management and surveillance of trans lives.[68] In other words, this book traces the interplay and collusion between public, legal, and state discourses in sanctioning and sometimes fortifying the surveillance, disciplining, and incarceration of trans people.

Discourses about trans people are imbued with power relations that actively constitute trans identity and define its subject position within a specific sociohistorical context: "Different discursive formations and apparatuses divide, classify and inscribe the body differently in their respective regimes of power and 'truth.'"[69] To analyze how certain transgender subjects are (re)produced through institutional discourses as deviant, disposable, and unworthy of care or protection, I merge Foucault's thinking about power and discourse with cultural studies frameworks that conceive of media as an "ideological state apparatus."[70] According to Stuart Hall, "the media serve, in societies like ours, ceaselessly to perform the critical ideological work of 'classifying out the world' within the discourses of dominant ideologies."[71] While the state sanctions and enacts violence against transgender people in multiple ways, it is precisely the "selective construction of *social knowledge*" about trans people by the media that allows for that violence to endlessly recur outside explicitly repressive and coercive state mechanisms.[72] Dominant ideologies permeating mass-mediated discourses racialize and criminalize trans people, especially those of color, as deceptive, deviant, and threatening, and in turn become the vehicle through which state-sanctioned violence against certain "aberrant" populations is legitimated and continuously allowed to occur.

The chapters on CeCe McDonald are not only informed by close readings of legal, news, and social media discourses circulating about her case between 2011 and 2014, but these chapters are also refracted through a queer ethnographic lens.[73] I had moved to Minneapolis to start graduate school just a few months after CeCe McDonald and her friends were attacked in the summer of 2011. When McDonald went to trial the following year, I paused for the first time to ponder what material consequences actually derive from increased LGBT visibility. I also began to scrutinize my own privileged white cis queer positionality more closely, as I initially had not followed what had happened to a poor trans woman of color walking down a street in a neighborhood not far from my own. While I have no intention of exceptionalizing McDonald's story, the writing of these chapters has certainly been a personal matter and has sharpened my sensibilities toward the blurred lines between scholarship and activism as well as the complex politics of allyship. My close interactions with McDonald supporters and my on-the-ground approach not only allowed me to gather data and insights that would have otherwise been foreclosed to me but significantly changed my own conceptualizations of the relationship between researcher and informant. I came to realize that "the ground" quite literally is "both our particular field site—the communities within which we study and about which we write—and also the epistemological ground on which we stake our claims."[74]

Although critiques of the hierarchies of knowledge production in academia have become commonplace in feminist writing, within communication and media studies such critiques remain scarce and are often dismissed as unsophisticated, not theoretical enough, or too "blinded" by political activism. Yet, María Lugones and Elizabeth Spelman's foundational questions about the ethics of knowledge production are a powerful reminder: "When we speak, write, and publish our theories, to whom do we think we are accountable? Are the concerns we have in being accountable to 'the profession' at odds with the concerns we have in being accountable to those about whom we theorize? Do commitments to 'the profession', method, getting something published, getting tenure, lead us to talk and act in ways at odds with what we ourselves (let alone others) would regard as ordinary, decent behavior?"[75] Academia historically privileges those doing the theorizing over those who are theorized about. After all, I knew that "sourcing" my interlocutors for knowledge and writing about communities that I myself am not a part of would help me to publish journal articles, finish my PhD, and apply for tenure-track jobs. I thus sought to be accountable to the communities that are the subjects of *Terrorizing Gender*. The people I spoke with were not merely informants, but they actively contributed to this book as research agents and have shaped its final form and content.[76] Part of *Terrorizing Gender*'s work explicitly follows a feminist commitment to move beyond the ivory tower and engage directly with community and activist spaces surrounding the walls of academia—such spaces remain often ignored and neglected as too distant others—in order to contribute to alternative epistemologies about the value of trans people's lives.

More importantly, I recognize how, despite my ability to critically reflect on my own subject positionality, the dangers of replicating a voyeuristic or patronizing gaze of marginalized communities—in this case poor trans communities of color—persists.[77] The "reflexive turn" in ethnography, that is, acknowledging the inherent subjectivity, situatedness, and partiality of all knowledge production, still functions as a double-edged sword as it strategically deploys this admission to justify its truth claims.[78] In other words, all ethnographic work and research is inherently contingent and messy.

Visibility for Whom?

Finally, let me address one obvious caveat: while I frequently deploy the more generalizing terminology *transgender visibility*, it is important to acknowledge that this book predominantly focuses on trans women. I had not planned on focusing exclusively on trans women, yet the media's current fascination with transgender people and issues tends to "depict the trans revolution in lipstick and heels," as trans rights activist Julia Serano puts it.[79] We have seen the occasional appearance of trans men on TV and in movies, yet representations of trans masculine people remains scarce.[80] More recently, Amazon's show *Transparent* received criticism not only for casting cis male actor Jeffrey Tambor in the role of late-life-transitioning Maura but especially for its joking depiction of trans man Dale (played by comedian and trans actor Ian Harvie), whose interaction with one of the Pfefferman daughters solely revolved around his "sexual deficiency" because he lacks a cisgender penis.[81] The few trans men that do garner media attention, such as trans model Aydian Dowling, who participated in *Men's Health* magazine's "Ultimate Guy" contest, or Shane Ortega, a prominent advocate for trans military inclusion, are typically represented in ways that (re)assert their (hyper)masculinity and heterosexuality.[82]

Why is there such a disparity in the amount of attention given to trans women versus trans men? One explanation may be that trans men do not have to endure the same objectifying gaze that trans women do. The media's fascination with trans women is not only indicative of the frequent sexual objectification of women on- and off-screen based on patriarchal and sexist attitudes but specifically a widespread "transmisogyny"—the intersection of cissexism and misogyny—that makes trans women particularly vulnerable. Serano observes that fetishizing media portrayals highlight trans women as hyperfeminine in order to assert the very inauthenticity of their womanhood.[83] It is, therefore, more likely that trans men tend to remain largely invisible in media and that the violence targeting transmasculine people often goes unnoticed because scrutinizing their gender transgressions would bring into question masculinity, patriarchy, and sexism itself.[84] Given the noticeable difference in mediated visibilities of trans feminine versus trans masculine people, I hope future scholarship will dissect more carefully visibility discourses generated specifically around trans men.

As the confines of "proper" visibility for trans and nonbinary people are arguably narrow, C. Riley Snorton and Jin Haritaworn remind us that "it is necessary to interrogate how the uneven institutionalization of women's, gay, and trans politics produces a transnormative subject, whose universalized trajectory of coming out/transition, visibility, recognition, protection, and self-actualization largely remains uninterrogated in its complicities and convergences with biomedical, neoliberal, racist, and imperialist projects."[85] While the purported "transgender tipping point" of 2014 heralded unprecedented legal protections for trans people under the Obama administration, it has also occasioned a reinvestment in the security state's surveillance and regulation of trans people. Even though transnormativity connotes self-realization, access to citizenship rights, and escape from violence for some, it simultaneously produces new contours of insecurity, vulnerability, neglect, and harm for other gender-nonconforming people. The promise of visibility as a crucial element in progress narratives about securing citizenship rights for LGBT people, therefore, does not necessarily lead to the promised land or outweigh its perils.

Given the current political climate in the United States, there is a renewed urgency for a critical queer and trans politics that evades the trap of visibility. The election of President Trump in 2017 has been accompanied by a resurgence in white supremacy with attempts to roll back various civil rights gains through concerted attacks on immigrant, gay, transgender, and reproductive rights. Such a critical politics must be invested in coalitional social justice work for not just the privileged few but for those most marginalized. In the book's coda, therefore, I engage Tourmaline's call for resistive "nobodies" to imagine different modes of recognition, collectivity, and belonging—modes that transcend the security state's life- and death-making capacities engendered by invisibility, visibility, and hypervisibility.

1

PATHOLOGIZING AND PROSECUTING
A (GENDER) TRAITOR

(In) our efforts to meet the risk posed to us by the enemy, we have forgotten our humanity. We consciously elected to devalue human life both in
Iraq and Afghanistan. When we engaged those that we perceived were
the enemy, we sometimes killed innocent civilians. Whenever we killed
innocent civilians, instead of accepting responsibility for our conduct, we
elected to hide behind the veil of national security and classified information in order to avoid any public accountability.

Chelsea Manning, pardoning request to President Obama, August 2013

On June 6, 2010, *Wired,* an online technology website that hosts blogs
on topics ranging from business, science, and transportation to security,
posted an article that announced the arrest of a U.S. Army intelligence
analyst, Private First Class Manning,[1] in the investigation of a video
leaked to the whistleblowing website WikiLeaks. The video depicts a
ruthless U.S. Apache helicopter strike in Baghdad in 2007, which killed
several unarmed Iraqi civilians, among them two war correspondents
working for Reuters.[2] The video, known as "Collateral Murder," had
garnered significant media attention upon its release by WikiLeaks
in April 2010 raising questions about U.S. war crimes and causing an
upheaval in U.S. foreign relations. Reuters had unsuccessfully requested
the release of the video footage under the Freedom of Information Act
in 2007. A statement issued by the Department of Defense shortly
after Private Manning's arrest on June 7, 2010, stated: "United States
Division-Center is currently conducting a joint investigation of Special-
ist Bradley Manning, 22, of Potomac, Md., who is deployed with Second Brigade 10th Mountain Division, in Baghdad, Iraq. He was placed
in pretrial confinement for allegedly releasing classified information

and is currently confined in Kuwait. The Department of Defense takes the management of classified information very seriously because it affects our national security, the lives of our soldiers, and our operations abroad."[3] No one could have predicted at that point that Private Manning would soon become implicated in the biggest leak of government secrets in U.S. history, comprising more than seven hundred thousand U.S. intelligence documents. WikiLeaks and its alleged source became one of the most prominent news stories of the decade.

In July 2010 WikiLeaks first released a set of classified U.S. military documents pertaining to the war in Afghanistan revealing details of civilian victims and alleged ties between Pakistani intelligence and the Taliban. These leaks were followed by the Iraq War logs in October 2010, containing four hundred thousand classified U.S. documents on the Iraq War from 2004 to 2009. Among other things, these logs chronicled the torture conducted by Iraqi forces with the silent approval of U.S. troops, checkpoint shootings of Iraqi civilians, and missile strikes accidentally targeting children. Last, in November 2010 WikiLeaks published a trove of State Department documents, colloquially referred to as "Cable Gate," revealing the secret dealings of behind-the-scenes international diplomacy, exposing blunt commentary from world leaders, and recounting U.S. pressure tactics overseas.[4] These materials painted a highly embarrassing portrait of U.S. might and imperialist foreign policy.

While WikiLeaks insisted on the anonymity of its source, it was an exchange between Manning and ex-hacker Adrian Lamo that ultimately led to her arrest in June 2010.[5] In an online chat room she wrote: "I'm sure you're pretty busy [but] if you had unprecedented access to classified networks 14 hours a day, 7 days a week for 8-plus months, what would you do?"[6] Lamo began logging their chats and notified the authorities. Lamo would later say that he was afraid Manning's leaking could put American lives at risk.[7] Manning stood trial in June 2013 for twenty-two violations of military law, eight of which fell under Article 104, "Aiding the Enemy," of the Espionage Act—a 1917 statute against sharing information with unauthorized sources, which became a key decree used by the Obama administration in what some viewed as a larger "war on whistleblowers." Although Manning was found not guilty of the aiding the enemy charge on July 30, 2013, she was convicted of twenty other charges, including six under the Espionage Act and sentenced to thirty-five years in prison.

From her arrest in 2010, the media attention surrounding Manning's case was driven by a quest for potential motives, focused on her difficult childhood, alleged mental instabilities, a narcissistic personality, and her experiences of being bullied when she identified as a gay man. In particular, Manning's announcement shortly after her sentencing in August 2013, in which she revealed her transgender identity and desire to transition, ignited an unprecedented public debate about the correct use of pronouns for trans-identified individuals and questions of gender self-determination. At its worst, the media whirl following her announcement contributed to the long-standing stigmatization and pathologizing of transgender identities as dangerous, deceptive, and terrorist. As Stryker and Currah have pointed out in their introduction to the inaugural issue of *Transgender Studies Quarterly*, "It is virtually impossible, in the wake of the Manning case, to ignore transgender issues or not to have opinions about them."[8] Manning's case also brought to the fore questions about unrestrained government surveillance and secrecy, the Obama administration's aggressive pursuit of whistleblowers, the humane treatment of detainees, and whether the military systematically fails to provide support to minority and LGBT soldiers.

This chapter illustrates that mainstream media's portrayal of Manning as "emotionally fractured" and plagued by "delusions of grandeur" provided a rationale for the state's extralegal—if not illegal—treatment of Manning by tying her alleged sexual orientation and gender nonconformity to mental instabilities that threatened state interests. More specifically, I argue that Manning's initial emasculation and feminization as a gay man in mainstream media reporting and the media's subsequent focus on her diagnosis with "gender identity disorder" perpetuates the military's traditional role as a heteropatriarchal institution—"a dominance inherently built on a gender binary system that presumes heterosexuality as a social norm" and that fundamentally privileges white hegemonic maleness.[9] Manning's leaking of classified information, which revealed the ugly operations of U.S. imperial expansionism, and her inability to embody and perform heterosexuality and hegemonic masculinity rendered her an alien enemy who both betrayed and failed to "properly" enact whiteness.[10] Manning's case shows how discourses of sexuality, gender, and race are constitutive of one another; specifically, Manning's whiteness must be understood through the logic of gender, which is in part contingent upon her ability to embody and perform heteromasculinity. Thus, the othering of Manning through her treatment as an alien enemy is also entangled with a process of racialization, demonstrating that white supremacy and heteropatriarchy remain vital logics for the building of U.S. empire.

The Traitor Is a "Sissy," a "Fag," and "Mentally Unstable"

While Stryker and Aizura contend in their introduction to the second edition of the *Transgender Studies Reader*, "with the pop cultural cachet of transgender phenomena seeming to increase with every new episode of *RuPaul's Drag Race*," the story of Chelsea Manning appeared on the media landscape at an unprecedented moment for trans visibility.[11] The media's fascination with transgender phenomena, however, is not new. In 1952 Christine Jorgensen was the first transgender person to receive significant media coverage for her successful gender-affirmation surgery. As Stryker notes in *Transgender History*, the media particularly focused on the fact that Jorgensen was an "ex-GI" who had been drafted into the army after high school, suggesting deep-rooted anxieties about masculinity and sexuality: "If a macho archetype such as 'the soldier' could be transformed into a 'blond bombshell,' what did that mean for the average man?"[12] Not surprisingly, fears about the undermining of heteromasculine militarism would also resurface in Manning's case. Some sixty years after Jorgensen's story made headlines, the dominant themes emerging from Manning's news accounts depicted similar anxieties about sexuality and gender. Manning was mainly pathologized for her gender nonconformity and her inability to "properly" perform heteronormative whiteness. I begin with a comprehensive analysis of the news media coverage surrounding Manning before I engage in close readings of court documents and legal discourses pertaining to her pretrial confinement and court proceedings.[13]

DAILY ☒ NEWS
NEW YORK'S PICTURE NEWSPAPER »

5¢

Vol. 34   No. 136   Copr. 1952 News Syndicate Co. Inc.   New York 17, N.Y., Monday, December 1, 1952   4¢ IN CITY   5¢ OUTSIDE LIMITS   CITY LIMITS

EX-GI BECOMES
BLONDE BEAUTY
Operations Transform Bronx Youth

Story on Page 3

A World of a Difference

George W. Jorgensen Jr., son of a Bronx carpenter, served in the Army [▲] for two years and was given honorable discharge in 1946. Now George is no more. After six operations, Jorgensen's sex has been changed and today she is a striking woman [◄—], working as a photographer in Denmark. Parents were informed of the big change in a letter Christine (that's her new name) sent to them recently.   —Story on page 3

Fig. 2. Christine Jorgensen on the front page of the *Daily News*, December 1, 1952. Courtesy of Getty Images.

First, it is noteworthy that the time period between Manning's arrest in June 2010 and her pretrial in December 2012 was marked by a glaring lack of media attention and coverage. Despite Manning's detainment on May 27, 2010, in Kuwait, major news outlets did not report on her arrest until June 7, 2010. While WikiLeaks published the Afghanistan and Iraq logs followed by a large trove of State Department cables throughout the second half of 2010, silence mostly surrounded Manning's case and whereabouts. If one wanted to keep up with Manning's numerous pretrial and motion hearings, also known as Article 32 hearings, which began in December 2011 one had to find alternative news outlets. Only a handful of independent journalists regularly attended, transcribed, and commented on her hearings.[14] Among those were Occupy Wall Street organizer Alexa O'Brien and Kevin Gosztola from the blog *Firedoglake*. These independent journalists were Manning supporters, as they considered her exposure of war crimes ethically conscious and heroic acts.

Later on in November and December 2012 when Manning's defense filed an Article 13 motion against unlawful pretrial punishment at the Marine Corps Brig at Quantico, Virginia, Margaret Sullivan, then the public editor for the *New York Times*, saw herself forced to call out her own paper for failing to send a reporter to cover Manning's compelling testimony over her harsh treatment:

> It was part of a fascinating few days in the history of the Manning story—resonating with implications for free speech, national security and the American military at war—but you wouldn't have known much about it if your only source of information was the *New York Times*. . . . As a matter of news judgment, giving so little coverage to the hearing is simply weird. This is a compelling story, and an important one. . . . Beyond the story itself, the *Times*, which considers itself the paper of record, had an obligation to be there—to bear witness—because, in a very real sense, Private Manning was one of its most important sources of the past decade.[15]

Sullivan's allusion to the seeming paradox of a glaring absence of coverage concerning Manning's pretrial hearings while the *Times* had simultaneously been one of the lead publishers of the WikiLeaks documents in question allows for several interpretations. One explanation for the lack of the newsworthiness of Manning's story may be found in the fact that with the continuous decline of print media and newspaper revenues, newsrooms have been facing drastic cuts to their budgets, and staff shortages are making it more difficult if not impossible to send their own reporters to cover a broad array of events. Thus, if the calculation was that "the *Times* did not think the hearing itself demanded coverage" since hours of pretrial hearings do not necessarily yield front-page news, it was certainly much cheaper to depend on wire-service articles from the Associated Press or Reuters if the event was to be covered at all.[16] The initial lack of Manning's coverage, therefore, points to some of the larger impacts of the political economy of the media, where downsized newsrooms severely undermine the ability of both traditional print and electronic news media to still function as a watchdog and as the Fourth Estate that monitors political processes and informs the public.

Whistleblower or Traitor

Once Manning was revealed as the alleged leaker of U.S. government documents, right-wing news outlets were quick to denounce and vilify her as a traitor. Only the British left-leaning newspaper the *Guardian* took a more sympathetic stance toward Manning's actions and critiqued her questionable treatment at Quantico early on. National newspapers shied away from taking specific sides on whether Manning was a whistleblower or a traitor and engaged mostly in factual, juridical recounting. An op-ed in the *New York Times* argued that Edward Snowden, with his revelations about the National Security Agency's surveillance practices and the PRISM program in 2013, was "not nearly as reckless as Bradley Manning, . . . who seemed not to know or care what secret documents he was exposing" and that there was "an unavoidable appearance of self-aggrandizement as well." Fox News described her as a "rogue GI," and Mike Huckabee argued that "anything less than execution is too kind."[17] On the *O'Reilly Factor*, Bill O'Reilly referred to "vile" WikiLeaks and asked Geraldo Rivera, "What did this weasel plead guilty to?" only to recount, "For those of you who don't remember Bradley Manning. He was in Iraq. He's some kind of gay, militant guy and I guess that was his beef; that he wasn't treated the way he wanted to be treated, but he leaked the information of Afghans helping the U.S. military and that got them killed." O'Reilly further asserted that "You make an example out of this guy; that's what you do."[18] Similarly, Adm. Mike Mullen, then chairman of the Joint Chiefs of Staff, told reporters that Julian Assange and his WikiLeaks sources "might already have on their hands the blood of some young soldier or that of an Afghan family."[19] These comments illustrate how the portrayal of Manning's actions as harming not only her fellow U.S. soldiers but also Afghani families reasserted and solidified a protective and patriarchal role that the United States ascribes to itself in an ever-recurring media narrative of justifying the wars in Afghanistan and Iraq as liberating Middle Easterners—especially brown women from their "oppressive" counterparts—in the name of freedom and democracy.

Contrary to the media discourses cited above, Manning herself revealed a grave concern over dubious U.S. military actions in Iraq in her chat logs with Adrian Lamo and subsequently in her pretrial statement to court on February 28, 2013. Manning claimed that she wanted people to see the truth and hoped that by revealing the gruesomeness of war, she could "spark a domestic debate on the role of the military and our foreign policy in general."[20] Manning displayed great frustration and disgust about U.S. military actions in Iraq that condoned, for example, the arrest of fifteen Iraqis by the Iraqi federal police for allegedly printing "anti-Iraqi literature," which turned out to be nothing more than a benign political critique of Iraq's then–prime minister Nouri al-Maliki. Referring specifically to the "Collateral Murder" video and its "war porn content," Manning was particularly disturbed by the dehumanizing treatment of Iraqi civilians at the hands of the U.S. aerial weapons team crew: "I wanted the American public to know that not everyone in Iraq and Afghanistan are targets that needed to be neutralized, but rather people who were struggling to live in the pressure-cooker environment of what we call asymmetric warfare."[21]

"WikiLeaks Suspect Manning: A Troubled Home Life"

Most prevalent across a variety of different news outlets was a focus on Manning's alleged "erratic behavior" and emotional problems, which ignored the possibility that Manning might have been motivated by a larger conscience. Initially, an emphasis on Manning's past struggles with her sexuality was frequently mentioned as being important to her decision to leak classified information. Manning, the daughter of a former naval intelligence operator, had developed an interest in science and programming early on. Born in Oklahoma, Manning had come out to her friends as gay at thirteen and was repeatedly teased during her high school years. After her father kicked her out of the house, she spent a few years adrift working across the Midwest. Manning joined the U.S. Army in 2007, which offered a new life and a way to pay for college. Manning's tiny physique at five feet, two inches, certainly made her an atypical soldier. In boot camp, she was persistently bullied and suffered anxiety attacks. Enlisting in the army also meant that Manning had to remain closeted due to the military's Don't Ask, Don't Tell policy, which prevented gay and lesbian soldiers from serving openly. Nonetheless, she attended a 2008 gay rights demonstration in Syracuse, New York.[22]

Describing Manning's time in the army, Barbara Starr on CNN emphasized that the "very low-ranking private" had "discipline problems" and "had been teased in the military for being gay."[23] The *Washington Post* frequently referred to her as a "young man adrift" and as "troubled," while a NPR report described her as "cherubic looking." In one of the first detailed profiles of Manning, Ginger Thompson from the *New York Times* asserted that Manning "barely looks old enough to drink" and wondered whether it was her desperation for acceptance or "delusions of grandeur" that caused her to leak the information.[24] Similarly, the Associated Press during pretrial hearings in November 2012 described a "compact, 24-year-old intelligence analyst [who] looked youthful in his dark-blue dress uniform, close-cropped hair and rimless eyeglasses" but spoke in "emphatic bursts, sometimes stumbling over his words."[25] A front-page article in the *Guardian* asked "Naïve idealist or notoriety seeker?" while in an opinion editorial, Bill Keller described the transcripts of online chats with Adrian Lamo as the only insights into Manning's psyche, which "portrays a young man, in his own words, 'emotionally fractured'—a gay man in an institution not hospitable to gays, fragile, lonely, a little pleased with his own cleverness, a little vague about his motives."[26] Responding to the fact that Manning had initially tried to contact the *New York Times* before handing the documents to WikiLeaks, Keller further surmised, "If Manning had connected with the *Times*, we would have found ourselves in a relationship with a nervous, troubled, angry young Army private who was offering not so much documentation of a particular government outrage as a chance to fish in a sea of secrets."[27] Interviewing several of Manning's friends, the *Guardian* ran a special investigation on the "beaten, bullied outsider who knew U.S. military's inner secrets" and reported that Manning "was far from typical soldier material. He was smart, gay, physically weak and politically astute."[28]

Focusing particularly on Manning's upbringing, numerous articles provided detailed accounts of her early dysfunctional family life: "Trial shows young man scarred by childhood neglect and loneliness[;] the army offered escape from early years blighted by parental alcoholism."[29] Even more tellingly, a story in the *New York Times* titled "Loner Sought a Refuge, and ended Up in War" alleged, "That story involved the child of a severed home, a teenager bullied for his conflicted sexuality whose father, a conservative retired soldier, and mother, a Welsh woman who never adjusted to life in Oklahoma, bounced their child back and forth between places where he never fit in."[30] What emerges from these dominant discourses is an attempt to explain and blame Manning's actions on her troubled childhood, which did not fit into the traditional "healthy" model of the stable, nuclear family. Media outlets conflated references to her childhood with mental health as well as gender and sexuality references to create a pathologizing narrative arc in which Manning's "broken childhood" was allegedly the cause for her mental instabilities, which in turn revealed themselves in nonnormative gender expressions and sexuality. This failure to "properly" perform heteronormativity then allegedly manifested itself in the betrayal of her country.

Although narratives of soldiers and veterans as "broken" and "injured" yet sacrificing themselves are frequently circulated and deployed by dominant media as a means to incorporate them into the national imaginary, Manning's failure to sacrifice herself for the nation was largely painted as a result of mental instabilities. According to this story arc, Manning's acts of whistleblowing were due to her own deviance, not to the failures of the security state in either its conduct of imperialist foreign policy or the military's lack of adequate mental health care and support for LGBTQ soldiers. This extensive focus on Manning's internal confusion about her gender and sexual identity, which was consistently framed as rooted in a troubled childhood and early emotional disturbances, diverted blame away from practices of U.S. imperialism and onto the individualized experience of homo- and transphobia, especially in the context of the military.

Similar to the framing of Manning's struggles with harassment and mental health as individual failure, in her analysis of media coverage addressing mass shootings on military bases, Ruth DeFoster observes that questions concerning access to mental health treatment are often displaced by media narratives upholding the primacy and nobility of the military.[31] Particularly insightful is DeFoster's comparative analysis of shootings on military bases committed both pre- and post-9/11. She demonstrates that since the beginning of the War on Terror, with its heightened sense of nationalism and patriotism, these shootings have been persistently framed by military and mainstream news coverage as tragic yet isolated and exceptional events, committed not by soldiers—i.e., one of the military's own—but by abject un-American "outliers" and "bad apples," those who never really belonged in the first place. Similarly, then–secretary of state Robert Gates was quick to point out that Manning's security leak should be viewed as an isolated incident and was not reflective of the majority of proud and honest service members.[32]

However, the fear generated by "effeminate" gay men "infiltrating" the military is certainly not new. During the "lavender scare" of the late 1940s and 1950s, the State Department relentlessly targeted gay employees who were seen as seductive, duplicitous, and posing a national security risk.[33] M. Jacqui Alexander and Chandra Mohanty point to this continuing state-generated discourse on gays in the U.S. military as reflective of a severe crisis in heteromasculinity. Their analysis of the initial institution of DADT in 1993 is worth quoting here:

Ostensibly, the purpose of this debate was to determine whether "effeminate" masculinity (practices, but not spoken) could be relied upon to undertake one of the most important tasks of citizenship: that of loyalty to and defense of one's country. The central preoccupation was whether such feminized masculinity (which was deemed neither masculine nor citizen at all) would jeopardize manly masculinity (heteromasculinity) as it undertook its job: defense of the imperial nation. After months of contestation (including predictable state lament over its own threatened identity in the context of a reduced military), heteromasculinity reasserted itself, rendered "gay" sexuality present yet silent, and erased lesbian sexuality almost entirely. Further, this conclusion premised homosexuality in whiteness, making it possible for "invisible" lesbian and gay soldiers to intervene in the Third World and within communities of color at home.[34]

Hegemonic news characterizations of Manning as an effeminate gay man who was repeatedly bullied by other service members retains and even strengthens these heteromasculinist discourses by allegedly proving the ineptness and profoundly treacherous nature of effeminate or queer soldiers. Tony Perkins, president of the conservative Family Research Council (FRC), for example, called Manning an "extreme homosexual activist" whose "fury over the services' homosexual policy" may have led her to publicize classified documents: "Unfortunately for all of us, Manning's betrayal painfully confirms what groups like FRC have argued all along: the instability of the homosexual lifestyle is a detriment to military readiness."[35]

But even more significantly, Alexander and Mohanty gesture toward the ways in which discourses of sexuality, gender, and race are constitutive of one another. Although not always articulated explicitly, Manning's case allows us to see that the process of sexualizing the other is always implicitly entangled with a process of racialization by positioning Manning and her actions as inherently un- and anti-American. As a white—initially gay-identified—intelligence analyst serving (silently, i.e., closeted) in Iraq, Manning was seemingly participating in nationalist and patriotic projects that justified the "defense of the imperial nation." However, Manning's whistleblowing on U.S. war crimes and her refusal to be further complicit in U.S. interventionism, which according to media discourses was motivated by her struggles with mental health and heteromasculinity, firmly framed her as an unpatriotic traitor and hence an enemy of the state, as I elaborate in more detail in the final part of the chapter. Manning's commitment to American nationalism and whiteness, therefore, was in part contingent upon her ability to act as the "manly man," in short, her performance of heteronormativity. The hegemonic media discourses surrounding Manning thus point to the ways in which refusals to adhere to traditional heteromasculine and heteronormative scripts in the context of the military are also entangled with a process of racial othering. In other words, Manning's case elucidates how the neoliberal U.S. security state strategically replaces the primacy of whiteness solely as phenotype with a manifestation of whiteness through the logics of heteronormativity and its commitment to furthering imperialist U.S. foreign policy. Manning's treatment and representation by the media reveal the contingency and fragility that characterize such exceptionalist modes of inclusion into U.S. nationalism—represented here by the violently heteropatriarchal institution of the military—for LGBTQ people and people of color.

"My Problem": Pronouns, Genitals, and Taxpayer Dollars

The media's belittlement and pathologizing of Manning's character heightened as she announced via her lawyer David Coombs on NBC's *Today Show* shortly after her sentencing on August 22, 2013, that "I want everyone to know the real me. I am Chelsea Manning. I am a female. Given the way that I feel, and have felt since childhood, I want to begin hormone therapy as soon as possible. I hope that you will support me in this transition. I also request that, starting today, you refer to me by my new name and use the feminine pronoun."[36] While Bob Schieffer from CBS's *Evening News* and newscasters from other cable news channels claimed that with this announcement Manning had "dropped a new bombshell," for those closely monitoring her case this information was anything but new.[37] In the infamous chat logs with Adrian Lamo, which *Wired* had fully published online by July 2011, one could read:

(1:47:01 p.m.) bradass87: im an army intelligence analyst, deployed to eastern baghdad, pending discharge for "adjustment disorder" in lieu of "gender identity disorder" ...

(10:19:00 a.m.) bradass87: im kind of coming out of a cocoon. . . . its going to take some time, but i hopefully wont be a ghost anymore

(10:19:53 a.m.) info@adrianlamo.com: You mentioned gender identity, I believe.

(10:19:59 a.m.) bradass87: ive had an unusual, and very stressful experience over the last decade or so

(10:20:53 a.m.) bradass87: yes. . . . questioned my gender for several years. . . . sexual orientation was easy to figure out . . . but i started to come to terms with it during the first few months of my deployment

(11:50:54 a.m.) bradass87: i wish it were as simple as "hey, go transition" . . . but i need to get paperwork sorted . . . financial stuff sorted . . . legal stuff . . . and im still deployed, so i have to redeploy back to the US and be outprocessed.[38]

In these chat logs Manning revealed a persistent discomfort with her masculine features. Furthermore, during Manning's first Article 32 hearings in December 2011, her lawyer had explained in great detail that the military had been well aware of Manning's struggles with gender identity yet failed to competently respond to her signs of distress by providing adequate counseling or support.[39] During her deployment to Iraq in 2009, Manning had begun to question her gender identity as she felt herself surrounded by "a bunch of hyper-masculine, trigger-happy, ignorant rednecks."[40] While on leave in the United States during the winter of 2010, she had spent a few days dressed as a woman, calling her female alter ego Breanna, and began to increasingly incorporate her female gender identity into her daily life.[41] Upon her return to Iraq in April 2010, Manning approached the sergeant in her chain of command with an email titled "My Problem" and enclosed a picture of herself as a woman:

> This is my problem. I've had signs of it for a very long time. Its caused problems within my family. I thought a career in the military would get rid of it. It's not something I seek out for attention, and I've been trying very, very hard to get rid of it by placing myself in situations

where it would be impossible. But, it's not going away its haunting me more and more as I get older. Now, the consequences of it are dire, at a time when its causing me great pain in itself.... I don't know what to do anymore, and the only "help" that seems to be available is severe punishment and/or getting rid of me. All I do know, is that fear of getting caught has caused me to go to great lengths to consciously hide the problem. As a result, the problem and the constant cover-up has worn me down to a point where it's always on my mind, making it difficult to concentrate at work, difficult to pay attention to whatever is going on, difficult to sleep, impossible to have any meaningful conversations, and makes my entire life feel like a bad dream that won't end.[42]

During Manning's court-martial in 2013, her supervisor, M.Sgt. Paul Adkins, testified that he still deemed Manning competent to perform her daily duties as an intelligence analyst, as she delivered good work products despite her documented struggles and emotional, at times even violent, outbursts. Asked by Manning's lawyer, David Coombs, why he did not forward Manning's email to the appropriate chain of command until three months later, Adkins responded: "I really didn't think at the time that having a picture floating around of one of my soldiers in drag was in the best interests of ... the intel mission, sir."[43] Adkins further acknowledged that since the unit was facing "manpower issues" and Manning was only one of two analysts tasked with the Shia insurgency, he felt "an indirect pressure knowing [that] ... the unit wanted to make sure that everyone who could possibly deploy would deploy."[44] These court documents reveal not only that the army knew about Manning's struggle with her gender identity and sexual orientation in advance of the leaks but that her chain of command deliberately chose to ignore warning signs about her mental health and failed to provide her with adequate treatment. As the military had been struggling with recruitment rates after the beginning of the Iraq War in 2003 and as many units were notoriously understaffed and overburdened, Manning's worthiness to the military consisted solely in her ability to consistently produce valuable intelligence. By prioritizing its mission over Manning's personal well-being, the military demonstrated little to no care for the individual soldier and (re)asserted its traditional role as a heteropatriarchal institution.

Manning's struggles with her gender identity were therefore well documented long before most mainstream media outlets caught on to it. And once media did catch on, they engaged in sensationalizing discussions about how these struggles were allegedly a major motive for Manning's disclosure of classified documents, what pronouns should be used to properly refer to her, whether she would be housed in an all-male correctional facility, and whether she could possibly get a "sex change" financed by taxpayer dollars.

Manning's request to be referred to by female pronouns left many editors rushing to their stylebooks and demonstrates the problematic use of gendered pronouns.[45] *The New York Times Manual of Style and Usage,* for example, states: "transgender (adj.) is an overall term for people whose current identity differs from their sex at birth, whether or not they have changed their biological characteristics. Cite a person's transgender status only when it is pertinent and its pertinence is clear to the reader. Unless a former name is newsworthy or pertinent, use the name and pronouns (he, his, she, her, hers) preferred by the transgender person."[46] Yet *Times* managing editor Dean Baquet argued that "readers would be totally confused if we turned on a dime overnight and changed the name and gender of a person in the middle of a major running news story."[47] A spokesperson for NPR declared, "Until Bradley Manning's desire to have his gender changed actually physically happens, we will be using male-related pronouns to identify him."[48] After some fumbling and pressure from advocacy groups such as GLAAD, several news outlets, including NPR, the Associated Press, and the *New York Times,* began switching to feminine pronouns and more gender-neutral references. However, several major news outlets refused to honor Manning's request and willfully misgendered her. CNN declared that it would continue to refer to Manning as male "since he has not yet taken any steps toward gender transition through surgery or hormone replacement therapy."[49] Fox News introduced a segment on Manning by playing Aerosmith's song "Dude (Looks Like a Lady)" in the background while juxtaposing a photograph of Manning in her military uniform with a grainy black and white photograph of her dressed in a wig and

Fig. 3. "Call Me Chelsea" segment on *Fox & Friends*, August 27, 2013. Screenshot.

makeup.[50] CNN showed the same photograph, arguing that "Manning is apparently a cross dresser ... a misunderstood, very confused young man who had some serious psychological issue."[51] And questioning court reporter Adam Klasfeld about Manning's gender identity on NPR's *Here and Now*, Robin Young prefaced their discussion with "a warning— [since the topic] may not be an appropriate conversation for all ears," only to emphasize that Manning was putting the military in "an awkward situation ... because they have an incoming inmate to an all-male prison, who has said she sees herself as a woman."[52] Manning's decision to transition elicited numerous transphobic responses from mainstream news outlets. Her request to respect her gender identity was ignored by most media; moreover, she was deliberately misgendered and psychopathologized as a mentally unstable threat to national security.

With sensationalized discussions, several media outlets immediately focused on whether Manning wanted "sex reassignment" surgery and whether taxpayers would have to cover the costs for her desired transition. In a *Today Show* interview, Savannah Guthrie repeatedly asked David Coombs: "Is it the bottom line you don't think she wants sex reassignment surgery or she doesn't think she'll be able to get it?" CNN ran numerous headlines over the following days announcing, "Manning wants sex change," "Is Bradley Manning entitled to gender change in prison?," and "Bradley Manning's sexual identity."[53] Similarly, the *O'Reilly Factor* deliberated whether Manning's demands for transgender health care could set a "dangerous precedent":

Bill O'Reilly: Chelsea, as the *New York Times* is now calling her, wants to set precedent bill. Wants to be the first person ever to have the U.S. government—

Lis Wiehl (Fox News legal analyst): —pay for the sex change. . . .

Kimberly Guilfoyle (Fox News legal analyst): He doesn't want equipment change[;] he just wants the hormones to become more feminine.[54]

These news commentaries not only reveal a typical tendency to conflate Manning's sexual orientation with her gender identity, but they further reflect the frequent media frenzy and sensationalism voiced around the idea of taxpayer money supporting transgender health care and an ignorant preoccupation with surgical procedures. They also reveal a deep-seated transphobic attitude toward gender-nonconforming people and continue the long-standing tradition of medicalizing trans identities as a psychological disease. While homosexuality was removed from the American Psychiatric Association's *Diagnostic and Statistical Manual of Mental Disorders* (DSM) in 1973, gender nonconformity is still listed in the current DSM as "gender dysphoria," previously known as "gender identity disorder." The erasure of Manning's transgender subjectivity and the prevalence of pathologizing and marginalizing discourses confirm the reduction, if not the outright denial, of gender fluidities that exist outside the traditional, hegemonically constructed gender binary.

The sensationalizing and ridiculing discourses surrounding Manning seem to follow a larger pattern of the media's tendency to specifically objectify transgender women. Julia Serano suggests that these discourses symbolize not only a persistent transphobia but more so a transmisogyny, precisely because the womanhood of trans women is not deemed legitimate.[55] These dominant representations of Manning speak not only to dehumanizing ways in which trans people are often characterized in the media but also to the ways in which cissexism—the belief that trans identities are somehow less authentic or inferior to those individuals whose gender identity matches the sex they were assigned at birth—and misogyny intersect in these discourses with severe effects on the lives of people identifying on the trans feminine spectrum. Unfortunately, few articles and broadcasts offered more nuanced coverage by explaining the difference between sexuality and gender identity or by contextualizing Manning's case more broadly with the widespread discrimination and disproportionate incarceration and criminalization that trans people, particularly those of color, often face.[56]

Finally, several news stories insisted that Manning and her defense team had deliberately used her gender identity struggles during her trial as an excuse for her actions: ABC reporter Josh Elliott proclaimed on *Good Morning America*, "The Army private who leaked thousands of secret government and military files to the website WikiLeaks now says that his gender identity crisis led him to do it."[57] And Richard Herman, a criminal defense attorney, debated with CNN anchor Fredricka Whitfield in the *Newsroom*, "He argued at trial that it was a defense. He said there was a connection. When he puts that wig and lipstick on, the guy's a dead ringer for Tonya Harding, isn't he? It didn't work. It was a silly defense, frankly."[58] Similar to the report from CNN's *Newsroom*, the prosecution around Maj. Ashden Fein emphasized during the closing arguments of Manning's court-martial that she was solely responsible for her own actions: "This is a case about PFC Manning, Your Honor. The army is not on trial. The command is not on trial. Mr. Adkins is not on trial. Behavioral health is not on trial."[59] Fein further proclaimed, "PFC Manning took an oath. He knew what he was doing. The army didn't abandon PFC Manning. PFC Manning abandoned the army. The army didn't betray PFC Manning, PFC Manning betrayed the army."[60]

Seizing on Manning's gender transition as a palpable explanation for her disclosures demonstrates the media's excessive psychopathologizing of her perceived gender deviance, "which makes perfect sense only if you blame the gender straightness of Bush and Blair for the invasion of Iraq,"[61] as civil rights attorney Chase Madar noted. Much more factual, however, is that neither Manning nor her defense team ever argued those struggles were relevant for her disclosure of the documents in question. During the defense's closing arguments, Coombs tried to paint Manning as an intelligent, caring, compassionate, and well-intentioned person who may have been a little naïve. Coombs explicitly stated that he was not offering these struggles as a mental health defense to excuse or "in any way to lessen PFC Manning's decisions on why he did what he did, but instead to explain the context, the circumstances surrounding it."[62] Moreover, in an apology statement to the court a couple of days later, Manning consciously declared, "At the time of my decisions, as you know, I was dealing with a lot of issues, issues that are ongoing and continuing to affect me. Although a considerable difficulty in my life, these issues are *not* an excuse for my actions."[63]

In their review of terrorism studies, Jasbir Puar and Amit Rai note how white mythologies of "pathological personalities" that emerge from negative childhood experiences, inconsistent mothering, and a damaged sense of self are frequently presented as psychological compulsions that determine and fix the mind of the terrorist.[64] As the detailed analyses of Manning's media coverage above reveal, similar pathologizing discourses ascribe meaning to Manning's actions, all reaching the conclusion that an internal confusion about her gender identity and sexuality led her to betray her country. Speculations about why Manning dared to send WikiLeaks the nation's "most closely guarded secrets" about U.S. carnage in Iraq and Afghanistan was frequently accompanied and explained by her portrayal as being unfit and not "man enough" for military service: in short, as someone who should have never been deployed in the first place, let alone given a top security clearance. Manning's initial casting as an effeminate gay man, a "sissy" who could not deal with the pressure and was mentally unstable aimed to feminize and discredit her. Moreover, the media's emasculating treatment continued even after Manning's transition because her womanhood was not deemed legitimate. As major news outlets focused on Manning's "gender identity disorder" portraying her as gender deviant, the press further psychopathologized her and actively worked to undermine the credibility of her actions and statements exposing U.S. military wrongdoing and abuse as a product of her mental health. This hegemonic portrayal of Manning exonerated the military from taking any responsibility for her or their actions, for example by acknowledging its systematic failures in providing support for soldiers struggling with sexuality and gender identity. Instead, news media actively fed into the racialization of Manning as an anti-American traitor. Additionally, the press's focus on Manning's gender identity as a motivation for her leaking classified documents, largely with the omission of her own account that she did so out of a "love for my country and a sense of duty to others."[65] This drew attention away from her questionable treatment in detention as well as her harsh sentence, paralleling the state's own conceptualization of Manning as an alien enemy and threat to national security.

The Haunting Ghosts of Guantánamo

Speaking truth and blowing the whistle on secretive and abusive foreign policy and military practices brought the wrath of the U.S. military judiciary upon Manning. While former JAG officer Tom Kenniff asserted on Fox News that "he's not a terrorist, he's a U.S. citizen, he's in uniform. He's entitled to all the rights anyone would enjoy in this trial,"[66] Manning's treatment in detention, the slow pace of the trial proceedings, and the Obama administration's vigorous pursuit of charging her with Article 104, aiding the enemy, have stirred debates about the transparency of the U.S. military justice system, the use of enhanced interrogation techniques and prolonged confinement practices, and statutory protections for whistleblowers. The state's constant surveillance, monitoring, and policing of Manning during her confinement and the denial of rights and privileges typically granted to U.S. citizens during trial proceedings together created Manning's status as a domestic alien enemy.

A Veil of Secrecy

Public access to Manning's pretrial hearings in 2011 was severely limited and put a questionable light on the transparency of the U.S. military justice system. During the pretrial proceedings, reporters were not allowed to carry any electronics into the courtroom, and wireless Internet service was disabled while the court was in session. Thus, reporters and activist bloggers had to rely mostly on their own handwritten notes to analyze and report about the proceedings. In October

2012 the Center for Constitutional Rights filed a lawsuit against the government for withholding basic court documents (including dockets of court activity, transcripts of the proceedings, and orders issued from the bench by military judge Col. Denise Lind) to seek greater public access. More than thirty news organizations also filed an amicus brief with the court protesting the restrictions. In February 2013 the Department of State finally announced the release of eighty-four out of roughly four hundred judicial court orders (some heavily redacted) for greater transparency and to circumvent the lawsuit. During Manning's actual court-martial from June through August 2013, the Freedom of the Press Foundation raised money to hire an unofficial stenographer to attend the trial and produce daily transcripts.

The lack of media coverage surrounding Manning's pretrial hearings mentioned earlier in the chapter was therefore partially due to restrictive media access. The redactions and extensive delays in releasing information from the trial proceedings further extended a veil of secrecy that deliberately prevented public access, which is a fundamental component of a public trial. This lack of public accessibility violated core protections provided to Manning by the First and Sixth Amendments, which guarantee both freedom for the press and the right to a public trial without unnecessary delay. David Carr aptly noted in the *New York Times* that "a public trial over state secrets was itself becoming a state secret in plain sight."[67]

Is Quantico the New Gitmo?

From the start of her confinement in June 2010 in Camp Arifjan, Kuwait, Manning, then only twenty-two years old, was repeatedly deprived of human contact and put on a "reverse sleep cycle" as part of "administrative segregation" (the military does not use the term *solitary confinement*). In July 2010 Manning was transferred from Kuwait to the Marine Corps Brig in Quantico, Virginia, and put on "suicide prevention":

I was also stripped of all clothing with the exception of my underwear. Additionally, my prescription eyeglasses were taken away from me. Due to not having my glasses, I was forced to sit in essential blindness during the day. . . . Under my current restrictions, in addition to being stripped at night, I am essentially held in solitary confinement. For 23 [hours a] day, I sit alone in my cell. The guards checked on me every five minutes during the day by asking me if I am okay. I am required to respond in some affirmative manner. At night, if the guards can not see me clearly, because I have a blanket over my head or I am curled up towards the wall, they will wake me in order to ensure that I am okay. I receive each of my meals in my cell. I am not allowed to have a pillow or sheets. . . . If I attempt to do push-ups, sit-ups, or any other form of exercise I am forced to stop by the guards.[68]

I had no personal items in my cell. If I wanted to use toilet paper, I had to ask for it from one of the Marines—then I had to return it when I was finished. I had no soap. I had limited access to toothpaste and a toothbrush—my teeth have been permanently damaged by this time period. And I had limited access to legal documents, books, or any other printed material.[69]

During pretrial hearings in November 2012, two psychiatrists who had evaluated Manning after her arrival at Quantico testified that brig officials repeatedly ignored their recommendations to remove her from suicide risk watch and subsequently from prevention of injury watch without further explanation, despite their assessment that she was not deemed a danger to herself or appeared depressed.[70] In March of 2011, P.J. Crowley, a State Department spokesperson and aide to Hillary Clinton, had to resign from office after calling Manning's treatment "ridiculous and counterproductive and stupid" and further arguing that the actions at the Quantico brig undercut the credibility and legitimacy of the prosecution.[71] Forced to respond to Crowley's comments, President Obama stated that the Pentagon had assured him that conditions of Manning's treatment were "appropriate."[72] Around the same time, Juan Méndez, the UN special rapporteur on torture, was denied a request for a private, unmonitored visit with Manning to investigate whether her treatment at Quantico amounted to torture. A statement by the Department of Defense (DoD) claimed: "As in the federal prison system, and for security reasons, DoD does not guarantee unmonitored communications with confinees except for privileged communications or in other special circumstances not present here."[73] The discourses surrounding Manning's treatment in detention disclose that the state deemed Manning a threat to national security that needed to be contained and warranted the military's use of extralegal forms of interrogation and confinement. These technologies of torture—constant observation and frequent interruption techniques—employed against her are well-worn tactics widely used on detainees in Iraq and Afghanistan, as well as in the infamous prison camp at Guantánamo Bay. Manning's treason and her alleged suicidal tendencies reduced her to alien status, rendering her undeserving of the rights conferred upon U.S. citizens and thus justifying her domestic treatment to mirror that of foreign terrorist others.

In 2011 a UN special report concluded that the U.S. government was guilty of "cruel, inhuman and degrading treatment" toward Manning. A similar conclusion was drawn by some 250 prominent lawyers, law professors, and legal scholars who published a letter in the *New York Review of Books* denouncing Manning's treatment as "illegal and immoral," violating the Eighth Amendment's prohibition of cruel and unusual punishment and the Fifth Amendment's ban against pretrial punishment.[74] An editorial in the *Nation* further asserted, "The treatment of Manning in Quantico, as well as the incarceration of inmates in CMUs [Communication Management Units] for no apparent penological purpose, demonstrates that the poisonous shards of Abu Ghraib are still with us." After nine months in solitary confinement, mounting public pressure, and negative press coverage, Manning was transferred to the Joint Regional Correctional Facility at Fort Leavenworth, Kansas. There Lt. Col. Dawn Hilton described her as a "typical detainee" who did not exhibit any significant mental health or behavioral issues after her arrival.[75] Yet, commenting on Manning's transfer, Jeh Johnson, then the Pentagon's general counsel, said: "Many will be tempted to interpret today's action as a criticism of the pre-trial facility at Quantico. That is not the case. We remain satisfied that Pte Manning's pre-trial confinement at Quantico was in compliance with legal and regulatory standards in all respects, and we salute the military personnel there for the job they did in difficult circumstances."[76] In January 2013 Manning was awarded with 112 days of credit for enduring unlawful treatment at Quantico. However, the judge denied a motion to dismiss all charges filed by the defense for lack of a speedy trial. Judge Colonel Lind further ruled that Manning's motive—prompted by the military's dehumanizing treatment of Iraqi and Afghani civilians and its strategic avoidance of public accountability for its morally and legally disputable actions by hiding behind classified information—was irrelevant to intent. This meant that the defense could not use motive during the merits portion of the trial—in other words, until Manning was found guilty or not guilty.[77] Nor was the defense allowed to elaborate on whether or not the WikiLeaks disclosures were actually damaging to U.S. national security. Precluding both of these issues severely limited the defense attorneys' ability to advance an argument about Manning's revelations as acts of whistleblowing in order to counter the prosecution's charge that she was deliberately aiding the enemy. Manning's actual court-martial proceedings finally began on June 3, 2013, after the now-twenty-six-year-old had spent more than one thousand days in pretrial detention.

Aiding the Enemy

Manning's othering was furthered by the government's insistence that with her disclosures, she actively and knowingly aided the enemy. Despite Manning's acknowledgment that while she could have sold the data to Russia or China to "make bank," she did not do so "because it's public data. . . . It belongs in the public domain,"[78] the prosecution's team around Maj. Ashden Fein was keen on portraying Manning as an arrogant, narcissistic anarchist who craved notoriety and had the deliberate, evil intent to share classified information with enemies of the United States, specifically Al-Qaeda: "Your Honor, PFC Manning was not a humanist; he was a hacker. . . . he was not a troubled young soul. He was a determined soldier with a knowledge, ability, and desire to harm the United States in its war effort. And, Your Honor, he was not a whistleblower; he was a traitor. A traitor who understood the value of compromised information in the hands of the enemy and took deliberate steps to ensure they, along with the world, received all of it."[79] The Obama administration's rigorous prosecution of whistleblowers under the presumption that leaking classified information to journalists or news organizations such as the *Guardian*, *Washington Post*, or WikiLeaks (which according to Yochai Benkler belongs to the "networked fourth estate") is tantamount to aiding the enemy is highly problematic as it attempts to inhibit the free flow of information. [80] Prosecutor Fein further emphasized that Manning's ruling should function to scare future whistleblowers, as "there is value in deterrence. . . . This court must send a message to any soldier contemplating stealing classified information."[81] Later on, a Department of Defense's review into the potential fallout from the WikiLeaks disclosures actually revealed that *not a single case* was found where an individual had been killed by enemy forces as a result of having been named in the leaked documents.[82] By leveling the aiding the enemy charge against Manning, the government painted her as someone who had willfully betrayed her country, and it foregrounded her status as a threat to national security—an alien enemy—who required immediate and permanent containment.

The case of Manning thus vividly illustrates how the use of the aiding the enemy charge, "enhanced interrogation techniques," and prolonged detention practices are grounded in discourses of a U.S. exceptionalism, ensuring that the security state does not have to adhere to the limits of juridical power because of the creation of a permanent "state of exception."[83] Manning's prolonged incarceration is a prominent example of how the operations of governmentality, understood as dispersed mentalities, rationalities, and techniques for governing individual bodies, territory, and populations within neoliberalism post-9/11 are increasingly extralegal without being illegal. Judith Butler argues that "when law becomes a tactic of governmentality, it ceases to function as a legitimating ground: *governmentality makes concrete the understanding of power as irreducible to law.*"[84] Indefinite detention practices and enhanced interrogation techniques thereby constitute an illegitimate exercise of power that has become part of a broader tactic to neutralize the rule of law in the name of security. These bio- and necropolitical mechanisms do not necessarily signify an exceptional circumstance, but rather the exception becomes established as naturalized norm in the state of emergency. Similarly, Giorgio Agamben emphasizes that "the exception does not subtract itself from the rule; rather, the rule, suspending itself, gives rise to the exception and maintaining itself in relation to the exception, first constitutes itself as a rule."[85] Manning becomes the *homo sacer*—the nonsubject excluded and banned not by being made indifferent and put outside of law but by being *abandoned* by it, exposed and threatened on the threshold in which life and law, inside and outside become indistinguishable.[86]

Conclusion

As the U.S. security state recycles and rearticulates discourses of exceptionalism through the War on Terror, the widespread acceptance of such techniques and practices employed against brown bodies abroad, whether in Abu Ghraib or at Guantánamo, now enables their use against U.S. citizens at home and allows Manning's domestic treatment to mirror that of foreign terrorist others. Perhaps even more importantly, Manning's case demonstrates that the process of effeminizing and sexualizing the other is always implicitly entangled with processes of racialization. Manning's "treason" and her ineptness to "properly" enact white heteromasculinity rendered her an othered alien enemy, a domestic nonsubject who was denied access to civil and human rights. While the security state shied away from imposing literal, physical death upon Manning, she is effectively caught in what Mbembe calls "death-worlds," wherein living conditions are so depraved, gruesome, and unbearable that their inhabitants are marked as "living dead."[87]

In her pardoning request to President Obama shortly after her sentencing, Manning carefully reflected on the United States' historically ambiguous relationship with patriotism: "Patriotism is often the cry extolled when morally questionable acts are advocated by those in power. When these cries of patriotism drown out any logically based dissension, it is usually the American soldier that is given the order to carry out some ill-conceived mission. Our nation has had similar dark moments for the virtues of democracy—the Trail of Tears, the Dred Scott decision, McCarthyism, and the Japanese-American internment camps—to mention a few. I am confident that many of the actions since 9/11 will one day be viewed in a similar light."[88] What the analyses of Manning's trial proceedings, court records, and mainstream media coverage between 2010 and 2014 demonstrate is that dominant discourses focusing on Manning's nonnormative upbringing and traits as a motivation for her leaking classified documents paralleled the state's own conceptualization of Manning as a traitor of the state. The media coverage provided a rationale for the state's surveillance and extralegal treatment of Manning by tying her sexual and gender nonconformity to mental instabilities that threatened state interests. Manning's case reasserts Lawrence Grossberg's observations that "peoples' identities are defined precisely by the complex articulations between their different positions in a variety of systems of social difference."[89] These articulations form a nexus of discourses that inscribe, produce, manage, and discipline transgender lives (and deaths) according to sexualized, gendered, racialized, and classed logics of what constitutes proper gender identity within the traditional gender binary and the state's conceptualization of safety and security. The next chapter interrogates more closely why Manning's revelations also rendered her a controversial figure within the LGBT movement, especially during a moment where national LGB(T) organizations were focusing significant energy and monetary investments on the repeal of DADT.

2

TRANSPATRIOTISM AND
ITERATIONS OF EMPIRE

WE are right at a point in HISTORY were many people are beginning to understand who we are as Transgender, DIVERSE, and that we are just like everyone else. WE ARE ONE. Now Manning just dirtied the hope of a truly FREE America. Dr. Martin Luther King Jr.['s] "I have a Dream" speech was 50 years ago. . . . I am still hoping for HIS dream of equality for ALL. America to be a beacon of Freedom and equality. . . . Manning is a tarnish on my dream, he [sic] is a tarnish on Dr. King['s] Dream.

Kristin Beck, former U.S. Navy SEAL and transgender veteran, in a Facebook post, August 22, 2013

On April 26, 2013, the San Francisco Pride Celebration committee retracted an earlier statement making Chelsea Manning a grand marshal for its annual parade, which usually honors celebrities, politicians, and community organizations for their contributions to LGBTQ communities, calling her appointment a "mistake" and "error." The official retraction statement released by then–SF Pride board president Lisa Williams emphasized the potential harm Manning's actions had inflicted: "Even the hint of support for actions which placed in harm's way the lives of our men and women in uniform—and countless others, military and civilian alike—will not be tolerated by the leadership of San Francisco Pride. It is, and would be, an insult to every one, gay and straight, who has ever served in the military of this country. . . . Bradley Manning will have his day in court, but will not serve as an official participant in the SF Pride Parade."[1] Echoing Williams's statement, Sean Sala, a prominent gay military activist in the Bay Area and navy veteran, threatened to launch a campaign to boycott the parade if Manning was honored: "San Francisco has spit in the face of LGBT Military by using a traitor to our country as a poster child." Sala further added, "Manning makes Gay military, the Armed Forces and cause of equality look like a sham. We have spent fifty years trying to garnish equality and Manning cannot and will not represent Gay Military patriots."[2] Similarly, Stephen Peters, president of American Military Partner Association, a group that advocates for same-sex military families, had called on the Pride Committee to rescind the invitation as "Manning's blatant disregard for the safety of our service members and the security of our nation should not be praised. . . . No community of such a strong and resilient people should be represented by the treacherous acts that define Bradley Manning."[3] Further labeling Manning's actions a "disgrace," Josh Seefried from OutServe-SLDN (Servicemembers Legal Defense Network) explicitly warned that after just winning the Don't Ask, Don't Tell repeal, honoring Manning would send the wrong signal to the military community that "we think he is some sort of hero."[4] Not surprisingly, then, Manning was replaced with safer and less contentious political choices reflecting the allegedly successful inclusion of LGBT people into the nation-state represented by various celebrities such as BeBe Sweetbriar, a popular San Franciscan drag performer, and Alex Newell, who is best known for his role as Wade "Unique" Adams on *Glee* (2009-15).

In recent years the LGBT movement has gained unprecedented legal victories, most importantly marriage equality, granting recognition and rights to certain gay and lesbian citizens. In sharp contrast, the retraction of Manning's nomination as a grand marshal for the SF Pride march in April 2013 and the disparaging media coverage surrounding her story—especially following Manning's public coming out as trans in her announcement in August 2013—provides insight into the many contradictions plaguing assimilationist, single-issue politics advanced by many national LGB(T) organizations and presents a significant moment for analyzing contemporary sexual and gender identity politics within the neoliberal security state.

In this chapter, I engage Manning's story to reveal how her "treacherous" and "terrorist" acts are incongruous with the assimilationist politics advanced by groups such as the HRC and break with idealized narratives of a U.S. sexual exceptionalism that promotes a seamless incorporation of queers into the workings of U.S. empire.[5] Manning's story points to the intricate ways in which the boundaries between discourses of gay and transgender identities cannot be neatly separated from one another but are inherently porous and oscillating. Yet there is a tendency among some scholars and mainstream LGBT organizers to eradicate the specificity of trans identities and experiences by using *queer* as a broad umbrella term to deflect attention away from a persistent investment in narrowly aligned gay and lesbian identity politics. Manning's case, therefore, not only highlights the importance of paying attention to the nuances and interplay between sexual orientation and gender identity; her story also induces us to ask whether transgender communities still remain a constituency outside of mainstream lesbian and gay politics.

In 2014 a special issue of *QED: A Journal in GLBTQ Worldmaking* assembled a diverse list of contributors, ranging from queer scholars, activists, and journalists to artists, to provide commentary on how mainstream LGBTQ politics turned away from Manning and her retraction as a 2013 SF Pride marshal.[6] While these articles succinctly identified the split between the mainstream gay rights movement and more radical, grassroots queer politics supporting Manning, I move beyond descriptions of her being caught between these tensions to specifically engage frameworks of U.S. sexual exceptionalism to theorize more thoroughly *why* she has been such a contentious figure for the LGBT movement.

Puar argues that contemporary forms of U.S. sexual exceptionalism rely not only on extraordinary forms of national heteronormativity but on the deployment of certain domesticated homosexual bodies to reinforce U.S. nationalism and patriotism—what she calls "homonationalism." Puar specifically suggests that "the Orientalist invocation of the terrorist is one discursive tactic that disaggregates U.S. national gays and queers from racial and sexual others," particularly Muslim others.[7] Manning's treatment demonstrates that the inclusion of some subjects into these exceptionalist frameworks is always provisional. I argue that Manning's revelations not only rendered her incompatible with homonational projects, but her actions and her fluctuation between gay and trans identities generated a new set of conservative, militaristic discursive formations that were promoted by other transgender veterans and that I call *transpatriotism*.

While Puar's work addresses the deployment of certain domesticated gay, lesbian, and queer bodies for the reinforcement of nationalist projects, she specifically acknowledges that "national homosexuality" does not include "two-spirit identity among other formations."[8] Because homonationalism leaves unexplored *if* and *how* trans and gender-nonconforming identities are deployed for similar purposes, I introduce the concept of transpatriotism to address this critical omission and to achieve a more concise mapping of the intersections between trans and gender-nonconforming identities, nationalism, and U.S. empire. By suggesting that current formations and modalities of U.S. empire are legitimated through transpatriotism, I trace how certain transgender subjectivities have been deployed for nationalist and militaristic means.

The rescinding of Manning's SF Pride nomination and the pathologizing of her as a deviant traitor indicate how easily particular subjects can be removed from the tenuous liberal representations of assimilationist politics. Such queer strivings for equality may weaken, if not deny, the legitimacy of more critical engagements with sexuality, gender, citizenship, and the state. This chapter, therefore, begins by scrutinizing the gay and lesbian mobilization against the military's DADT policy to reveal how homonormative quests for gay military inclusion elide any acknowledgment of the imperialist workings of the military-industrial complex. I then contrast Manning's story with DADT poster child and gay "model minority" Dan Choi as well as transgender veteran Kristin Beck to critique formations of homonational and transpatriotic discourses that uncritically support the incorporation of queer and trans people into U.S. empire. I conclude with a critique of the current push for trans inclusion in the military as an extension of transpatriotic discourse, and by highlighting the most recent developments in Manning's case, most notably President Obama's commutation of her sentence in 2017.

From Grassroots Struggle to Queer Domestication and War Participation?

Arguably, the exigencies of the LGBT movement have changed substantially in the past fifty years, as sexual politics has devolved from a grassroots struggle for liberation into an increasingly liberal program of social assimilation. *Queer* once described activism that critiqued a range of institutionalizations, normalizations, and exclusions while arguing for more radical forms of social justice. The term is now often used in conjunction with a particular type of gay and lesbian politics narrowly aligned with economic interests in neoliberalism and whiteness. SF Pride, for example, which has been held annually since 1971 and is one of the country's largest and most renowned pride festivals, has become increasingly commodified and corporatized over the past few years, straying away from its roots of proud political dissent as voiced in Compton's Cafeteria riots in 1966.[9] Potentially losing key corporate sponsors, such as Clear Channel, Bank of America, and Hilton Hotels and Resorts, may well have played a role in the decision to drop Manning as a grand marshal in 2013. Indeed, it may seem as if SF Pride nowadays is really all about "selling as much Absolut vodka as possible," as one commentator on Facebook responded to SF Pride board president Williams's statement.[10]

Unfortunately, with an agenda dominated by same-sex marriage and military inclusion—the Few, the Proud, the Gays, to adapt the U.S. Marines' famous recruitment slogan—the *en vogue* language of gay rights distorts and erases the historic alliance between radical politics and queer politics, at whose core has been a struggle for sexual freedom and challenges to the status quo. Thus, the emergence of homonormative, assimilationist single-issue politics since the 1990s and the "gains" achieved for U.S. LGBT citizen-subjects—for example, via increased media representations of and niche marketing for LGBT people, the possibility for gay marriage and adoption, the passing of the Matthew Shepard and James Byrd Jr. Hate Crimes Prevention Act, or the repeal of DADT—must be read within larger neoliberal, capitalist, and imperial contexts, especially the 1996 Welfare Reform Act and expansionist U.S. foreign policy conducted in the wake of 9/11.[11] Chandan Reddy identifies this contemporary political moment as a "freedom with violence"—a unique structure of state violence integrated with social emancipation. According to Reddy, in arguments for citizen rights LGBT advocates have appealed to the liberalism of the state under the rubric of equality, positioning the state as the ultimate enabler and guarantor of equality: "Even if this standpoint identifies the state as the source of grievance, injury, or horrific exposure to arbitrary violence, its epistemological assumptions ultimately affirm the value of that very state formation." David Eng aptly describes this confluence of political and economic conditions that form the basis of liberal inclusion, rights, and recognition for particular gay and lesbian U.S. citizens as a "queer liberalism."[12]

In their efforts to overturn the military's DADT policy, national LGBT groups such as GetEQUAL or the Lambda Legal Defense and Education Fund emphasized that the discriminatory policy actually damaged military readiness, effectiveness, and national security.[13] These groups maintained that openly serving troops would have no negative effect on unit cohesion, recruitment, and retention, which a report commissioned by the Department of Defense in 2010 had concluded as well.[14] The arguments advanced in favor of repealing DADT are emblematic of a queer liberalism, invoking narratives of inclusion and progress, promoting domestic and international security, and implicitly affirming imperialist U.S. foreign policy.

The public discourse surrounding DADT had changed substantially in the last decade with 67 percent of Americans saying that they would vote for a law allowing gays and lesbians to serve openly in the U.S. military in 2010.[15] Numerous LGBT groups such as the HRC and the SLDN heightened their lobbying efforts and monetary investments in 2010 for "gays in the military" by joining forces with a "Countdown 2010" grassroots campaign to push for the passage of the DADT Repeal Act. Their campaigns effectively characterized DADT as discriminatory by emphasizing humanizing narratives of gay and lesbian service members who were facing discharge under the policy.[16] However, what was left unaddressed in these campaigns was the fact that due to the involvement in two costly wars in Afghanistan and Iraq, the military was facing recruitment shortfalls and in desperate need for more personnel in the expanding global War on Terror. In their zealous efforts pushing for DADT repeal, many LGBT groups as well as gender and sexuality studies scholars failed to acknowledge important oppressive intersectionalities entrenched in military service. For example, the military remains the nation's largest employer and job program for poor and working-class people and often the only means for access to better living standards; African American women were disproportionally discharged under DADT; and military enlistment is advertised as an expedited "pathway to citizenship" for undocumented immigrants.[17]

On September 20, 2011, President Obama announced the end of DADT, emphasizing that the repeal would "enhance our national security, increase our military readiness, and bring us closer to the principles of equality and fairness that define us as Americans."[18] Because the promotion of homonormative enterprises and strategies, such as the SF Pride Celebration or the repeal of DADT, do not challenge the interdependence of the homo- and transphobic, racist, sexist, classist, and imperialist operations of the U.S. military-industrial complex, or seek to alleviate economic injustice, it is essential to ask: what is really to be gained from LGBT military inclusion? Manning's case, as analyzed in the next section, demonstrates that this supposed inclusion in the service of U.S. imperialism is contingent and often fleeting. Moreover, these discourses of sexual and, as I argue, gendered exceptionalism that advertise inclusion actually serve to maintain the oppression of marginalized communities both inside and outside the United States.

Fractures in Homonationalism

Observing in particular the LGBT media's reception of Manning, Victoria Brownworth notes that Manning's story never became a cause célèbre for major LGBT publications. Covering Manning's case for the *Advocate*, Brownworth frequently heard that "there's no real LGBT/local angle here," which contrasted starkly with mainstream media's pathologizing focus on Manning's alleged sexual and gender transgressions.[19] At a time when national LGBT organizations were rallying for DADT repeal and LGBT media were filled with heart-wrenching discharge stories, Manning's revelations presented an unpredictable liability. LGBT outlets seemed aware that giving Manning's story a platform could undermine these lobbying efforts. As mainstream media reports pathologized Manning as a mentally unstable "freak" and as the legal system arguably failed her, which I demonstrated in the previous chapter, Manning's immediate retraction as grand marshal for the SF Pride Parade in 2013 and the silence around her case from major

LGBT advocacy groups is indicative of how easily one can be removed from the spectacle of gay pride and how tenuous these liberal models of inclusionary politics are. Manning's story thus illustrates that the inclusion of particular subjects into what Puar terms "homonationalism" is always provisional.[20]

No commentary better encapsulates the schisms between a mainstream LGBT movement that feels compelled to condemn homophobia *abroad* but fails to recognize its own complicity in oppressive mechanisms and institutions *at home* than a two-minute outburst by conservative gay columnist James Kirchick on the Kremlin-financed news channel Russia Today during live coverage of Manning's court-martial in August 2013: "I'm not really interested in talking about Bradley Manning; I'm interested in talking about the horrific environment of homophobia in Russia right now, and to let the Russian gay people know that they have friends and allies and solidarity from people all over the world, and that we're not going to be silent in the face of this horrific repression that is perpetrated by your paymasters, by Vladimir Putin. That's what I'm here to talk about."[21] Kirchick's staunch display of patriotic homonationalism vowing to support and stand up for gay Russians facing prosecution under Putin illustrates his investment in exporting an often paternalizing Western "gay rights are human rights" agenda. Manning's case on the other hand does not easily lend itself to advance such (neo)imperial projects. As we find ourselves at a juncture in contemporary LGBT politics where certain racially and economically privileged, homonormative, able-bodied, middle-class queers are gaining access to rights associated with citizenship and their humanity is recognized, a whole group of nonsubjects is created as well. The granting of constitutional rights to certain queer bodies and identities comes at a time when the United States is in a state of perpetual war, waged predominantly against bodies of color at home and abroad: while killing hundreds of thousands of civilians in recent conflicts and ongoing counterterrorism operations, domestic prisons function as the "new Jim Crow" for the containment of the "detritus of contemporary capitalism."[22] Given this context, the question is: whose bodies must be criminalized and obliterated in order to produce the good, homonormative, queer subject at home?[23]

The figure of Chelsea Manning presents a clear contrast to Lt. Dan Choi, an infantry officer with a deployment to Iraq, who was discharged under DADT in 2009 after coming out on *The Rachel Maddow Show*:

> By saying three words to you today, I am gay, those three words are a violation of Title 10 of the U.S. Code. It's a code that is polluted by the people who . . . want us to lie about our identity. It is an immoral code and goes up against every single [thing] that we were taught at West Point with our honor code. The honor code says a cadet will not lie, cheat, steal. . . . Being an Iraq combat veteran, an Arabic linguist, a West Point graduate, I come back to America as a second-class citizen who's forced to lie because of this rule, because of this law.[24]

Homonationalism became a key sentiment invoked in the dominant media discourses surrounding Dan Choi, whose charisma, articulateness, and outspokenness gave a voice and face to the DADT repeal campaign. By handcuffing himself to the gates of the White House in protest of his discharge, Choi quickly became a cover model for patriotic gays everywhere and the "darling" of groups such as GetEQUAL and the HRC. Over the next year, Choi's story could be found in major newspapers and magazines and on numerous networks, including a feature in the *Atlantic* that declared him a "brave thinker" as well as appearances on ABC News, NBC's *Nightly News*, Al-Jazeera, and CNN's *Anderson Cooper 360*. Choi repeatedly toured the country, attending gay rights rallies and lecturing on college campuses. Choi, a Korean American, thereby presented the ideal image of the patriotic homonational West Point graduate (with degrees in Arabic and environmental engineering), feeding into discourses surrounding Asian Americans as the hardworking model minority.

In public interviews lobbying for the repeal of DADT, Choi frequently insisted, "war is a force that gives us meaning. War is a force that teaches us lessons of humanity."[25] But he also asserted, "I've never been incarcerated, and for something that I thought was not my country's mission. I know my country's mission is not to make an entire group of people into second-class citizens."[26] Despite lamenting, "It's hard to know that all of a sudden, I'm the terrorist," Choi maintained a strong devotion to the country he once pledged to die for: "I still love

Fig. 4. Dan Choi in *The Atlantic*'s "Brave Thinkers" special issue, November 2010. Courtesy of Ben Baker/Redux.

free speech, and I still love America"—"those feelings don't go away because you were betrayed."[27] Dan Choi's story mirrors other narratives of patriotic gay and lesbian service members that have proliferated in homonationalist discourses used to reinforce national authority and coherence in the wake of 9/11.

While Choi encountered racism firsthand in the military as a group of cadets during rifle training announced that the target was "'a chinky-eyed, flat-faced gook in North Korea on the DMZ [demilitarized zone],'" he seemed unable to understand the interconnections between military racism, homophobia, and the enduring War on Terror.[28] Given the disproportionate use of violence enacted by the military against poor people and people of color both within the United States and abroad, the public discourse surrounding Choi erases the paradoxes of an Asian American gay soldier who considers himself a second-class citizen of the United States living under "the oppression of 'Don't Ask, Don't Tell'" while his sexuality was deployed to support the global War on Terror.[29] Unreflectively seeking such institutional inclusion represents a commitment to an uncritical agenda that fails to see how traditional logics of sexuality and gender are strategically deployed by the security state in the service of colonialism, racism, and militarism. While Choi's exemplar status as a model minority and gay patriot was celebrated and provided at least temporary incorporation into U.S. exceptionalism, Manning's lack of such patriotic devotion and her "ultimate betrayal" of the homeland and (both hetero- and homonormative) whiteness, meant that she was ostracized as the alien enemy.

However, since his crusade for DADT repeal, Dan Choi has had to reckon with intersecting oppressions that have isolated him from family members and the mainstream LGBT movement. Choi's "fall from grace" shows the contingency of his acceptance into the nation. In an article for the *American Prospect* from December 2013, Gabriel Arana alleges that by conflating activism with celebrity, Choi "had fallen in love with his own martyrdom."[30] Arana chronicles Choi's struggles with mental breakdowns and burnouts since the end of the DADT campaign, accompanied by drug use and treatment for his bipolar disease. According to such media discourses, Choi's sexual identity still causes him to be shunned by his Southern Baptist family, who disapproves of his lifestyle. While Choi was initially included in and praised by LGBT advocacy groups and numerous liberal mainstream media outlets for exemplifying homonationalism, his story is much more complex than the discourses surrounding him during the DADT repeal campaign suggest. Choi's temporary inclusion based on his sexual identity through the challenge to DADT was limited because of the oppressive intersectionalities he is subject to—racism, homophobia, and ableism. Choi's claim to inclusion through an assertion of his homomasculinity still left him open to extraction from that narrative and thus excluded from the nation-state. In other words, Choi's professing his gayness does not necessarily open a pathway for cultural citizenship. The dominant discourses encompassing Choi make explicit that people in and of themselves are not homonational but are discursively constructed as such through powerful media narratives—a process that is never quite complete and always conditional.

Importantly, Choi, who also served in Manning's unit in Iraq (though at a different time), has been a staunch supporter of her. When Choi was attending a pretrial military hearing for Manning in December 2011, he was pinned down by military police because he was allegedly disrupting the court hearing. In an interview with *Democracy Now!*, Choi later explained that his attendance at the court hearing in uniform as an Iraq vet and someone who proudly served was meant to show support for Manning, which presented a clear provocation to the army.[31] When asked about his support for Manning, Choi praised Manning's ethical righteousness that demanded the support from "patriotic Americans" and emphasized that he did not stand up for her because they shared an "identity as gay Americans" but because Manning was "a good soldier—in fact, the only soldier in his entire chain of command who did the right thing."[32] Choi's reflections attest to an interesting moment of affinity between the discourses of liberal inclusion, equality, and Manning's actions, which disrupted the imperialist workings of the military-industrial complex. Choi also pointed to the fact that none of the national LGB(T) organizations had spoken out for Manning. Choi empathetically asserted that the gay community "is the only community in the entire world that bases its membership, the price of admission, on *integrity* and *telling the truth* about ourselves, essentially declassifying something that people deserve to know, that's important to our soul, our community, exactly who we are. And when we hide that, that's what damages not only the *safety, but the reputation and the security, of our entire society*."[33] The values of integrity and ethical responsibility that Choi repeatedly evokes in the interview and that guided Manning in her decision to release the documents were omitted from mainstream media coverage. Moreover, Manning's failure to enact homonormative whiteness rendered her unworthy of attention by other national LGB(T) groups, such as the HRC, SLDN, or Lambda. Despite John Pilger's aptly titled commentary in the *New Statesman*, "Never forget that Bradley Manning, not gay marriage, is the issue," none of these groups that had been actively involved in the DADT repeal issued a single statement concerning Manning's case during her trial proceedings.[34]

Shortly after Manning announced her desire to transition in August 2013, HRC's then–vice president Jeff Krehely released a statement urging the media to treat her transition with dignity and respect and advocated for appropriate medical care and protection in prison. However, he concluded by emphasizing that "there are transgender service members and veterans who serve and have served this nation with honor, distinction and great sacrifice. We must not forget or dishonor those individuals. Pvt. Manning's experience is not *a proxy* for any other transgender man or woman who wears the uniform of the United States."[35] Reasserted here is an image of honorable, self-sacrificing trans people who proudly serve, an image Manning apparently does not reflect. Failing to advance narratives of homonationalism, Manning's story therefore encourages us to look more closely at current iterations of U.S. empire that legitimate themselves through the fairly recent emergence of transpatriotism, engendered through exceptional forms of transnormativity that are grounded in an unmarked whiteness and a reassertion of the gender binary.

Transpatriotism

While "trans people have often been positioned as the innocent Other of homonationalism" and on the receiving end of the War on Terror, transgender veterans' responses to Manning's actions and her coming out bolstered support for U.S. empire and revealed complicit participation in its expansion, predicated on narratives of diversity and colorblindness.[36] Brynn Tannehill, a trans woman and former lieutenant commander in the navy who serves as spokesperson for SPART*A, a group representing mostly active-duty LGBT service members, exclaimed that "our view is Manning's gender identity—no matter what it is—does not justify what he did."[37] Similarly, Autumn Sandeen, a navy veteran and trans activist wrote on the *TransAdvocate* blog, "I'm cognizant that Chelsea didn't respect the trans community—the trans community of which I am a part—in how she came out. . . . There is no honor in harming the community to which you are entering. . . . Chelsea, as a sibling in both military and trans community, hasn't earned my respect."[38] Former U.S. Navy SEAL Kristin Beck, who came out as transgender in June 2013 and received much publicity for her memoir *Warrior Princess: A U.S. Navy SEAL's Journey to Coming Out Transgender* and the documentary *Lady Valor: The Kristin Beck Story*, also accused Manning of using her gender identity as an excuse to act badly: "What you wear, what color you are, your religion, race, ethnicity, sexual orientation, gender identity has no basis on whether you are a CRIMINAL or NOT."[39]

Despite Manning's taking full responsibility for her actions and asserting that her struggles with mental health and gender identity were "not an excuse," the foregoing statements questioned Manning's gender identity as legitimate, sutured her actions specifically to her trans identity, and simultaneously revealed a broader contempt for identity politics in this current moment.[40] However, this disavowal of Manning's gender identity precisely calls attention to the norms of "the trans community." The construction of this community relies on the logics of the gender binary as well as the implicit whiteness bestowed on those who help to further the hegemony of U.S. empire. The trans community that Beck articulates and that Manning is excluded from is an expression of transpatriotism.

In her memoir, which is full of accounts of military prowess and heroism, Beck makes several problematic nationalist statements, for example, about the Taliban in Afghanistan being "the worst women haters in the world," and upon recounting an incident where she was harassed and kicked by a group of African American teenagers, Beck writes, "There was something very ironic . . . about black kids attacking [me] for being a 'minority.' *Fucking prejudiced bigots*."[41] Beck's transpatriotism is rooted in a xenophobia that accuses Afghanis and ethnic minorities of harboring profound (trans)misogynist attitudes. In what can only be described as a vicious tirade, Beck continued to describe Manning as a liar, thief, and traitor who allegedly came out as trans in order to stay alive in prison:

> Let me pose a scenario. . . .
> LEVANWORTH-very tough place with a lot of Marines and others who defended AMERICA and are spending a year or two there for mistakes and bad conduct. Minor sentences, but still loyal to American interest.
> GENERAL Prison population: Tough place to be in any prison.
> MEDIA: Manning is know[n] to every person in the prison.
> SOLITARY: option for Manning to stay alive, but very lonely and its punishment.

TRANSGENDER: Most prisons have special accommodations to ensure safety for that person.

OUTCOME: Manning shows one photo or a few "Halloween" photos o[f] him and some of his friends dabbled? These photos are released and a story is unfolded. . . . He is Chelsea and protected in special accommodations.

He will not be in general population where his life expectancy would be about a year tops. . . . He is now using something AGAIN for his own gain.[42]

Not only do Beck's accusations match those of right-wing conservative talk show hosts that consistently misgendered Manning, but her claim that transgender people receive "special accommodations" in prison to protect them presents a problematic and flawed belief in the military and in the realities of the prison-industrial complex. By alleging that solitary confinement is a benign means to protect Manning from other inmates, Beck ignores the fact that prisoners frequently face violence at the hands of correctional guards, that prolonged isolation poses significant mental and psychological harm to prisoners, and that trans people of color are disproportionally criminalized and incarcerated to begin with.[43] Beck's assertion that Manning's actions sullied "many other transgender people who are beacons of righteousness" and the "hope of a truly FREE America" as she "is a tarnish on Dr. King's Dream," signals the emergence of transpatriotism.[44]

The evocation of a "truly free America" and of Martin Luther King Jr. demonstrates how the discourse of transpatriotism is predicated on a narrative of American progress and equality that signals entry into an allegedly colorblind society. Transpatriotism, which symbolizes the presumed inclusion of marginalized trans communities into the national imaginary, thus functions to legitimize U.S. empire. Such comments from transgender veterans like Tannehill, Sandeen, and Beck reveal that in order to be recognized as a member of the trans community it is essential to perform nationalism and proudly display patriotic devotion. For transgender veterans, patriotism indicates not only a cultural and social belonging within the nation but the right to represent the nation as a patriot. *Both* homonationalism and transpa-

Fig. 5. Kristin Beck speaking at a conference about perspectives on transgender military service in Washington DC in 2014. Courtesy of Nicholas Kamm/Getty Images.

triotism allow subjects to become part of U.S. sexual exceptionalism, a discourse firmly grounded in the gender binary, heteronormativity, and U.S. imperialism. *Both* homonationalism and transpatriotism ruthlessly police boundaries of acceptable racial, gender, sexual, and class performances by exceptionalizing certain subjectivities vis-à-vis modes of racialized, sexualized, and pathologized othering. But, while homonationalism is primarily concerned with bolstering heterosexuality as the norm rather than upending it, transpatriotism specifically functions to (re)assert the gender binary, negating any (gender) fluidity. To be a true transpatriot one must adhere to and uphold that binary.

Enabled through the security state's imperial warfare since 9/11 and drawing on hetero- and homonormative ideals of securing citizenship rights, transpatriotism allows for the inclusion and recognition of certain privileged white normative trans bodies into assimilationist frameworks of liberal equality and U.S. exceptionalism at the expense of marginalized trans communities, particularly those of color—a process that is inherently racialized despite occurring in a putatively free and equal society. Anna Agathangelou, Daniel Bassichis, and Tamara Spira argue that the (re)consolidation of empire works through the constant demonization and demolition of the racially and sexually aberrant. While certain classes of subjects are invited into the folds of empire (e.g., Dan Choi or Kristin Beck), there are always othered bodies of (non)subjects (e.g., Chelsea Manning) "whose quotidian deaths become the grounding on which spectacularized murder becomes possible."[45] While these patriotic transgender veterans deny Manning a right to her subjectivity, it is important to acknowledge that Manning's whiteness still provides her with privileges, recognition, and media visibility compared to trans women of color who are disproportionately victims of violence. I therefore want to differentiate Manning's racialization—a result of her nonnormative sexual and gender identity, as explained in the previous chapter—from other processes of racialization that trans people of color face.

The discourses surrounding Manning reflect how within contemporary neoliberal societies freedom, rights, and citizenship for certain queer and trans people are simultaneously tied to institutionalized and legitimated violence enacted against others. Transgender veterans who ostracized Manning for allegedly betraying national security rendered her a treacherous black sheep of the trans community who deliberately used her struggles with gender identity as a pretext for her deeds. Along with a number of media commentators, these trans veterans deem Manning to be worthy neither of U.S. exceptionalism nor of the rights and privileges—for example, to a fair and speedy trial—granted to other U.S. citizens. Manning becomes the nonsubject against whom the security state enacts legitimized violence. Her case vividly demonstrates how transpatriotism reasserts the hegemony of white heteromasculinity, heteropatriarchy, and U.S. imperialism.

Trans Inclusion in the Military? Final Lessons from Assimilationist Politics

Despite receiving multiple nominations for the Nobel Peace Prize and the prestigious Sam Adams Award, which honors intelligence professionals who have taken a stand for integrity and ethics, Manning was sentenced to thirty-five years in prison in August 2013, concluding the

U.S. government's case against her. A total of 1,294 days were deducted from her sentence for her time spent in military custody, and she was "compensated" with another 112 days for harsh treatment endured at the Quantico marine base. Manning's sentence represented the longest ever handed down for a leak of U.S. government information and would have put her behind bars for most of her adult life. An editorial in the *Guardian* called the sentence "both unjust and unfair," as her prison term far exceeded other military convictions.[46] Charles Garner, for example, received a ten-year sentence for his role in the Abu Ghraib scandal.

After sentencing her, the security state expanded its violent repression of Manning's gender identity by denying Manning access to hormone therapy treatment. In September 2014 the American Civil Liberties Union (ACLU) filed a suit on behalf of Manning demanding that she receive treatment for her official diagnosis with "gender dysphoria," including psychological treatment, hormone therapy, and gender-affirmation surgery.[47] In February 2015 *USA Today* obtained an internal military memo that approved Manning to receive hormone therapy treatment.[48] She was, however, still prohibited from engaging in "female hair grooming," and the military persistently failed to follow recommendations made by its own medical providers. Although Manning had already legally changed her name to Chelsea in April 2014, it took until March 2015 before an army appeals court ordered the military to stop referring to Manning as male and employ either gender-neutral language or use feminine pronouns in all its legal filings.[49] The military's tentative decision to finally recognize Manning's gender identity presented a small victory. Yet due to lack of adequate care, Manning was living, in her own words, through "a cycle of anxiety, anger, hopelessness, loss, and depression" and attempted to die by suicide in July 2016.[50] The military further punished Manning for attempting to take her own life by placing her in solitary confinement, where Manning "tried it again because the feeling of hopelessness was so immense" and began a hunger strike.[51] Manning's ordeals inside the U.S. Disciplinary Barracks speak volumes about the military's lack of adequate mental health care and points to the tremendous state violence and bureaucratic hurdles that many incarcerated trans people face.

As Manning's gender nonconformity and framing as an alien enemy continued to cast her as a threat to the nation-state and national security, warranting her permanent containment, what, then, is the real liberatory value of a gay and trans rights agenda that seeks acceptance by and entrance into repressive state systems? Addressing Manning's case from a critical queer and trans politics perspective forces an acknowledgment, not only of the specific discriminatory policies of the military, but also of the very purpose of the military and its conditional incorporation of certain nonnormative groups for the purpose of U.S. expansionism. Writing editorials from prison in 2014, Manning voiced her grave concerns about the possibility that an eruption of civil war in Iraq would necessitate a potentially renewed U.S. intervention. She specifically blamed limitations on press freedoms and excessive government secrecy "for making it impossible for Americans to grasp fully what is happening in the wars we finance."[52] Despite Manning's concerns, the push for transgender inclusion in the military has been the most recent hot agenda item for many mainstream LGBT organizations—many of those, such as the HRC, are the very organizations that were unsupportive of Manning during her trial and have well-documented histories of ignoring trans people and trans issues in their advocacy.

Notwithstanding the repeal of DADT in 2011, the military has continued to ban transgender soldiers from serving, citing medical reasons. In recent years, trans inclusion advocacy initiatives have gained prominence, spearheaded by billionaire investor and longtime service member Col. Jennifer Natalya Pritzker, who announced her transition in 2013 and is an heir to the Hyatt Hotel fortune. In July 2013 Pritzker's well-endowed Tawani Foundation awarded a $1.35 million grant to the Palm Center, a think tank that played a crucial role in DADT repeal and conducts research around gender and sexuality in the military, to launch a multiyear research initiative about trans military inclusion.

Because of the ban on trans soldiers, studying transgender service members and veterans has been notoriously difficult. As part of the Palm Center initiative, Brandon Hill and his colleagues conducted one of the few studies exploring mental and physical health differences between transgender active-duty U.S. military personnel and trans veterans. Their results revealed that depression and anxiety followed by PTSD were the most commonly reported conditions among trans people in the military, findings that parallel the mental health patterns of cisgender military personnel. The study's authors concluded that "taken together, these results do not support the notion of poor mental or physical health as primary grounds for excluding or discharging transgender people from active-duty service."[53] Similarly, a 2014 report sponsored under the same initiative pointed out that the ban on transgender military service was not based on sound medical reasoning.[54] Commission member Gen. Thomas Kolditz specifically claimed that allowing trans people to serve openly would reduce assaults and suicides while enhancing national security: "When you closet someone, you create a security risk, and we don't need another Chelsea Manning."[55] In June 2016 then–secretary of defense Ashton Carter announced: "Effective immediately, transgender Americans can serve openly, and they no longer can be discharged or otherwise separated from the military just for being transgender." He justified his decision by referencing the need tap into a wide recruitment pool for the United States' all-volunteer force: "The Department of Defense needs to avail ourselves of all talent possible, in order to remain what we are now: the finest fighting force the world has ever known."[56]

However, with the ascent of the Trump presidency in January 2017, a new series of transphobic policies and executive orders were rolled out with the explicit intent of undoing much of the Obama era's "progressivism." On July 26, 2017, Trump tweeted, "After consultation with my Generals and military experts, please be advised that the United States Government will not accept or allow Transgender individuals to serve in any capacity in the U.S. Military. Our military must be focused on decisive and overwhelming victory and *cannot be burdened with the tremendous medical costs and disruption that transgender* [sic] *in the military would entail.*"[57] Trump's announcement of this major policy revision via Twitter not only caught the Pentagon off-guard but led to widespread confusion and a resurgence of trans military inclusion advocacy. Since a tweet in and of itself cannot constitute legal action, Trump formally signed a presidential memorandum a month later, which officially reinstated the original ban of transgender service members. In the memo, Trump argued that further studies are necessary to conclude whether trans service members would "hinder military effectiveness and lethality, disrupt unit cohesion, or tax military resources."[58] While the memorandum unequivocally banned all new transgender recruits, it provided Secretary of Defense James Mattis some discretion over trans people already serving in the armed forces. The memo further instructed the Pentagon to stop paying for any trans-related medical treatments, including gender-affirmation surgeries, "except to the extent necessary to protect the health of an individual who has already begun a course of treatment to reassign his or her sex."[59]

Trump's insistence on the alleged costliness of transgender health care for the military is grossly exaggerated. A study conducted by the RAND Corporation on transition-related treatment costs predicts a $2.4 to $8.4 million increase in the military's healthcare expenditures, which represents merely 0.005 to 0.017 percent of the $49.3 billion of the Department of Defense's overall health-care costs.[60] Trump's framing of trans health care as a significant burden on taxpayer money is thus false. While the financial basis for Trump's claims have been discredited, his concerns about military effectiveness, unit cohesion, and deployability have also already been disproven under the various Palm Center studies. The reinstatement of this ban is, therefore, wholly based on discrimination, as it either seeks to prevent trans people from joining in the first place or discharges them based solely on their gender identity. After the U.S. Supreme Court had vacated the injunctions issued by two federal appeals courts, which were temporarily blocking the implementation, Trump's ban on transgender military service officially went into effect on April 12, 2019

For many critical queer/trans scholars and activists, Trump's ban illustrates a tension between the necessity of critiquing U.S. militarism and imperialist expansionism while also recognizing that the ban on trans service members is discriminatory. How can we reconcile critiques of the military with the fact that trans service members continue to rely on it for their livelihood? Considering open trans military service a "worthy fight," trans veteran Brynn Tannehill, for example, proclaimed that "military service is one of the most time-honored ways to better yourself in America. For many LGBT folks, the military is a pipeline out of poverty, violent homes, homelessness, and hostile communities. Service gives people access to a livable wage and education. Right now these are paths that privilege white, straight, cisgender males. Working on equality issues in the military does not harm civilian movements for equality; it provides greater options for trans persons."[61] The transpatriotic narratives favoring and advocating for transgender inclusion in the military advanced by Tannehill, Beck, and others follow a familiar line of reasoning advanced to end DADT, namely that eligibility for military service is an essential means for marginalized communities to gain equality, recognition, and access to full U.S. citizenship rights.

However, Dean Spade asks us to consider "how . . . trans issues [are] being used politically" and whether or not the debate about trans inclusion in the military "is really about trans people's well-being."[62] In other words, access to health care, education, and stable employment for trans people should not only be achievable through the possibility of military employment. Similarly, Aaron Myracle, a former member of the U.S. National Guard and one of the few trans veterans who publicly supported Manning, has explicitly spoken out against the push and (re)allocation of resources for trans inclusion in the military. Myracle considers trans inclusion in the military a misguided step and notes that it "is not a push for trans inclusion. It's a push for binary-identified trans people inclusion."[63] The transpatriotism undergirding the push to end the ban not only relies on a nationalist and patriotic rhetoric but seeks to integrate gender-nonconforming individuals into the military by neatly (re)boxing them into the traditional gender binary. Furthermore, homologous to the repeal of DADT, the current push for trans inclusion in the military elides any acknowledgment of the imperialist workings of the military-industrial complex, particularly the fact that the continuous global War on Terror is mainly deployed against bodies of color—as evidenced by ongoing drone strikes and counterterrorism operations in the Middle East.

Despite SF Pride's public apology to Manning and reinstatement of her as an honorary grand marshal in 2014, Manning's story specifically and the investment in trans military inclusion more broadly reflect the persistent chasm between a critical queer politics and mainstream gay rights organizations, which continue to sideline transgender issues unless they are explicitly in accord with the capitalist and geopolitical expansion of the security state. Along with the Against Equality collective and other critical scholars and activists, I advocate for a coalitional, social-justice-oriented queer politics—one that weighs the costs of seeking equality, inclusion, and recognition by state institutions more carefully.[64] Instead of arguing for trans inclusion in the military— where LGBT people can be just as aggressive in carrying out missions and killings as their heterosexual counterparts—such a critical politics prioritizes the numerous other urgent social justice issues facing trans communities: disproportionate rates of criminalization, imprisonment, and violence, the denial of urgently needed medical care, and placement in gender inappropriate facilities, just to name a few.

Conclusion

During President Obama's final months in office in the fall of 2016, Manning's supporters initiated a final attempt to commute her sentence. In a personal statement accompanying her clemency application, Manning reiterated taking full responsibility for her actions, which did not intend to harm the interests of the United States or any service members but were made "out of concern for my country, the innocent civilians whose lives were lost as a result of war, and in support of two values that our country holds dear—transparency and public accountability." Manning further emphasized that she "pleaded guilty without the protection of a plea agreement because I believed the military justice system would understand my motivation for the disclosure and sentence me fairly. I was wrong." Recounting the mental and physical toll the military's harassment and denial of health care had on her, Manning concluded her statement with the plea: "I am merely asking for a first chance to live my life outside . . . as the person I was born to be."[65] By December 2016 a "We the People" White House petition had garnered more than one hundred thousand signatures and the hashtags #FreeChelseaNow, #TimeServed, and #HugsForChelsea were trending on Twitter.

On January 18, 2017, Obama commuted all but four months of Manning's remaining prison sentence into time served with a scheduled release for spring 2017 instead of 2045. Commenting on his decision, Obama asserted that Manning had taken responsibility for her actions and "has served a tough prison sentence," which, he acknowledged, was disproportionate relative to what other leakers had received. Given that she had already served a significant amount of time, according to Obama, "it made it sense to commute—and not pardon—her sentence."[66] While Obama's commutation is laudable, let us not forget that his administration is the one that kept Manning in prison for all these years and sanctioned the questionable if not illegal treatment Manning had to endure. This decision points to the many ambiguous legacies that the Obama administration has left behind: on the one hand, his administration advocated for the enactment of unprecedented federal transgender rights protections, but on the other, his aggressive pursuit of whistleblowers as well as the embrace of drone strikes and deportations have further cemented U.S. imperialism. As Bay Area activist and prison abolitionist Eric A. Stanley tweeted, "When someone kidnaps and tortures your friends, when they finally escape, we ought not to thank their kidnappers. #WelcomeHome @xychelsea <3."[67]

In May 2017 Manning was officially released from Fort Leavenworth. After dictating tweets over the phone for years, Manning instantly took to social media to begin documenting her first steps of freedom: eating a slice of pizza and toasting to her release with a glass of champagne. On May 18, 2017, she announced: "Okay, so here I am everyone!! =P," showing herself to the world for the first time in a new profile picture. For years, news media had either relied on the grainy selfie of Manning in a wig or her official military photo that was so violently incongruent with her own gender self-identification. With her new profile picture on Twitter and Instagram, Manning self-confidently reclaimed the personhood that state institutions had been denying her for years. Since then Manning has been active on social media, providing commentary on numerous sociopolitical debates. Many of her tweets specifically criticize the military- and prison-industrial complex. For the first time, Manning is able to assert her own voice loud and clear.

Fig. 6. Manning (@xychelsea) tweets "Okay, so here I am everyone!! =P,"
May 18, 2017. Screenshot.

Since her release, Manning has participated in several high-profile
interviews, including a profile in the *New York Times Magazine*, an interview on ABC's *Nightline*, and a *Vogue* spread depicting her in a red
swimsuit photographed by Annie Leibovitz.[68] While these articles
tended to report on Manning in a favorable light, right-wing trolls on

social media and conservative commentators continue to depict her as a "deranged" traitor. President Trump referred to Manning in a tweet as an "ungrateful TRAITOR, who should have never been released from prison," and in an op-ed for the *New York Times*, aforementioned James Kirchick reiterated false claims that Manning's leaks had allegedly put innocent lives at risk and harmed U.S. national security.[69] Besides lambasting *Vogue* and other outlets for giving "such a morally compromised figure" such a "positive reception," Kirchick was particularly enraged about "Manning's embrace by large swaths of the L.G.B.T. community," which according to him discredits the LGBT cause for gay and trans people to serve openly.[70] For Kirchick, LGBT activists celebrating Manning while simultaneously critiquing Trump's trans military ban attests to a "cognitive dissonance" that unwittingly reasserts cultural myths that LGBT service members are not to be trusted and endanger national security. Kirchick provocatively ended his op-ed alleging that with "transgender being the liberal cause du jour," it is precisely Manning's "atypical identity" that "adds a frisson of subversion to her already subversive acts. Transgender, it would appear, trumps treachery."[71] Kirchick's commentary illustrates how the very same media discourses that originally surrounded Manning's arrest and trial continue to operate post Manning's release.

Similar to the homonational patriotism Kirchick had voiced years earlier about Putin's human rights violations against gay and lesbian Russians, his commentary here expresses a strong nationalistic devotion, one that aligns with the transpatriotic commentary of veterans such as Kristin Beck and Brynn Tannehill who also sought to disavow Manning's gender identity as incompatible with the "true" values of other patriotic trans service members. In Kirchick's view, the American left's "obsession" with identity politics has led to a point where celebrations of diverse and minoritarian identities are strategically used to eclipse the severity of betrayal and the endangerment of U.S. national security. Yet as I have argued throughout this chapter, a critical queer and trans politics must precisely identify the violence such homonational and transpatriotic equality rhetorics perpetuate. Instead, viewing Manning's leaks through the lens of a critical queer politics has the potential to disrupt the imperial motivations of the U.S. security state—which only contingently includes those minority groups who are willingly participating in its expansionism but actually does not care about their health and safety.

Despite Manning's freedom, a commutation means that her court-martial conviction will remain on her record indefinitely, with far-reaching implications for her future well-being: it comes, for example, with a punitive discharge, a rank reduction, and the loss of veteran's benefits, which will further impede her access to health care. Manning was also notified by Canadian custom officials that she "is inadmissible on ground of serious criminality" when she applied for a visitor visa in late September 2017, based on her convictions under the U.S. Espionage Act.[72] Her felony record is thus effectively preventing her from traveling outside of the United States. During the same month, the prestigious Kennedy School of Government at Harvard also invited Manning as a visiting fellow to campus, only to rescind its invitation two days later amid intense pressure from CIA officials, including Mike Pompeo, the newly appointed CIA director under Trump. In a repeat of the 2013 SF Pride debacle, the school declared, "designating Chelsea Manning as a Visiting Fellow was a mistake."[73] Michael J. Morell, a former CIA deputy director under Obama, resigned as a senior fellow, arguing, "I cannot be part of an organization . . . that honors a convicted felon and leaker of classified information" and will help "in her long-standing efforts to legitimize the criminal path that she took to prominence." Preemptively fending off accusations of transphobic motivations, Morell concluded his letter, "It is important to note that I fully support Ms. Manning's rights as a transgender American, including the right to serve our country in the U.S. military."[74] In response to Harvard's disinvitation, Manning pointedly tweeted that she felt "honored to be [the] 1st disinvited trans woman visiting @harvard fellow. . . . they chill marginalized voices under @cia pressure."[75]

Despite the obstacles and hostilities she has been facing since her release, for trans rights activist Chase Strangio, who was also part of Manning's legal team, this moment nonetheless represents something hopeful: "Instead of certain death, it will be a chance at life."[76] Demonstrating that she is not easily intimidated by the powers that be, in early 2018 Manning announced her run for a Senate seat in Maryland.[77] However, in March 2019 a federal judge found Manning in civil contempt of court and sent her back to jail after she refused to testify before a secret grand jury, which is widely believed to be investigating charges against Julian Assange over the 2010 WikiLeaks disclosures. Manning has publicly stated that she already provided answers to the pertinent questions during her 2013 court martial and that compelling her to testify would be "duplicative of evidence already in the possession of the grand jury." [78] At the time of this writing, Manning was still jailed. Manning's ongoing struggles should encourage critical queer and trans scholars as well as activists *not* to sit comfortably on assimilationist "victories of equality" but to dismantle a prevailing logic of "how can you not want rights?" and continue voicing dissent against the intersectionalities of the prison-industrial complex, racist immigration policies, imperialist warfare, trans- and homophobia in the military, and the disturbingly high rates of sexual assault and harassment that affect *all* service members, straight, queer, and trans people alike. Sometimes we need to be reminded that "we have more power than they do," as Manning often concludes her day on Twitter.[79]

3

BLIND(ING) (IN)JUSTICE AND THE
DISPOSABILITY OF BLACK LIFE

When I reached the courthouse the morning Chrishaun "Cece" McDonald was supposed to have her pre-trial hearing on a charge of second-
degree murder, I saw news trucks lined up at the curb. Wow, I said to
myself. Someone is finally paying attention to CeCe McDonald. I was so
naïve. They were there for the Amy Senser trial, which started that day.
They were continuing their endless coverage of a rich white woman who
allegedly struck and killed an innocent pedestrian and drove away. The
level of media interest is very different when it comes to a young, poor,
black transgender woman who gets involved in a desperate midnight fight
over in my part of town.

Haddayr Copley-Woods, Minnesota Public Radio reporter

The scales of justice have got a blindfold on them for a reason, and we try
to follow that.

Michael Freeman, Hennepin County Attorney

On the night of June 5, 2011, Cece McDonald, an African American
trans woman, and a group of her friends, all LGBTQ people of color, had
been enjoying a quiet night barbecuing and spending time together at
McDonald's apartment building in South Minneapolis. Around 11:30
p.m. they decided to take a short walk over to Cub Foods, a local twenty-
four-hour grocery store, to pick up some groceries. On their way to
the store, the group was racially profiled and harassed by police as a
squad car pulled up to them and asked what they were doing out on
the street; a "noise complaint" had been made in the neighborhood.
After several minutes of trailing them, the police car pulled away. As
McDonald and her friends kept walking along East Twenty-Ninth

Street, they passed the Schooner Tavern and began hearing catcalls from across the street.[1]

After making a visit to the Schooner Tavern on an early October evening in 2014, I would describe the tavern as an average neighborhood bar that offers cheap drinks, live music, and pool tables and seems to attract a primarily white, blue-collar, working-class, and biker crowd in an ethnically diverse, lower-income neighborhood. The tavern borders a mall complex in the midst of a rather oddly placed commercial and industrial section bisected by light rail tracks. This commercial section is straddled by the considerably wealthier and more gentrified neighborhood of Longfellow to its south and, to its west, Powderhorn Park, which is traditionally working-class, predominantly inhabited by people of color, and known for higher crime rates. The Schooner is also directly located off Lake Street, a major, bustling thoroughfare in Minneapolis that is home to many immigrant populations from Latin America and East Africa, including the city's large Somali population. On its website the Schooner prides itself for being conveniently located with easy access to public transportation, "ample lighted parking," and "friendly, safe, cab service."[2]

However, what McDonald and her friends encountered outside the Schooner that night was not the friendliness and hospitality of a neighborhood bar but an onslaught of racial, homophobic, and transphobic slurs from some of the white patrons smoking and drinking outside the bar. Among those were Dean Schmitz, his ex-girlfriend, Molly Flaherty, and his current girlfriend, Jenny Thoreson. What exactly was exchanged that night is still up for debate. However, McDonald and her friends testified that Schmitz and his group assaulted them with numerous slurs, calling them "faggots," "nigger lovers," "tranny," and "a bunch of nigger babies."[3] Schmitz allegedly yelled: "Look at that boy dressed as a girl, tucking his dick in!" and "You niggers need to go back to Africa!"[4] In a later interview McDonald remembered, "The incident in it itself was so complex. We dealt with race. We dealt with sexual orientation. We dealt with transphobia and transmisogyny. We dealt with homophobia. . . . You don't know what part of you that you're defending. I didn't know if I was fighting for myself because I was black. I didn't know if I was fighting for myself because I was trans. But it all coincided."[5] How the two groups became involved in a physical altercation remains unclear; however, all parties agreed that Molly Flaherty first threw her glass tumbler at McDonald, causing a gash, which later required eleven stitches to repair. McDonald recalled: "She had a glass tumbler—as I was turning she threw her drink in my face. All her liquor went into my eyes. And then I felt the glass shards break into my face. And it was really an excruciating pain and instantly I was covered with blood, and I was really scared and I couldn't see because there was liquor in my eyes. After she hit me with the glass, she decided to pull me into the street by my hair and show how strong she was."[6] As people piled onto Flaherty, a security guard from the Schooner walked out of the bar and saw how Schmitz was trying to shove McDonald off his ex-girlfriend. Schmitz and McDonald both stepped away from the group. According to the bar's security guard, McDonald was holding onto a pair of fabric scissors while Schmitz was clenching his fists and approaching her before he suddenly fell over and exclaimed, "You stabbed me!"[7] McDonald herself testified that she did not jab Schmitz but was trying to defend herself: "I had some scissors in my purse, just to be on the safe-side cause I never know. I pulled them out. He came towards me, but ... I didn't stab him, it was like he ran into the scissors, because [crying/sighing] it's like he was trying to get me; like he really just wanted to hurt me so bad. ... I was ... only trying to protect us, myself."[8] Despite conflicting eyewitness accounts, police later arrested McDonald, considering her both the instigator of and aggressor in the attack.

In this chapter, I take up Julia R. Johnson's call for communication studies scholars to engage with transgender people and issues through an intersectional and interdisciplinary lens to intercede in the violence against and criminalization of trans people.[9] Building on Johnson's initial analysis of McDonald's case, I scrutinize how local media affirmed the state's refusal to acknowledge the lived experience of a transgender woman of color defending her life as she was publicly harassed and targeted in a racist and transphobic attack. Drawing on critical race theory and intersectionality, I argue that the dominant framing of McDonald's gender nonconformity as deceptive and threatening in conjunction with the state's refusal to grant McDonald a right to self-defense illustrate how both the media and the state reinforce the justice system's self-professed color and gender blindness, masking the state's ongoing investment in and protection of whiteness. As *both* local news media and the state failed to recognize and acknowledge McDonald as an intersectional subject, the assertion of a colorblind rhetoric enabled McDonald's a priori criminalization and the state-sanctioned violence enacted against her. I conclude this chapter with broader observations about hate crime legislation to interrogate whom these laws are actually designed to protect and how the justice system's alleged impartiality continues to deny legal protections to both people of color and transgender communities long after the end of Jim Crow. The overlap and interplay of mediated and legal discourses are indicative of the intricate operations of state power and systematically reinforce the categorization of certain racialized populations as always already criminal, deviant, and, therefore, disposable. In so doing, this chapter points to the limits of relying on mass media visibility and the law as avenues for achieving social justice.

Local Crime Reporting: Transgender Violence and White Victims

Analyzing several local print and broadcasting outlets in Minneapolis reveals the prevalence of derogatory and insulting language used to discuss McDonald—if her story was even deemed newsworthy at all.[10] The quote from Haddayr Copley-Woods, a contributor to Minnesota Public Radio (MPR) News, in the epigraph to this chapter concisely describes the crux of the matter: while news outlets meticulously covered the high-profile, celebrity trial of the wife of a former Minnesota Vikings football player who was convicted in a hit-and-run that killed a prominent Asian American chef around the same time McDonald was facing charges for second-degree murder, they differed drastically in their coverage of the story of a poor, young, black trans woman defending her life. The *Saint Paul Pioneer Press*, the second largest newspaper covering the Twin Cities, did not publish a single article on McDonald's case. When local news media did cover McDonald's story, they mainly sensationalized her gender nonconformity, repeatedly misgendered her as male, and were dismissive of and/or oblivious to the racial and transphobic motivations behind the assault and thus unwilling to recognize the intersectional nature of the violence and discrimination at work in her case.

Initial news reports on the stabbing broke under crime reporting sections, and all identified McDonald as a *male* suspect: "A 23-year-old man has been charged," "He is accused in the death of 47-year-old Dean Schmitz, who died after an altercation at The Schooner Tavern," or "A 23-year-old man fatally stabbed a bar patron in the midst of a melee outside the Minneapolis tavern." The local NBC affiliate, KARE 11, closed its initial report on the stabbing with "McDonald is currently in custody at the Hennepin County Jail. Police say his mug shot is unavailable as the investigation continues."[11] While law enforcement typically releases mug shots of individuals who are arrested and under suspicion of having committed a crime, the Minneapolis Police Department's delay in providing news stations with her mug shot raises several questions: Did the police hide McDonald's gender identity and the stab wound prominently displayed on her face to divert attention from the fact that the altercation was much more complicated than a brawl that had gotten out of hand? Did KARE 11 and other news stations demand from the police to explain the absence of the mug shot in the alleged murder case? Did the news station not fulfill its journalistic watchdog function to follow up and question state authorities in its investigative reporting on the case, or did KARE 11 not deem the absence of McDonald's picture worthy of inquiry? While the police's motive cannot be established beyond a doubt, hiding and delaying the release of the mug shot rendered McDonald's intersecting identity categories, especially the intersections of her gender identity and race, invisible.

Most of the early stories focused solely on the "victim," Dean Schmitz. The local Fox affiliate ran the headline "Man Faces Murder Charge in Minneapolis Bar Stabbing" without mentioning the racist and transphobic slurs that initiated the altercation between the two groups.[12] Instead, in an effort to sanitize Schmitz's death and elevate his role as the victim, Fox 9 presented sound bites from mournful family members emphasizing what a caring and loving person Schmitz had allegedly been, as he "would give the shirt off his back to help people."[13] None of the channels mentioned Schmitz's extensive criminal record that contained convictions for drug possession and domestic assault. Schmitz's ex-wife Tammy Williams was "hoping for justice" and asserted, "Whoever did this left my kids without a father, and to me, that's devastating."[14] In a later interview during McDonald's sentencing, the *Star Tribune* further cited Schmitz's family, saying, "With all of the focus on McDonald, Schmitz, a father of three, has been forgotten as the true victim," and quoting his ex-wife: "Dean loved his children, and at the hands of Chrishaun McDonald, he can never tell them again."[15] Schmitz's unexpected death not only confronted his loved ones with the painful experience of suddenly losing him, but his dead body was specifically (re)constructed in news narratives to idealize and mobilize an imagined white fatherhood to secure the cultural and sociopolitical capital of white heteronormativity, thus absolving Schmitz of any blame. As E. Cram contends, the violence directed against queer and trans bodies is often portrayed as "the result of a personal moral failing on behalf of the perpetrator and as the fault of the victim, rather than as an offense necessitating reflection of a wider community."[16] More specifically, the local media's valuing of Schmitz's life simultaneously depended on the immediate criminalization and othering of McDonald because of her gender nonconformity.

On May 9, 2012, Minneapolis's *City Pages*, a weekly paper, published a cover story under the sensationalizing title, "The Edge of Doubt: When a Transgender Woman Stabs a Man Tattooed with a Swastika, How Will Justice Be Served?"[17] The title and accompanying story reinforced the notion that McDonald's gender nonconformity rendered her deviant and threatening. The cover art intensified the perceived threat by depicting scissors, the alleged murder weapon, cutting through a black and white face. Reminiscent of the movie *Basic Instinct* (1992), a noir erotic thriller portraying a bisexual woman (Sharon Stone) as a murderous, narcissistic psychopath, the cover art gracing *City Pages* played into long-enduring stereotypes and fears of queer and trans people as deceptive and dangerous. While the full-length feature acknowledged the racialized and transmisogynist motivations behind the attack, it was full of hyperbole describing the incident,

MAY 9–15, 2012 | VOLUME 32 | NUMBER 1640   CITYPAGES.COM | FREE

CITY PAGES

THE
EDGE
OF DOUBT

When a transgender woman stabs a man tattooed
with a swastika, how will justice be served?

By ANDY MANNIX

Fig. 7. Front page of *City Pages*, "The Edge of Doubt," May 9, 2012. Illustration by Mike Kooiman. Courtesy of *City Pages*.

particularly a graphic recount of the stab "slowly staining" Schmitz's shirt "red from the geyser of blood."

The article was also extremely dismissive of the organizing work that was happening on McDonald's behalf; author Andy Mannix not only alleged that McDonald's supporters were exceptionalizing her by treating "her as a folk hero of sorts, a transgender Matthew Shepard," but concluded that a plea deal offered to McDonald was "generous." Mannix further suggested the inevitability of violence against trans women, as "the tragedy outside the Schooner Tavern may have been bad timing more than anything else. It was the chance meeting of two people who couldn't have been more different. Together, they were primed to explode."[18] Despite the *City Pages*' explicit acknowledgment of the racial and transphobic comments inciting the brawl, by suggesting that the fatal outcome in the incident at the Schooner Tavern was merely due to "bad timing" and that McDonald was simply at the wrong place at the wrong time, Mannix individualized and exceptionalized the Schooner patrons' actions and insinuated that the violence committed against McDonald and her friends was an isolated incident.

Not once, for example, did Mannix contextualize McDonald's case with the nationwide increase in violence committed against trans people, especially trans women of color; instead, he paired McDonald's gender nonconformity with Schmitz's white supremacist background as symmetrically powerful forces whose convergence caused a violent eruption. In so doing, Mannix implicitly blamed McDonald's otherness for how the events unfolded and implied that gender-nonconforming people are inherently threatening. This effectively worked to gloss over and erase long and systemic strains of white supremacist violence enacted against LGBT communities and people of color in U.S. history. By idealizing Schmitz as a loving father figure, enforcing his heteronormativity, and absolving him of any blame or responsibility for the incident, the *City Pages* article, similar to the news reports mentioned earlier, cast the white, racist perpetrator getting killed as a tragedy that needed to be properly mourned and recuperated into the national imaginary; conversely, it presented a trans woman's fight and courage to survive as an anomaly. Schmitz became a loving white father figure precisely through his encounter with a person racialized and gendered as a violent other. With its coverage, *City Pages* actively (re)created discourses that describe trans people as impulsive, inherently violent, unpredictable time bombs ready to explode at any moment. In short, the paper systematically used the othering of McDonald to absolve and rehabilitate white supremacist violence into national belonging.

During McDonald's pretrial proceedings and later her sentencing, local media coverage also frequently justified the state's decision to hold her in solitary confinement and isolation "because of safety concerns related to gender-transition status" and "the well-being of others." In his news column for the *MinnPost*, a nonprofit, nonpartisan, web-based publication, Brian Lambert later commented on McDonald's sentencing with the headline, "She's man enough to do her time in the boy's prison."[19] The *Minnesota Daily*, the University of Minnesota's student-run newspaper, addressed McDonald's case only in its editorial and opinion pages and condemned McDonald's assignment to an all-male facility, asking, "How does a community of people who do not fit within a binary gender prison system receive proper punishment fairly under the law?" While the student paper's efforts urging legislators and correctional facilities "to find a safe place for its transgender inmates and understand their needs" are laudable, these editorials viewed McDonald's solitary confinement as a benign means to keep her safe and presumed she was guilty.[20] However, as my analysis of Chelsea Manning's treatment in detention in chapters 1 and 2 demonstrated, solitary confinement presents another means in the state's inventory of detention practices to further surveil, silence, discipline, and repress individual prisoners. Several civil rights organizations, including the Sylvia Rivera Law Project and the Center for Constitutional Rights, assert that "solitary confinement is torture" because it violates constitutional rights against cruel and unusual punishment.[21] Putting prisoners in so-called Special Housing Units or Security Housing Units to supposedly protect them from other inmates without justification, due process, or outside oversight also ignores the fact that prisoners frequently face violence at the hands of correctional guards and that prolonged isolation poses significant mental and psychological harm to prisoners.[22] Similarly, in their analysis of the legal rhetoric surrounding gender identity on death row, Peter Odell Campbell and Cory Holding point out that cisnormative capital punishment in the United States primarily operates "through laws and procedures whose de jure purpose of protecting vulnerable prison populations works as a cover for the laws' de facto function of acting as a transgender death penalty."[23] The few articles that sought to shed light on the precarious status of transgender prisoners because of their incarceration in correctional facilities based on their birth-assigned sex, therefore, neglected to critically interrogate the state's deceitful use of solitary confinement. These articles still deemed McDonald's incarceration as just and failed to critique the general functions of the U.S. prison-industrial complex and the systemic inequalities of the justice system, as I will elaborate in the chapter's second section.

Reporting "Dilemmas," Compelled Disclosures,
and Transgender Style Guidelines

The Minneapolis *Star Tribune*, the largest newspaper covering the Minneapolis–Saint Paul metropolitan area, particularly stood out with its sensationalistic and derogatory reportage of McDonald's case.[24] The *Star Tribune* continued to misgender McDonald well after her self-identification as a trans woman was known and framed her as a murderer. Articles frequently referred to McDonald by her birth name and described her as "Chrishaun Reed 'CeCe' McDonald, 23, who is a person in transition from a man to a woman" or as "McDonald, who is transgender and lives as a woman."[25] By consistently misgendering her, the *Tribune* belittled McDonald's gender identity and denied her transgender subjectivity as well as her right to self-determination. These news reports discursively upheld a fixed, normative gender binary (where one is always either male or female but can never be fluidly in between or change from one end of the spectrum to another). Similar, to Barker-Plummer's observations surrounding news coverage of the murder of Gwen Araujo in 2006, the *Tribune* and other local news organizations marked only McDonald's transgender identity, instead of attaching, for example, the label "cisgender" to the patrons McDonald and her friends encountered outside the Schooner.[26] Headline after headline felt it necessary to point out that McDonald was trans, sensationalizing her gender nonconformity: local CBS affiliate WCCO, for example, ran the headline "Transgender woman gets 41 months after accepting plea deal," and MPR reported, "Transgender woman gave up self-defense claim in plea deal."[27]

Studies show that crime coverage in news media disproportionately highlights the ethnicity of a perpetrator if the offender belongs to a racial minority (often in conjunction with racializing labels such as "super predators" and "gang members").[28] Similarly, McDonald's trans identity received such heightened scrutiny whereas cis identity, just like whiteness, remained invisible. While the *Tribune* repeatedly fetishized McDonald's trans identity, it refused to discuss how the intersection of her trans identity and identity as a poor woman of color affected the circumstances of the case. By reasserting cisgender identity and the gender binary as the norm, local media failed to recognize McDonald as an intersectional subject and concurrently obscured the material and structural inequalities she faced.

Despite the *Star Tribune*'s early reporting that "McDonald and a witness said Schmitz incited a melee after midnight when he made racist and gay-bashing remarks toward McDonald, who is black," the paper's succeeding articles were quick to label and criminalize McDonald as "a transgender murder suspect" whose alleged "pent-up fury exploded" from the "pressures of being transgendered [*sic*]."[29] The *Tribune*'s fetishizing of McDonald's gender nonconformity not only sought to render her deviant but, as had other local news outlets, deliberately reinforced a representation of McDonald as threatening and violent precisely because she was transgender. Invoking deep-rooted tropes of black rage and black criminality, the local media coverage of McDonald's case repeatedly suggested that the "pressures" of being transgender inevitably result in violence (or as I have demonstrated in the chapters on Manning, in the leaking of government documents threatening the nation-state and national security). These portrayals of McDonald as dangerous and threatening, therefore, invalidated her claims to self-defense.

While local outlets fetishized McDonald's transgender identity, they typically ignored or omitted altogether the fact that she was African American. Not once, for example, did an article in the *Star Tribune* refer to her as "a transgender woman of color" or "a black trans woman." On those rare occasions when local outlets did point out McDonald's racial identity, it was treated as separate from her transgender identity: "The group that included McDonald, all of them black, crossed the street to confront the bar crowd."[30] At the same time, Schmitz's whiteness remained unmarked and was only occasionally implied by acknowledging that racially, homophobically, and transphobically charged verbal assaults had preceded the altercation. The media coverage surrounding McDonald refused to acknowledge that race played a role in the incident, let alone how race intersected with gender. Local news media thereby failed to take into account and acknowledge how multiple identity categories relating to race, gender, sexuality, and class present intersecting systems of oppression and that these oppressions do not function separately from one another.[31] McDonald and her friends were targeted not only because of their race or class or their sexual orientation or their gender nonconformity—one did not trump the other—but because these oppressive systems were intertwined and mutually constitutive of one another in shaping the groups' experiences—forming a "matrix of domination."[32]

The *Star Tribune* later became directly involved in McDonald's pretrial proceedings. Under the Minnesota Free Flow of Information Act, the paper was ordered to disclose a letter that McDonald had sent to the paper shortly after her arrest.[33] In the letter, which the *Star Tribune* referenced several times in its coverage, McDonald described her initial confession of stabbing Schmitz as a "mistake" and claimed that she made admissions to the police to cover up for a friend. The prosecution asserted that the letter was "relevant to the prosecution of a serious felony, cannot be obtained by alternative means, and there is a compelling interest in obtaining the letter to prevent injustice." While attorneys for the *Star Tribune* argued that newspapers should not be treated as a repository of information for litigation purposes, the court granted the prosecution's request and ordered the *Star Tribune* to disclose the letter to better weigh McDonald's believability: "In a case where the defendant has noticed his [*sic*] intentions to rely on self-defense, the issue of credibility and the defendant's state of mind are paramount. This is not a case of 'who done it.' It is a case where the central issue will be whether the death of D.S. [Dean Schmitz] was justified."[34] The judge's order to disclose the letter points to the fragility of the freedom of the press guaranteed by the First Amendment. The leaks of classified documents by WikiLeaks in cooperation with newspapers such as the *New York Times* and the *Guardian* in 2010 have also renewed debates about the use of subpoenas to force journalists to disclose confidential news sources and unpublished information. As the state explicitly compelled the *Star Tribune* to cooperate, the disclosure of the letter further reinforced the ostracizing, criminalizing, and demonizing of McDonald as a deceptive murderer.

Because the *Star Tribune* received criticism from local community organizers for its derogatory coverage of McDonald, I directed several inquiries to staff reporter Paul Walsh, who initially covered her case, about whether he would be willing to share his experiences. However, I received in response only a one-line email wherein Walsh indicated, "Sorry, I won't be able to help you."[35] Similarly, Abby Simons, another staff writer, tried to deflect any responsibility for the paper's derisive coverage arguing—inaccurately—that "the heat the *Star Tribune* took" for reporting on McDonald with male pronouns occurred before she started covering the case.[36] Simons's statement, however, is inconsistent: despite interviewing local activists and organizers supporting McDonald, *Star Tribune* articles still used the wrong pronouns and omitted important context about the daily street violence and harassment trans women of color often face. Lex Horan, a member of McDonald's Support Committee recalled: "At the time what they told us is that *Star Tribune* policy was that they couldn't use female pronouns ... for CeCe. I think clearly what was happening was, Abby [Simons] was as sympathetic as a reporter we could have gotten, but the editorial board was shutting her down."[37] How could reporters have spoken differently about McDonald's gender nonconformity? Would it have made a difference if the *Star Tribune* and other outlets had not repeatedly reminded readers of McDonald's anatomy through fetishizing and insulting phrases, for example, by simply stating that she was "identifying as a woman"? Local reporters could have consulted GLAAD's Media Reference Guide on transgender issues or made an effort to follow the advice from local community organizers about how to properly refer to McDonald.[38]

After contacting the *Star Tribune*'s senior editor about whether the newspaper adhered to any style guidelines in its reporting on McDonald, I received a note from the managing editor for operations, Duchesne Drew, who informed me that the paper did not have one during the time of McDonald's pretrial hearings but had adopted an official transgender style guideline in June 2014. Drew confirmed that the style guide was developed directly in response to the paper's initial treatment of McDonald: "The McDonald case led to discussions here and those discussions led us to come up with a style guide entry."[39] Some excerpts from the guidelines follow:

> Transgender (adjective) is a term for people whose gender identity differs from that typically associated with their sex at birth. Cite a person's transgender status only when it is pertinent and its pertinence is made clear to readers. Use the name and pronouns preferred by the transgender person, regardless of whether they have changed their biological characteristics . . . In court cases, where it is necessary to use a transgender person's legal name, use his or her preferred name on first reference, and preferred pronoun in all cases. Include the person's legal name at some point in the story, along with an explanation of his or her gender status: "McDonald's legal name is Chrishaun R. McDonald. The transgender woman was born male but now identifies herself as female."[40]

Although it may appear admirable that the *Star Tribune* recognized the flaws and demeaning language it used in covering CeCe McDonald by consciously misgendering and repeatedly fetishizing her gender nonconformity, it is important to consider the actual effects of institutionalizing transgender identities through the use of an official transgender style guide. I do not want to dismiss the importance of a media organization's minimizing sensationalism around trans people and raising awareness about using an individual's preferred pronouns or gender-neutral language; however, to simply be content with using the right pronouns to address someone appropriately makes it all too easy to overlook how media institutions continue to reinforce the state's othering of trans people, particularly trans women of color. McDonald's case shows how local media participated in dehumanizing her and actively sanctioned the state's violence enacted against her.

The use of style guidelines does not solve the problem that visibility for trans people still carries mostly negative implications; despite proper acknowledgment of a trans person's gender identity, such visibility does not necessarily lead to justice. On the contrary, this superficial inclusion and acceptance of trans identities through visibility politics only further works to hide a variety of injustices. As Horan carefully observes: "The prosecution used the right pronouns for CeCe all the time and they never made a mistake on that. They called her 'Ms. McDonald' and that's insidious because it is a very multicultural framework because 'if we call you the right thing and don't use insulting language than this immense violence that we are doing against you by trying to lock you up in prison for the rest of your life becomes totally invisible' and I think that was . . . happening in the media in general."[41] Today, rhetorics of colorblindness and multiculturalism promoted by dominant media and state actors allege that race and gender disparities in the United States no longer exist. After all, the election of Barack Obama as the first black president, Eric Holder's nomination as the first African American attorney general, Sonia Sotomayor's appointment as the first Supreme Court justice of Latinx descent, Oprah Winfrey's ever-expanding media empire, Indra Nooyi's successful tenure as the CEO of Pepsi, and LeBron James's rule over the NBA allegedly prove that race or racial difference no longer matter. This deeply flawed belief in colorblindness and racial indifference as a sociopolitical governing principle not only presents a conservative investment in individualism and self-responsibility that privatizes race (back to the promise of the American Dream that "everyone can make it, you just have to pull yourself up by your bootstraps"), but this prevailing multicultural consensus in public discourse also masks the importance of the continued enactment of racialized violence for U.S. capitalist expansionism. As Jodi Melamed cogently notes, "Multicultural reference masks the centrality of race and racism to neo-liberalism."[42] More specifically as legal scholar Michelle Alexander argues, turning a blind eye toward the realities of race in U.S. society has facilitated the emergence of a "new caste system for social control"—racialized mass incarceration: "In the era if colorblindness, it is no longer socially permissible to use race, explicitly, as a justification for discrimination, exclusion, and social contempt. So we don't. Rather than rely on race, we use our criminal justice system to label people of color 'criminals' and then engage in all the practices we supposedly left behind."[43] Just as the prevailing discourse of a diverse, post-racial America belies persistent systemic inequalities and racial injustices, so too does the increased visibility of transgender people and their current "hipness" in popular culture not necessarily result in improved material realties for those communities or in greater care for and protection of trans lives. On the contrary, similar to the flawed notions about transgender visibility, the color-blindness invoked by both dominant media and state actors mainly functions to conceal the disposability of and state violence committed against gender-nonconforming and nonwhite communities.

The local media coverage initially denied McDonald's trans subjectivity, labeling her as male, only to subsequently sensationalize her for being trans without providing any context for the lived experiences of trans people. The press systematically refused to question the prosecution's pursuit of the case, nor did it alert its audience and readers to the intersectionalities of race, class, gender, and sexuality, all pertinent factors in the assault. The portrayal of McDonald as a racialized, gender-nonconforming threat directed blame for the attack away from Schmitz, elevated his white innocent victim status as a loving father, and erased the historical context of racialized and gendered violence committed against LGBT and people of color communities. The media's elevation of Schmitz's victim status thus rendered his death grievable and relied on McDonald's criminalization to strategically foreclose any empathy from the public. Local news organizations framed the case as an isolated incident, thereby colluding with the state in criminalizing McDonald. Furthermore, news media created a color- and gender-blind public narrative about McDonald, which bolstered legal discourses about the justice system's alleged impartiality. These mechanisms not only allow for the disposal of stigmatized and criminalized populations as unworthy of legal protections, but they justify and reinforce state-sanctioned violence enacted against marginalized communities—an assumption I unpack in the following section.

Transgender Subjectivity and the Law

In September 2011 CeCe McDonald was offered a plea bargain, which she rejected. In response and what her supporters and defense viewed as a "retaliatory move," the prosecution added a charge of second-degree murder *with intent* to the previous charge of second-degree murder *without intent.*[44] Although a county attorney spokesperson insisted that there was "nothing unusual about" adding a second charge after the failed settlement negotiations, the prosecution's amendment of the original charge without including any new evidence pertaining to the case seemed to be a reprisal against McDonald for exercising her constitutional right to go to trial and putting the burden of proof upon the state.[45] Alexander has aptly chronicled the widespread practice of overcharging, in which prosecutors are "free to file more charges against a defendant than can realistically be proven . . . as long as some probable cause arguably exists."[46] According to Alexander, this tactic of overcharging is often employed to coerce people into taking deals, whether they are actually guilty or not, rather than to give them the benefits of a "fair and speedy trial" under the Sixth Amendment. Because McDonald rejected the original plea deal, the prosecution's swift response to add a second charge of murder *with intent* presented another punitive measure that sought to intimidate McDonald and to brand her as a murderer who had intentionally caused the death of Dean Schmitz.

In the following months, McDonald's defense team was repeatedly unsuccessful in filing motions to admit additional evidence that would have helped to contextualize the racism and transphobia surrounding the case, and which were relevant to McDonald's self-defense claim.[47] For example, a motion to admit testimony from a representative of Outfront Minnesota, a local nonprofit organization working toward LGBT equality, and Dean Spade, a law professor and cofounder of the Sylvia Rivera Law Project, to dispel common myths about transgender people and to provide background on the violence trans people disproportionally face was rejected. McDonald's lawyer, Hersch Izek, also sought to admit the expert testimony of toxicologist Leo Sioris, who had conducted a toxicology screening that revealed significant levels of alcohol, cocaine, and methamphetamine in Schmitz's blood at the time of the stabbing. Known to be "powerful stimulants," these drugs have been linked to aggressive behavior with a "high risk potential for unpredictable and sudden violence."[48] Yet the court denied the relevance of the toxicologist's testimony as pertinent to Schmitz's state of mind during the incident.[49] Furthermore, Schmitz had an extensive criminal record including charges of burglary and drug possession and prior convictions for domestic assault, including hitting and injuring his then-girlfriend's fourteen-year-old daughter.[50] McDonald's defense, however, argued in vain that Schmitz's "assaultive nature" was significant to his intent at the time of the stabbing.[51] Ironically, not bringing in a victim's background or sexual history originated in rape shield statutes in the 1970s (culminating in a federal rape shield law with the Violence Against Women Act in 1994), which were meant to limit the ability of a defendant to introduce evidence of a victim's past sexual behavior, history, or reputation during a rape trial. In McDonald's case such thinking, however, was applied in reverse and actively undermined her ability to claim self-defense.

The defense was also unsuccessful in arguing that McDonald was "incapable of making a knowing, intelligent, and voluntary waiver of her constitutional rights against self-incrimination" during the initial police interrogation at the night of the stabbing due to the injuries that she had sustained from the altercation and her prolonged, isolated detention that night.[52] After McDonald was brought to the Hennepin County Medical Center around 1:00 a.m. to stitch the laceration on her cheek, she was discharged and returned to the Minneapolis Police Department around 4:50 a.m., where she was kept in isolation before she was interviewed three hours later, around 8:00 a.m. During the interrogation, McDonald initially denied stabbing Schmitz but subsequently altered her account. She stated that she did not intend to stab Schmitz but that he ran into the pair of fabric scissors that she was holding.[53] McDonald mentioned during the interview that she was trying to listen despite her wound bleeding. The two sergeants, Christopher Gaiters and John Holthusen, continuously questioned McDonald's motive and alleged that they did not believe that she was a reckless and "hard core" person but someone who had "made a mistake" and now needed to own up to that mistake: "We deal a lot of times with cold-blooded murderers . . . that don't give a shit about anyone. They hurt people. They sexually assault people. They hit people, they do whatever, they don't care about people. I don't think you are that type of person. I don't buy it. . . . But I get the feeling that you got incredibly angry tonight and you made a mistake, and things got way out of hand.

And I'm guessing that if you could, I'd bet you anything, you wish you could take some stuff back."

McDonald repeatedly insisted during the interview that she did not intentionally stab Schmitz and acted out of self-defense: "I didn't have no motive to stab nobody. And that's what it seems like y'all are trying to get me to say. . . . My motive was to . . . protect myself. When it's a . . . over six foot person weighing 220 pounds chasing after me, . . . my only defense is to defend myself."[54] Ultimately, the court determined that the "temperate and courteous" behavior of the investigators as well as the length of the interview were within legal bounds and that McDonald's injuries did not render her statements involuntary; all were thus admissible as evidence: "Sgt. Gaiters did not use any overly aggressive tone, make any promises to the Defendant or mislead her in a coercive way. . . . [The] Defendant was aware, responsive and cognizant of her *Miranda* rights. . . . The Court concludes that Defendant's statements were voluntary and the totality of the circumstances do not suggest her will was overborne by investigators."[55]

However, the investigators' skillful yet deceptive techniques of "extracting" a confession from McDonald are highly problematic. Although the transcript of the interview is indeed devoid of any directly coercive language, the investigators repeatedly insinuated that they did not consider McDonald a "criminal" but were rather sympathetic to her as a person "who had made a mistake" and that she could trust them. They provided her with a false sense of security and access to legal protections as long as she was truthful and cooperative. Holthusen and Gaiters unremittingly pushed McDonald to recount the events over and over, seemingly discontent with her initial accounts. This silently functioned to undermine her willpower, intimidate her, and provoke differing statements that would later be used against her to render her testimony not credible and deny her a right to self-defense. As these confessional practices reappear endlessly in every television crime drama, from CSI to *Law and Order*, we have become conditioned to accept them as normal and unproblematic. Yet such acceptance only further reflects and feeds into the "state of exception"—wherein the state's extralegal violence and interrogation techniques are sanctioned as I outlined with Manning's case in chapters 1 and 2.

While McDonald supporters focused much of their efforts on getting the Hennepin County lead prosecutor Michael Freeman to drop the charges, arguing that McDonald was the victim of a hate crime fueled by racism and transphobia, Freeman was unrelenting. In an interview, Freeman stated that it was "a tragedy that somebody [had] died" but argued that McDonald did not fulfill her duty to retreat as outlined by Minnesota State law in order to claim self-defense:

> Self-defense cases are when the person is defending her own person against the person who is causing the present harm. And there is no indication, fact that we have today that the victim was a threat to Ms. McDonald other than the fact that he was in the middle of the group of people that occurred when these two groups met. If you are outside of your home and you are out on the street, you have a duty to flee if you can; but if the threat is so profound that you cannot do that then you have the right to use the force necessary to protect yourself including deadly force. Evidence here does not reflect self-defense. She didn't, she stepped forward to thrust the weapon into a person who had not assaulted her. That to me just doesn't fit.[56]

Despite conflicting eyewitness accounts and McDonald's own statement, the prosecution did not acknowledge that Schmitz's aggressive and violent behavior toward McDonald constituted an imminent danger to her life. For the state, the precarity of McDonald's life was not worthy of recognition or protection. Both the news media and the county prosecutor asserted that the death of Dean Schmitz was a tragedy and a punishable crime; they thus granted Schmitz the status of victimhood, validating his as death grievable while undermining McDonald's right to protect her own life.[57] The fact that McDonald survived the attack meant she was incapable of claiming self-defense from a hate crime. Denying McDonald a right to self-defense should induce us to ask how the state generally treats violence committed against people of color and what this says about both the justice system's alleged impartiality and the apparent disposability of people of color and transgender lives. Whose lives count as livable and whose lives are worthy of legal protection? Because both the local media and the state failed to recognize and acknowledge McDonald as an intersectional subject, the assertion of a colorblind rhetoric enabled the violence enacted against her after her arrest.

The Blindfolds of Justice

The prosecution in McDonald's case repeatedly emphasized its commitment to colorblindness and neutrality. Freeman was eager to deny that race, gender, or socioeconomic status played any role in the prosecution's pursuit of the case: "We see all kinds of crime by all sorts of people and to the best way humanly possible we try to review it as racially blind, as sexual-orientation blind, as economic-blind as we could be. The scales of justice have got a blindfold on them for a reason, and we try to follow that. . . . It doesn't matter what her record was [indicating that McDonald had once been convicted for writing a bad check], and it doesn't matter what her sex is, and it doesn't matter what her race is, none of that matters."[58] However, these identity categories clearly did matter, especially their intersectionality. When crimes are committed because of and in direct relation to these intersecting identity categories, how can the criminal justice system ignore them? The prosecution and the state drew on the blindfold metaphor to obfuscate the workings of white supremacy and to hide the violence committed against a black trans woman. As with so many others, what we witness with McDonald's case is that race, gender, sexuality, and class are incriminating identity categories that are still permeating the rule of law as critical race and legal scholars have repeatedly pointed out.[59]

The abolition of Jim Crow segregation laws with the enactment of the Civil Rights Act in 1964 rejected white privilege accorded as a legal right and created a "race-neutrality in law," which is supposed to guarantee "objectivity" over "subjectivity" and the "impersonal" over the "personal" in the justice system. However, the legal system's neutrality remains deeply flawed because "Blacks and women are the objects of a constitutional omission that has been incorporated into a theory of neutrality," as Patricia Williams asserts. Even when the law recognizes one identity category, legal discourses still do not acknowledge systemic structures and the intersecting oppressions of multiple identity categories. Kimberlé Crenshaw, for example, has demonstrated how dominant conceptions of antidiscrimination legislation are based on an understanding of subordination as occurring along a single categorical axis only.[60] Analyzing several Title VII cases, Crenshaw notes that the paradigm of sex discrimination is typically based on the experiences of white women, while the model of race discrimination tends to be based on the experiences of the most privileged blacks: "Notions of what constitutes race and sex discrimination are, as a result, narrowly tailored to embrace only a small set of circumstances, none of which include discrimination against Black women."[61]

Furthermore, legal scholar Cheryl Harris observes in her important essay "Whiteness as Property" that de facto white privilege continues to function as a property interest worthy of protection:

> In ways that it is rarely apparent, the set of assumptions, privileges, and benefits that accompany the status of being white have become a valuable asset that whites sought to protect. . . . Whites have come to expect and rely on these benefits, and over time these expectations have been affirmed, legitimated, and protected by the law. Even though the law is neither uniform nor explicit in all instances, in protecting settled expectations based on white privilege, American law has recognized a property interest in whiteness that, although unacknowledged, now forms the background against which legal disputes are framed, argued, and adjudicated.

Despite the end of de jure segregation, the material inequities produced by institutionalized white supremacy, racism, and economic exploitation—"the status quo of substantive disadvantage"—have been ratified as an accepted and acceptable "neutral base line" that continues to bestow legal and societal privilege upon whiteness.[62] Thus, prosecutor Freeman's reference to the blindfolds of justice illustrates how whiteness initially constructed as a racial identity has evolved over the centuries from a privileged identity to a vested interest as a form of external property protected in both explicit and implicit ways by U.S. law and society through a theory of neutrality and colorblindness.

Justice's purported blindness also explains why the court did not acknowledge Schmitz's swastika tattoo as representative of the violent histories of white supremacy. Photographs from Schmitz's autopsy depicting a four-inch swastika tattoo placed prominently on his chest were not deemed "relevant and probative in nature" and thus were not admissible in court.[63] While legally a tattoo cannot stand in as a sign of intent, I am interested here in the ways in which the law's internal logic ends up privileging hegemonic points of view, in this case how the ideology of colorblindness masks the continued operations and privileges of whiteness. In a memorandum Judge Daniel Moreno explained:

> The Court cannot be sure ... what the symbol represented to D.S. [Dean Schmitz], whether it represented a belief in the elimination of non-White races or a belief in the separation of Whites from other races, or whether the symbol reflects a hatred of all non-White races or a hatred of specific non-White races. And, while we might assume that an individual with a swastika tattoo subscribes to certain beliefs, the tattoo itself is not evidence that D.S. subscribed to any belief. Specifically, evidence of the tattoo does not establish that D.S. intended to threaten, fight or kill anyone.[64]

On its face, Moreno's reasoning seems to be logical. A swastika tattoo such as Schmitz's may be a symbol of many different kinds of beliefs and without any further context or explanation, showing a picture of his tattoo to a jury may indeed have been inflammatory and prejudicial; however, Moreno's conclusion that the tattoo was "not relevant to establish [the] Defendant's intent or state of mind" is based on several faulty assumptions.[65] Primarily, he assumes that McDonald's attorney would not contextualize Schmitz's tattoo in light of other evidence of his beliefs or statements about race, something her attorney could have done simply through the questioning of witnesses. Moreover, Moreno's decision to declare the tattoo irrelevant was only made possible after he had already found other pieces of contextual evidence inadmissible, such as witness statements that Schmitz and his friends used racist and transphobic slurs to refer to McDonald and her friends before the fight started.[66]

By ruling irrelevant Schmitz's swastika tattoo as well as evidence of his intoxication and previously violent behavior toward women, the court turned a blind eye toward how Schmitz's beliefs and state of mind may have influenced and instigated the altercation. Systematically declaring these pieces of evidence irrelevant or prejudicial reinforced an insidious investment in whiteness on the state's part, rendering the justice system's purported colorblindness functionally meaningless. This rhetoric of colorblindness is the premise upon which the U.S. legal system has operated since the 1960s and therein has invested white subjects, intentionally or not, with operative special benefits, rights, and privileges.[67] The court's decision about the tattoo not only furthers such hegemonic discourses about the law's alleged impartiality and colorblindness, but it does so at the same time that black and trans defendants are disproportionately arrested and convicted.

Colorblindness also allowed the court to later prohibit McDonald supporters from wearing buttons that alluded to the racial issues at play in the case. McDonald's courtroom supporters had worn buttons depicting a red "X" crossing out a swastika symbol, but these were deemed "inflammatory" and "inherently prejudicial posing an unacceptable threat to the right to a fair trial" as well.[68] In this instance, too, the justice system's self-professed blind eye functioned to blind a potential jury to any of the ways racial difference continues to operate in society, including how race motivated and drove Schmitz's assault of McDonald. This post-racial legal framework, which effectively obscures the tremendous violence and systemic injustice the state continues to commit against black and brown bodies long after the official end of Jim Crow, not only prevented McDonald from mounting an effective defense but silenced those who would expose the continued operations of white supremacy. In other words, by asserting colorblindness, the state furthered white privilege and white supremacy demonstrating that "whiteness has value, whiteness is valued, and whiteness is expected to be valued in law."[69]

Local news coverage also evidences the power of the colorblind mentality to privilege whiteness. The *Star Tribune* noted Schmitz's swastika tattoo only once in its entire series of articles covering the case, quoting Schmitz's friend Thomas Nelson, who claimed that the swastika tattoo was "a key to survival in prison, but . . . didn't represent who either of them were later."[70] By reporting an apparent justification and absolution for Schmitz's swastika tattoo without even mentioning the racist and transphobic declarations of Schmitz and his friends before the fight, the local media, like the court, operated on a colorblind logic that functioned to reinforce white supremacy.

The Disposability of Black Lives

In her letters from prison, McDonald frequently referenced the killing of African American teenager Trayvon Martin to highlight and reflect upon the legal system's treatment of people of color:

> We all . . . know that this whole situation, from the incident itself to the trial, is all based on race—racial profiling and racism spewing from it all. . . . I know that people have been comparing my case to Zimmerman's, and yes it's obvious that laws are biased. But even I can say I came out blessed knowing that (a) the system was against me to begin with, and that (b) looking at other cases similar to mines, I didn't have to spend extensive time—even decades—in prison. People don't understand that I actually feel a guilt for that. I know that nothing beyond the incident and getting arrested was in my control, as it is for anyone who is a victim of the system.[71]

In February 2012 Trayvon Martin was killed by self-declared neighborhood watchdog George Zimmerman in a gated community in Sanford, Florida. When Zimmerman spotted Martin walking away from a convenience store, he called 911 and reported a "suspicious guy" in a "dark hoodie" who "look[ed] like he [was] up to no good or he [was] on drugs or something."[72] Despite being explicitly told by the dispatcher not to follow Martin, Zimmerman continued to do so and ended up shooting the unarmed seventeen-year-old.[73] The local police initially did not arrest Zimmerman, arguing that they had no evidence to dispute his claim that he had acted in self-defense.

Florida is one of more than twenty states that has adopted a "stand your ground" law, which exempts those with reason to believe their lives are endangered from any legal obligation to attempt to retreat outside their homes before resorting to deadly force. While McDonald's claim to self-defense was invalidated by the prosecution's assertion that she did not attempt to retreat, this was not the case for Zimmerman, whom a jury later acquitted of all charges. In 2015 the Justice Department also failed to indict Zimmerman of hate crime charges because it could not prove that Zimmerman had willfully deprived Martin of his civil rights or killed the teenager because of his race: "A comprehensive investigation found that the high standard for a federal hate crime prosecution cannot be met under the circumstances here."[74] This points to the difficulty of successfully prosecuting hate crimes. Zimmerman's acquittal and his ability to successfully claim self-defense speaks directly to McDonald's case in that it illustrates how little value our society and legal system give to black lives. The killing and disposal of black lives is sanctioned by stand-your-ground laws, which protect white perpetrators from facing legal prosecution and render white violence permissible.

In sharp contrast to the Zimmerman case, Marissa Alexander's conviction of aggravated assault for firing a warning shot into the ceiling to stop her abusive husband from attacking her in 2010 also speaks to the intersections of race and gender affecting who is granted access to legal protection and who is not. Alexander, a woman of color, was assaulted, strangled, and held against her will by her estranged husband in her home. As she fled to the garage and realized that she was unable to escape without the keys to her truck, she reached for her registered weapon and reentered her house to either find another exit or get her cell phone.[75] Alexander, who had a concealed weapon permit, also attempted to invoke Florida's stand-your-ground law, but a pretrial judge ruled that she could have escaped from her home. Similar to the prosecutor in McDonald's case, Alexander's right to self-defense remained unacknowledged because she allegedly failed to retreat properly. Alexander, who had no previous convictions and whose estranged husband had a well-documented history of domestic abuse, received a mandatory minimum sentence of twenty years in prison for discharging her firearm into the ceiling.[76]

Another case, that of the so-called New Jersey Four, also reveals salient parallels to McDonald and Alexander's cases. In 2006 a group of young African American lesbian-identified friends were walking in New York's West Village as they were harassed with sexually explicit and homophobic slurs by an African American street vendor who threatened them with corrective rape: "I'll fuck you straight, sweetheart!" An argument erupted that escalated into physical violence and left the vendor with a lacerated liver.[77] Paralleling a "reverse racism" rhetoric, New York's tabloid papers framed the incident as a "hate crime against a straight-man" and used the women's nonnormative gender expressions and working-class backgrounds from Newark to dehumanize, bestialize, and demonize them. A *New York Post* article opened with the headline "Attack of the Killer Lesbians" to claim that the victim was encircled by "seven bloodthirsty young lesbians" and beaten by "a seething sapphic septet."[78] The *Daily News* ran the headline "'I'm a Man!' Lesbian Growled during Fight" and reported on the sentencing: "Lesbian wolf pack guilty[;] Jersey girl gang gets lockup in beatdown."[79] An all-white jury later found all four women guilty of second-degree gang assault, and the women received sentences ranging from three and a half to eleven years despite contradictory statements and unsubstantiated evidence.[80] All of the women also knew and went to school with Sakia Gunn, a fifteen-year-old African American lesbian who was sexually harassed and stabbed to death at a bus stop in Newark in 2003 after refusing advances by two men.[81] Gunn's case is yet another one paralleling that of the New Jersey Four and McDonald.

While George Zimmerman took the life of an unarmed teenager who allegedly presented a danger to him was found not guilty by a Florida jury, Alexander and the New Jersey Four, who were fighting for their lives in a fashion strikingly similar to McDonald, received long-term sentences for defending themselves from violent attackers.[82] These cases illustrate that the application of stand-your-ground laws and the right to self-defense is arbitrary as well as race- and gender-biased. Zimmerman's ability to claim and embody white heterosexual masculinity enabled him to craft a narrative of self-defense and access to citizenship rights when facing an unarmed black teenager. Zimmerman's passing as white, partially enabled by the physical invisibility and unmarkedness of his Latinxness as well as his investment in the security state by protecting his neighborhood's "borders" as a citizen watch-

Fig. 8. "Honor Our Dead and Fight Like Hell for the Living" by Micah Bazant, 2013. Courtesy of the artist.

dog, demonstrates that in the era of colorblindness, the stigmatizing of racial groups no longer has to perfectly concur with a phenotype or color line.[83] Certain formerly stigmatized and devalued racial groups can now attain legal privileges and protections in exchange for their investment in and promotion of the U.S. security state. According to Grewal, fears of the waning of U.S. global dominance as well as the loss of white supremacy and white patriarchy have not only produced new racisms and new racial identities, but they produce the "shooter," such as Zimmerman, as an exceptional citizen who exerts his violent sovereignty as a means to save the imperial security state from its decline.[84] This privileged status, however, is always contingent and fleeting.

By retelling the stories above, I do not mean to exceptionalize them; instead, I want to demonstrate that the parallels between the cases of Marissa Alexander, the New Jersey Four, and CeCe McDonald point to the gendered and racialized logics permeating stand-your-ground self-defense laws and even hate crime laws. As both dominant media discourses and the state frequently invoked the long-ingrained stereotype of the "angry black woman" when ostracizing, criminalizing, and demonizing Alexander, the New Jersey Four, and McDonald as impulsive threats to society, these women's cases demonstrate how judicial and mediated discourses repeatedly converge in (re)victimizing and traumatizing survivors of domestic abuse and hate crimes. As mediated and legal discourses collude in positioning black (trans) women as the perpetrators, they generate a public discourse that condones the (white) victim status of the attackers and thus grants them legal protections while the lives and survival of these women of color do not matter at all. The cases referenced above also warrant a closer scrutiny of the passage of the Hate Crimes Prevention Act in 2009, which explicitly seeks to take into account certain identity categories to examine who can invoke hate crime statutes and whom those hate crime laws are designed to protect.

"Their Laws Will Never Make Us Safer"

The passing of the Matthew Shepard and James Byrd Jr. Hate Crimes Prevention Act (HR 1592) was widely celebrated as a milestone by national LGBT organizations and purported to increase public consciousness about the violence committed against members of the LGBTQ community by providing specific legal protections for marginalized groups.[85] In what Chandan Reddy calls "an act of genius," the bill was passed in large part because it was attached to a military appropriations bill—the $680 billion National Defense Authorization Act to cover the expense of President Obama's hundred-thousand-troop surge in Afghanistan—that made it impossible for social conservatives to oppose it and simultaneously prevented leftists from combining it with antiwar legislation.[86] The act expanded the 1968 U.S. federal hate crime law that applies to people attacked because of their race, religion, or national origin to include crimes motivated by a victim's actual or perceived gender, sexual orientation, gender identity, or disability. It also mandates the FBI to track statistics on hate crimes against transgender people. However, this newfound queer investment in the expansion of punitive systems and the neoliberal carceral state is highly problematic.[87] There is little if anything about the Hate Crimes Prevention Act that is actually prevention oriented.[88] Since hate crime legislation only seems to be invoked effectively for victims of violence who die, not for survivors like McDonald, who sought to protect herself from a hate crime by acting in self-defense, those cases require us to ask what the expansion of hate crime legislation is really meant to do and whom it is actually designed to protect.

While hate crime legislation explicitly attempts to account for race and ethnicity, gender, and sexuality among other categories, its legislative logic is equally flawed and problematic because, as Crenshaw observed about antidiscrimination legislation, it depends on the mobilization of discrete identity categories and is unable to address a larger context of structural, institutionalized violence against people interpellated by multiple intersecting identity categories. The rhetoric of hate crimes activism strategically isolates specific instances of violence against LGBT people and categorizes them as acts of individual prejudice but fails to critique the systemic discrimination and biases permeating and upholding the justice system.[89] The media's sensationalizing coverage of McDonald and the New Jersey Four and neglect to carefully scrutinize the legal system's treatment of people of color illustrates how the Hate Crimes Prevention Act (re)constructs the raced homonormativity of a white, middle-class, gay male subjectivity that is deserving of legal protections and valued, while racialized, gender-nonconforming bodies are left for disposal and to wither away. Because hate crime legislation relies on the mobilization of a discrete identity category, it remains unable to adequately address intersecting oppressions produced by multiple identity categories.

In stark contrast to the media's and the state's treatment of these black women, the murder of Matthew Shepard in 1998 and the suicide of Tyler Clementi in 2010, both young, middle-class, white gay college students, generated a tremendous amount of sympathetic media coverage calling on the legal system to deliver justice in these "hate crimes." The deaths of Shepard and Clementi managed to generate unprecedented national debates about anti-LGBT bullying, harassment, and violence that led to legislative action with the expansion of the Hate Crimes Prevention Act and the proposed Tyler Clementi Higher Education Anti-Harassment Act precisely because the media gravitated toward these subjects, deeming them valuable and deserving victims.[90] In Clementi's case in particular it is noteworthy that his bullies were both students of Asian descent whom dominant media discourses were quick to paint as intrinsically homophobic. In so doing, these discourses recirculated long-held stereotypes alleging that people of color communities are more homophobic than white ones. Without mounting pressure from media institutions, the state would have been much less likely to directly address homophobia through legislative measures in efforts to quell the public outcry.

Who is capable of claiming the status of a victim in a hate crime thus depends on racialized and gendered conceptions of who counts as a deserving or undeserving victim. Black and brown people, as always already racialized and criminalized—Trayvon Martin's hoodie in conjunction with his skin color, for example, rendered him a "thug" in Zimmerman's eyes, and McDonald's racialized gender nonconformity rendered her threatening in Schmitz's eyes—remain rightless, not deserving of victim status but of death. Similarly, the execution-style shooting of three Muslim students in their apartment in Chapel Hill, North Carolina, in February 2015 was initially dismissed by local prosecutors as an incident that had erupted over a parking-lot dispute, not because of pervasive Islamophobia in the United States: "Yesterday's events are not part of a targeted campaign against Muslims in North Carolina."[91] Contrary to this claim, witness accounts asserted that the alleged white shooter Craig Steven Hicks had previously threatened the students with a gun and had made Islamophobic remarks about the women's hijabs.[92] Interpellated by intersecting oppressions, these marginalized subjects are unable to evoke media attention or sympathy and are left unprotected by the state. As ethnic studies scholar Lisa Cacho notes, these undeserving populations are left to decay; they are marked for "social death": "As targets of regulation and containment, they are deemed deserving of discipline and punishment but not worthy of protection. They are not merely excluded from legal protection but criminalized as always already the object and target of law, never its authors or addressees."[93]

Many LGBT proponents of hate crime legislation have argued that hate crime laws can intervene in the devaluing of queer and trans lives by law enforcement and state prosecutors, evident for example, in the lack of investigations of and convictions rates for trans murders. Yet McDonald's case and those of others show that attempts to reform the justice system only deflect attention from the raced and gendered violence perpetrated and sanctioned by the security state against subordinated communities. Instead of conceptualizing alternatives to crime and punishment models and mending a broken and deeply biased justice system, these hate crime laws further legitimate and enhance what the criminal justice system in the United States is designed to do: target and incarcerate the very people these laws are meant to protect. Despite hate crime legislation claiming to protect marginalized groups, the continued racialization and criminalization of these populations presents their de facto exclusion from state and legal protections. And worse, hate crime laws further expose vulnerable populations to the state's increased surveillance, discipline, and punishment apparatus. In so doing, they funnel primarily minorities, poor people, and people with disabilities, whose disproportionate incarceration in the United States has been extensively documented, into the prison-industrial complex.[94] Hate crime statutes, therefore, have become another political and legal mechanism by which the security state and its politics of colorblindness masks an ongoing investment in white supremacy.

Conclusion

Because numerous motions filed by CeCe McDonald's defense team were dismissed and because the prosecution added a second manslaughter charge, it was not surprising that McDonald ultimately agreed to a plea deal shortly before her case was set to go to trial. In May 2012 McDonald was sentenced to forty-one months in prison for a reduced charge of second-degree manslaughter due to negligence and received credit for 275 days already served. She was additionally ordered to pay $6,410 in restitution for Schmitz's funeral expenses.

Beginning with the attack at the Schooner Tavern in 2011, McDonald has experienced various forms of violence: from the all too common racial profiling and police surveillance practices witnessed by McDonald and her friends shortly before the incident at the Schooner as a squad car followed them, to the verbal and physical assault erupting outside the bar because McDonald and her friends were perceived as "different," to the purportedly benign intentions of correctional facilities to keep her in solitary confinement, to the deceptive behavior of police investigators' extracting a confession from her, to local media's racialization of McDonald's gender identity, and finally to the prosecution's denial of self-defense. Because *both* dominant news stories and the prosecution failed to recognize McDonald's own intersectional subject position as well as the intersectional nature of the incident itself, it was especially the assertion of a colorblind rhetoric that enabled the multidimensional violence enacted against her.

As I originally began to write this chapter in early 2015, a grand jury in Ferguson, Missouri, had just failed to indict police officer Darren Wilson in the shooting of Michael Brown. A few days later, a grand jury in New York cleared an officer in the chokehold death of Eric Garner, which was caught live on camera.[95] Both events reignited national protests that originally began with the hashtag #BlackLivesMatter after Trayvon Martin's death in 2013 seeking to affirm the lives of black people. These events have also renewed debates about racial profiling, police brutality, mass incarceration, and systemic inequalities perpetuated by the legal system. But while the deaths of black men have been increasingly documented, there is still much silence around the violence against (trans) women of color. Communities are mourning the lives of Ciara McElveen, Tiffany Edwards, Zoraida Reyes, Mia Henderson, Kandy Hall, Terrell Anderson, and Miriam Carey, to name a few. The mother of Islan Nettles, a twenty-one-year-old black trans woman who was attacked in Harlem and beaten to death in 2013, had to wait until the spring of 2015 before her daughter's murderer faced charges. Whether we look at the CeCe McDonalds, the Trayvon Martins, or the Marissa Alexanders, we see that the U.S. justice system deliberately fails transgender and people of color and is rife with racial, gender, and class biases.

What I have sought to point out more precisely with this chapter is how the interplay and collusion between mediated and legal discourses powerfully fortifies and sanctions the targeting, disciplining, and incarceration—in short, the state's multifaceted violence—enacted against racialized and a priori criminalized populations, especially trans and gender-nonconforming women of color. A prevailing public discourse thereby is (re)produced in which these populations are only recognizable as already marked for disposability. The local media's complicity in condoning the state's treatment of McDonald and that of so many other (trans) people of color illustrates the complex operations of state power and how bio- and necropolitical violence is dispensed at different sites and discursive spheres, even when the state is not always necessarily its primary or direct agent. It no longer suffices to simply be critical of explicit state violence; what is necessary is to highlight the intricate interrelations between legal and mediated discourses to account for the propagation and amplification of these complex processes of violence and disposability in an age of neoliberal colorblindness.

As media-generated and legal discourses feed off each other to systematically devalue the lives of certain populations, media studies scholars and activists must engage more critically with questions of visibility: what does visibility actually afford and what does it not afford? While visibility is often actively sought by subjugated communities in their efforts to gain access to civil rights, the visibility politics surrounding CeCe McDonald point to the ways in which visibility might actually result in detrimental effects by further harming marginalized communities, especially those experiencing intersecting oppressions. Analyzing the local media coverage of McDonald, which reinforced problematic stereotypes about trans people and did not generate any progressive elements of trans visibility—just as hate crime laws purporting to protect marginalized communities may further aid in their vilification and surveillance—illustrates that utilizing mass-mediated discourses and legal avenues for social justice and social change is limited.

While McDonald's trial and treatment in local media outlets speaks volumes about the discriminatory practices of the justice system and hegemonic media's corroboration in othering and demonizing trans people, McDonald's story also presents hopeful insights into grassroots organizing and social justice activism that relies particularly on social media to challenge the prevalence of harmful and derogatory discourses surrounding trans women of color. In the next chapter, I highlight the formation of the CeCe Support Committee and its use of social media as a means of garnering support for McDonald and catapulting her story to national attention. I also contextualize her story with ongoing social justice hashtag activism to explore the practices, possibilities, and limitations of social media activism more broadly.

4

MATERIALIZING HASHTAG ACTIVISM
AND THE #FREECECE CAMPAIGN

!!ALERT!! Cece was just informed she has a court appearance tomorrow, 12/20/11 at 2pm. We need as many folks to come out to show support as possible. We need to show this "justice" system that she has community support even at the last minute. Let's meet at the inside fountain at the Hennepin County Courthouse, 1.30pm tomorrow. See you there community!

FreeCeCe McDonald Facebook post from December 19, 2011

We believe that to achieve safety, community, leadership and liberation for trans youth of color, we need to work against racism, adultism, misogyny and violence. In many of our hearts and bodies, this is common sense. In the world we live in, it's a revolutionary message. Please continue to carry this message in your hearts, we always will.

Jahleel Arcani, Jakob Rumble, La'Niya Dixon, and **Tayvon Caples,** Trans Youth Support Network codirectors in their final newsletter, January 2015

After CeCe McDonald's arrest in June 2011, queer and anarchist communities in Minneapolis and Saint Paul were quick to organize an astounding level of support around her case. In particular, the Trans Youth Support Network (TYSN), a local nonprofit organization working for transgender youth, and several of its members became crucial figures in organizing support for McDonald.[1] According to Lex Horan, a TYSN board member and one of the cofounders of the CeCe Support Committee, TYSN was frequently "a catching point for crises that are coming and going within that community."[2] It was thus not surprising that McDonald's story was brought to the attention of Katie Burgess, TYSN's executive director at the time.

As the events surrounding McDonald's arrest rapidly unfolded, community meetings generated large turnouts and stirred fertile conversations and exchanges about formulating a concerted response. Resulting from these initial meetings was the ad hoc formation of a CeCe Support Committee. Horan, a seasoned community organizer with experience in prison abolition and student organizing, acknowledged the difficulty of turning this "big mobilization . . . into a body that can do organizing together" to arrange and voice a unified community response to McDonald's case.[3] Although the organizational structure of the Support Committee would remain rather loose and change over time and despite significant political differences between members, a core group of people soon crystallized that began to rally support for McDonald: "We knew that . . . CeCe's fighting that she was doing on her own needed reinforcement from a broader community and so the way that ended up coalescing was through a formalized support committee but then also just tons of strands of connections to broader community."[4] As the committee coalesced, the group sought to achieve two key goals: first, to get McDonald the best outcome possible in her own case and second, to build broader activism around the prison-industrial complex, particularly its violence against trans women of color.[5] To achieve these goals, the committee's use of social media, in addition to more traditional media work, became increasingly important as the campaign progressed.

In this chapter, I illustrate how the formation of the CeCe Support Committee and its use of social media present important lessons for effective grassroots organizing, which is fueled by and increasingly reliant upon social media for advancing social justice. Social media tools enabled the committee to challenge the state's violence enacted against McDonald and local media's framing of her black gender nonconformity as deceptive and threatening. However, I also argue that although social media allowed for a broader reach and raised public consciousness about the devaluation of trans women of color, they do not miraculously provide transformative political engagement because intersecting oppressions, particularly the centrality of whiteness, continue to permeate online activism. Employing a micro-level ethnographic approach to the #FreeCeCe campaign complicates current understandings of social media activism (which are driven largely by quantitative, big data network analyses) by highlighting the complex and arduous communicative on-the-ground processes of meaning-making and collective organizing that traverse online and offline spaces.

I begin with a brief review of convergence culture scholarship and the rise of networked social movements before turning to the do-it-yourself (DIY) mentality informing the CeCe Support Committee's media work. I then explore the committee's use of social media to create counternarratives to change the dominant framing of McDonald's story and to pressure the state to recognize her humanity. Finally, I revisit some of the conclusions drawn in the previous chapter about the disposability of black transgender lives by considering how socioeconomic stratification factors impact intersectional and coalitional grassroots activism and participatory media more broadly.

Convergence Culture

Since the early 2000s, the rise of new media technologies and increased "media convergence" have prompted both dystopic and utopic responses about the potential of new technologies to enhance the agency of media consumers and improve participatory democracy. These responses have ranged from claims about social media's capability to enhance freedom and democracy (the "Twitter Revolution"), to accusations about their feel-good, weak-tie, and low-risk "slacktivism," and most recently about their ability to skew political elections through the circulation of "fake news."[6] Henry Jenkins's optimistic formulation of the term *convergence culture* has been especially influential in media studies. Convergence describes the multi-platform flow of media synergies between media industries as well as increased participatory opportunities. According to Jenkins, media are thrown into flux, "expanding opportunities for grassroots communities to speak back to the mass media."[7] For Manuel Castells the surge of digital social networks in the early 2010s has resulted in "networked social movements" such as the Arab Spring and Occupy movements, which have drastically expanded the capacity of social actors to challenge state power: "Historically, social movements have been dependent on the existence of specific communication mechanisms: rumors, sermons, pamphlets and manifestos, spread from person to person, from the pulpit, from the press . . . In our time, multimodal, digital networks of horizontal communication are the fastest and most autonomous, inter- active, reprogrammable and self-expanding means of communication in history. . . . This is why the networked social movements of the digi- tal age represent a new species of social movement."[8] Although mass media are largely controlled by governments and corporations, Cas- tells believes that autonomous "mass self-communication" processes enabled by social media "offer the possibility for largely unfettered deliberation and coordination of action."[9] The prominence of network approaches to the study of digital social movements, as exemplified by Castells, has also been accompanied by a prevalence of quantitative, macro-level big data analyses of recent protest movements.

Particularly W. Lance Bennett and Alexandra Segerberg's concep- tualization of "connective action," which asserts the neoliberal logic of individual agency over collective solidarity, has been well received among scholars.[10] Analyzing the Occupy and Spanish Indignados movements, the authors argue that traditional logics of collective iden- tity formation and action are replaced by connective action, which is characterized by personalized logics of participation and sharing across media platforms. This transition from "collective" to "connective" is possible as social media become "organizing agents" themselves. But despite advancing our understandings of the internal workings of digital social movements, these empirical, quantitative analyses tend to result in "static overviews of protest activity (action as fact) while neglecting the micro-dynamics of collective action (action as process)," as Paolo Gerbaudo and Emiliano Treré note.[11] Approaching and eval- uating the #FreeCeCe campaign through an ethnographic approach illustrates what these large-scale empirical data analyses often omit and are unable to capture—namely, the material constraints on social media activism.

While some scholars emphasize the merits and potentials for dem- ocratic participation through converged media, most do not consider the political economy of the media or the power struggles historically reinforced by the digital divide. Other scholarship has illustrated how the assumed equation of interactive technologies and participatory usage with DIY citizenship is ignorant of how these technologies not only potentially silo and seclude communities but also allow for a consolidation of state power, increased state violence, and surveillance and self-regulation practices.[12] For example, in March 2018 it was revealed that Cambridge Analytica, an election consultancy hired by Donald Trump's 2016 election campaign had harvested data on eighty-seven million Facebook users to map their personality traits and then attempted to influence voter behavior with targeted digital ads. Undoubtedly, new interactive media technologies allow for increased participation in media, yet convergence culture cannot be understood to function separately from the sociopolitical, cultural, and economic processes in which they are embedded. For Nick Couldry it is more plausible to see "convergence" as "a medium of longer-term stratification" once we acknowledge how race, gender, class, and other identity layers hierarchize the spaces in which convergence is practiced.[13]

Feminist media scholars have specifically pointed out that labor divisions and gender inequalities continue to permeate converged media and undercut their participatory potential.[14] Recent scholarship has paid close attention to the surge in feminist hashtags that attempt to mobilize feminist communities across different spaces. For example, in her analysis of the framing of SlutWalk London, Keren Darmon illustrates that feminist messages circulating online do not necessarily travel intact into the larger public sphere; instead they are often (re)articulated by mass media through a "post-feminist tinted lens."[15] Other scholars have critiqued the continued hegemony of Western feminist discourses that produce (self-)orientalizing accounts and white rescue narratives within hashtag activism.[16] But while racism and sexism continue to flourish and are reinforced online—presenting a serious obstacle to equal participation, especially for women, people of color, and LGBTQ folks—social media are also known to cultivate a politics of resilience in the face of sexual assault and rape culture, as demonstrated, for example, with the rise of the #MeToo movement in the fall of 2017.[17]

Because "new media are increasingly sites of struggle over control, surveillance, and monetization, as well as sites of struggle over meaning, representation, and participation," I take to heart Larisa Kingston

Mann's call for interventionist feminist analyses in the visibility and participatory politics of these new social media platforms.[18] I situate the #FreeCeCe campaign within this strand of feminist critique to offer insight into the simultaneously promising yet precarious capabilities of social media to produce social change. My analysis contributes a more refined understanding of the different modes, material practices, and political impacts of the "participatory turn" engendered by social media. Social and political realities of the modern world do not simply disappear with the uptake of social media. My examination of McDonald's case highlights that intersecting oppressions are maintained and can even be exacerbated in the move to social media, which are, therefore, not a catchall solution for social movements. While identifying the shortcomings of overly enthusiastic interpretations of social media, I also recognize their unique capabilities for mobilizing a broader constituency by actively shaping public conversations about the value and disposability of trans women of color's lives.

Do-It-Yourself Grassroots Organizing

Unlike Castells's and Jenkins's views that networked social movements consist predominantly of (white) tech-savvy, highly educated, young middle-class professionals—the CeCe Support Committee comprised a multiracial group from working- and middle-class backgrounds with varying educational levels (some held college degrees, others did not).[19] The committee members' levels of experience working with traditional media differed, and the development of media strategies was strongly informed by a DIY mentality and ties to face-to-face networks already existing within left, anarchist, and queer communities. The media and organizing experience of some of the members of the notorious 2008 RNC Welcoming Committee proved particularly invaluable.[20] Although the National Center for Transgender Equality (NCTE) later provided media training for the Support Committee, the committee was mainly reaching out to local community members that enabled it to gain the necessary skills, knowledge, and resources to organize online and offline support.

Lex Horan remembered writing the group's first press release "before any of us knew how to write a press release." Similarly, Billy Navarro

Jr., a local trans activist working for the Minnesota Transgender Health Coalition who was instrumental in building and coordinating the committee's social media presence, had no prior professional media experience and developed the necessary technological skills and expertise as the case progressed. Navarro's "soft leadership" skills as a social media administrator became crucial for guiding and coordinating the committee's social media work. Katie Burgess, then TYSN's executive director, became the committee's most recognizable face as she participated in interviews with media organizations and led many rallies and fundraising efforts.

Because most committee members held regular day jobs, the majority of organizing work for McDonald was done during their spare time, consisted of unpaid labor, and made use of limited financial resources. The committee's strategies were never solely spontaneous and unplanned; instead, their mobilization efforts were achieved through carefully orchestrated and persistent strategies, what Gerbaudo calls "choreographies of assembly," which often did not lead to immediate results.[21] Every tactic underwent thoughtful deliberation from McDonald and the committee's core members, enacting a certain level of leadership. Without these preexisting face-to-face networks and soft-leadership directives, the committee would have been unable to create the effective "backstage" communicative dynamics that were central for generating collective momentum and achieving the committee's goals.[22]

The grassroots activism around McDonald illustrates that movements cannot be sustained solely within and by social media but instead must be combined with traditional media to be effective. From the beginning, the group was conscious of media framing and made sure to provide standard pieces of traditional media work, including press releases and official statements. The committee recognized the need to build relationships with reporters from local news outlets, such as Abby Simons from the *Star Tribune* and Andy Mannix from *City Pages*. In response to the condescending *Star Tribune* coverage described in the preceding chapter, the committee organized a letter to the editor campaign, but none of the letters were ever published. Horan also recalled the committee's disappointment after working on the cover story for the *City Pages*: "We spent *a ton* of time and energy working with Andy [Mannix] in the lead up to the trial and during [pre]trial, and the story they ended up putting out was shitty. . . . We felt like we got really burned after putting in so much time on the story."[23] As media and state institutions both criminalized McDonald's gender nonconformity to produce her as a threatening subject whose actions did not rise to the level of self-defense, the Support Committee started using social media channels to create counternarratives.

The Slow Spread of the Low-Hanging Fruit

The Support Committee was fully aware that the only way to exert pressure on the state and the prosecution to drop the charges against McDonald was to provoke a public debate about the disposability of a black trans woman trapped in the justice system. According to Horan, the committee knew that its power within the courtroom was always going to be immensely less than its power outside the courtroom and the media: "What was going to happen to CeCe was really going to rest on how much of the context we could get incorporated into the story and get into the court room if possible, but if not—just get present in a public narrative. Because we knew that, we were never calling for a fair trial for CeCe. We knew that there was no such thing [as] a fair trial for anybody in the U.S., let alone a black trans woman in the U.S."[24] The committee deliberately reached beyond Minneapolis's local media outlets to seek footholds wherever possible in national, independent media and with sympathetic bloggers. After continuously sending press releases and making phone calls, this tireless and tedious work cumulated in the "very slow build of the low-hanging fruit" as Horan described it:

> We had been sending releases to all those folks forever. And we were trying forever to get into the *Huffington Post*, and we were trying forever to get in touch with *Democracy Now!*. And finally, I think as CeCe's trial approached, and . . . as the critical mass of the smaller media outlets started to rise and started to cross the desks of those slightly larger outlets a little bit more—that was when we started to finally get calls but it didn't, this sort of sense of getting a flurry of coverage, wasn't until April, maybe even May [2012] after CeCe's [pre]trial.

Specifically, the retweeting of McDonald's story through the hashtag #FreeCeCe on Twitter became crucial for building this slow but steady momentum. The creation of the #FreeCeCe hashtag allowed for an effective indexing and inter-discursive hyperlinking of various information pertaining to McDonald's case.[25] As her case went to trial in the spring of 2012, the Support Committee urged supporters to "retweet, post, repost, tumble, forward, spread far & wide" her story.[26] The support of writer and trans rights activist Janet Mock (as well as the followers of her #GirlsLikeUs hashtag), activists from the Sylvia Rivera Law Project, and Laverne Cox further helped to propel McDonald's story onto the radar of national LGBT and media organizations.[27] By April 2012 McDonald's story frequently made national headlines in a variety of alternative and special interest outlets, with mentions on Melissa Harris-Perry's show on MSNBC, *Democracy Now!*, articles on *Colorlines*, the *Advocate*, *Huffington Post*, and *Mother Jones*, as well as Marc Lamont Hill's essay "Why Aren't We Fighting for CeCe McDonald?" on Ebony.com (see fig. 9).[28]

The committee's continuous efforts to reach out to larger national news organizations until McDonald's story was finally deemed nationally newsworthy complicates uncritical social media scholarship alleging that new media technologies easily enable messages to go viral and spread. For example, Jenkins and his colleagues assert in *Spreadable Media: Creating Value and Meaning in a Networked Culture* that the concept of "spreadability"—describing how the elements of the media environment, texts, audiences, and business models work together to facilitate easy and widespread circulation of mutually meaningful content within a networked culture—offers potential "for renegotiating the social contract between media producers and consumers in a way which may be seen as legitimate and mutually rewarding to all involved."[29] However, McDonald's case shows that content that explicitly addresses the intersections of racial injustice, homophobia, and transphobia is harder to digest and, therefore, less spreadable. It took the committee months of building slow momentum through repeated press releases and social media messages, yet the delayed spread of McDonald's story did not mean that it was dead. The fact that McDonald's story did manage to capture the attention of promi-

Janet Mock ✔
@janetmock

Following ⌄

@kenyonfarrow thanks for your @Colorlines piece on #FreeCeCe and the need to stand in solidarity with her: ow.ly/1LM4lU #girlslikeus

10:11 AM - 6 May 2012

Fig. 9. Janet Mock (@janetmock) tweeting in support of McDonald, May 6, 2012. Screenshot.

nent outlets such as *Democracy Now!* and *Huffington Post* through slow grassroots activism indicates that Jenkins's work ignores the political and economic power structures undergirding corporate media outlets and their influence on what is considered "mutually meaningful and rewarding content."

The initially slow uptake of the story by national news media is indicative of Bruce Williams and Michael Delli Carpini's apt description of the operations of the "media regime" as a "historically specific, relatively stable set of institutions, norms, processes and actors that . . . determine . . . the gates through which information about culture, politics and economics passes, thus shaping the discursive environment in which such topics are discussed, understood, and acted on."[30] The slow spread of McDonald's story is, therefore, illustrative of the socio-economic and cultural stratification processes that not only impact access to communication technologies in general but determine who gets to participate in the process of deciding and shaping what is considered spreadable, valuable, and newsworthy.

The media landscape of Minnesota is a microcosm of these processes. The ownership structures of Minneapolis's and Saint Paul's corporate media organizations and the increased concentration of the area's metropolitan media market are reflective of larger national trends concerning the political economy of news media. The *Star Tribune* and *Pioneer Press* (the latter of which, as I mentioned in the previous chapter, did not publish a single article on McDonald) functioned as gatekeepers and bottlenecks for the local media market, often setting the agenda for major news stories. Both papers have changed owner-ship several times in the past ten years (ranging from private equity firms and shareholding companies to the *Star Tribune*'s current own-ership by a former Republican Minnesota state legislator and wealthy businessman who also owns several professional sports teams) and are known to be fairly conservative in their reporting. In times when newspapers especially are facing continued pressure to increase prof-its with steadily declining readerships and downsized newsrooms, the old slogan "if it bleeds it leads" (at least if the bleeding person is white) seems more relevant than ever.

Despite the fact that socially disadvantaged communities are most likely the ones utilizing social media for activist purposes, gate-keeping practices in mainstream media continue to influence what spreads and what types of stories are highlighted. Although marginalized commu-nities have increased access to smart phones (and thus social media), corporate media outlets still reinforce racist, transphobic, and other problematic standards in their reporting.[31] For example, because the national Black Lives Matter movement is a product of those socially disadvantaged communities (of color, lower class, etc.), mainstream media often portray that movement not as activist but as criminal, its members engaged in "rioting" and "looting."[32] Thus, while hashtag activism since the early 2010s has allowed marginalized and oppressed communities to document incidents of state-sanctioned violence and to contest racialized media representations, it is also important to keep in mind that social media platforms are themselves corporate entities that police and surveil their users.

Users from disenfranchised groups are often differentially targeted as objects of surveillance on social media. Citing the story of a Canadian woman who lost her disability insurance because her insurer argued she looked "too happy" (to be depressed) in her Facebook pictures, Lisa Nakamura demonstrates the constant need for women to self-regulate online to avoid violating heteropatriarchal norms: "Our identities are inextricably attached to the cultural contingencies of our gendered bodies."[33] Similarly, while Facebook was lauded for introducing more inclusive gender options for its users in February 2014, the company has repeatedly shut down profiles of Native American, drag queen, and transgender users for allegedly violating their "authentic names policy."[34] Moreover, despite the availability of fifty-six "custom" gender options, Facebook's software remains coded to misgender users and reassert the gender binary once it translates those identities into storable data points. Rena Bivens argues that offering advertisers, marketers, and other third-party clients profitable data about gender only comes in one format: binary. Under a seemingly "progressive surface," Facebook thus intentionally continues to misgender users driven by corporate monetizing logics.[35] In December 2014 participants in a nonviolent Black Lives Matter protest at the Mall of America in Minneapolis were not only aggressively confronted by law enforcement in riot gear, but local organizers and Black Lives Matter groups on social media were also, as it turned out, preemptively spied on and surveilled by local police and the FBI Joint Terrorism Task Force.[36]

In McDonald's case the judge partially granted the prosecution the use of several statements from the Support Committee's blog and McDonald's personal Facebook account relating to the stabbing. The court admitted, for example, the following Facebook exchange: asked by a Facebook friend "wat you kill?," McDonald responded, "A PERSON . . . BUT IT'S HARD TO EXPLAIN . . . AND I DNT THINK I SHOULD TALK ABOUT IT OVER FB" and later added, "WHY AM I THE ONLY PERSON BEING CHARGED FOR DEFENDING MYSELF????"[37] Unbeknownst to McDonald at the time, the court later declared these electronic materials relevant "because they tend to prove or disprove Defendant's self-defense theory."[38] Monitoring McDonald's private Facebook account and the Support Committee's blog are examples of how law enforcement agencies commonly access personal conversations online (often with the complicity of social media site operators). These tactics demonstrate not only the widespread surveillance on social media but how easily data and information gathered on these sites can be used against unwary users. After having identified some of the pitfalls of social media as activist tools, next I illustrate that social media *did*, however, provide platforms for mobilizing broad support for McDonald. I examine social media as tools for social movements, both small and large, as a complex interaction between dominant formations and the agency of individual groups or coalitions.

Grassroots Power-Building through Social Media

In addition to Twitter and the #FreeCeCe hashtag, the committee's creation of the blog *Support CeCe* as well as Facebook and Tumblr pages administered by Billy Navarro Jr. proved crucial in generating national and even international support beyond the Twin Cities. Building a social media presence was not just a way to connect supporters and activists online and offline, but in conjunction with more traditional media work such a presence became a powerful tool for achieving the committee's goals. The committee's use of social media demonstrates many of the possibilities for subversive, bottom-up tactics that can be harnessed and implemented strategically by marginalized and oppressed communities to circumvent traditional media gatekeepers and to apply pressure on state institutions.

Spurred by frustrating interactions with local journalists, the committee deliberately deployed Twitter to call out derogatory local media coverage and voice calls to action. For example, the committee called out *City Pages* for its sensationalistic storytelling by alerting readers to the potential triggers of "white supremacy, racism, descriptions of physical and verbal violence, trashy tabloid writing, [and] total lack of tact."[39] Moreover, the committee used Twitter to successfully urge supporters to directly comment on the online version of *City Pages* cover story. As a result the paper changed the article's original headline—"The Edge of Doubt: When a Transgender Woman Stabs a Man Tattooed with a Swastika, How Will Justice Be Served?"—to "CeCe McDonald Murder Trial: Behind the Scenes of the Transgender Woman's Case."[40] However, the paper's editors did not make any changes to the article's original content or apologize for its problematic coverage and tone.

The *Support CeCe* blog, a simple WordPress website, became a platform for supporters to provide updates on the trial proceedings and post press releases, flyers, and videos. A petition, which demanded Hennepin County prosecutor Michael Freeman to drop all charges, generated almost nineteen thousand signatures.[41] The website encouraged active involvement and applied direct pressure tactics announcing "pack the courtroom" rallies and call-in campaigns to the prosecutor's office. The committee also organized several community events and

FreeCece McDonald
@Free_CeCe

Photo: Demand that Chrishaun Cece McDonald be administered the 20 milligrams of hormones that she is... tmblr.co/ZzRafvO-ZQwq

10:03 AM - 9 Jul 2012

Fig. 10. Tweet from the CeCe Support Committee (@Free_CeCe) demanding hormones for McDonald, July 9, 2012. Screenshot.

asked supporters to fill out posters inscribed with "I stand with CeCe because ___." These posters were then faxed to Freeman's office with the intention to clog his fax and phone lines. Similarly, the committee organized a successful call-in campaign to the Saint Cloud correctional facility, where McDonald was transferred after her sentencing. The Saint Cloud facility initially administered only six milligrams of hormones to McDonald, instead of the twenty milligrams she was prescribed.[42] Through widespread social media alerts on various platforms, supporters rallied behind McDonald and bombarded the prison's directors with phone calls requesting the appropriate dosage. Under the tab "CeCe's Blog," the committee also published correspondence it received from McDonald during her incarceration. In her letters, McDonald addressed numerous topics (for example, the Zimmerman trial mentioned in the preceding chapter) and wrote thoughtfully about her experiences as a trans woman of color facing daily street harassment and violence (see fig. 11).

The Support Committee saw the blog as a means of truly enabling McDonald to fight for her own life and have her voice heard, piercing the silencing walls of the prison-industrial complex. She also acted as an advocate for other trans women of color who were subject to similar experiences. As Horan noted, "CeCe was ready to take all the risks that she needed to take to speak out and to really call on people to step-up for her and that level of leadership that she took enabled everything else that happened. And she couldn't have done that on her own. There were a lot of people, a core group of people in the Support Committee and then thousands and thousands of supporters around the world who stepped-up behind her. And I think those two things were both totally necessary."[43] Social media were one piece of a larger puzzle that allowed McDonald to raise her own voice and to narrate her life and its conditions, what Judith Butler describes as "giving an account of oneself," whereby the "I" is always addressing an other while simultaneously being interpellated by normative structures and other subjects.[44] For Butler, the self is inherently relational and certain norms will always determine the limits of who is recognized as a subject and who is not. Social media gave the committee the ability to bypass mainstream media gatekeepers—these tools presented what Benkler terms "feasibility spaces" for social practice and action that produce effective counternarratives through social peer production rather than hierarchical knowledge production steeped in corporate market forces.[45] Social media specifically challenged colorblind discourses that denied McDonald's transgender subjectivity and the violence committed against trans and people of color communities.

The committee's organizing work is, therefore, exemplary of Nick Couldry's call to *value* voice appropriately as the rationalities of neoliberalism deny, exclude, and undermine voice and forms of its expression. These hegemonic rationalities have led to a crisis of voice, not just in economic but also in political and cultural realms, as the dominant view of politics as (free) market trumps all other concerns. For Couldry expanding on Butler, "voice" is, therefore, not just the process of giving an account of oneself, but also the value given to that process: "The fundamental deficit in neoliberal democracies is, then, not one of voice but ways of valuing voice, of putting voice to work within processes of social cooperation."[46] The committee's social media activism gave McDonald the necessary social and material support to make her voice matter—to not just give an account of herself but to give value and recognition to her voice, to validate her lived experience as a trans woman of color and to influence the knowledge production around transgender lives. However, it is important to note

Fig. 11. The *Support CeCe!* blog, November 5, 2014, www.supportcece
.wordpress.com. Screenshot.

that while the committee's social media activism was crucial for generating broader awareness about McDonald, such activism does not consistently translate into material change without a basis in traditional activist strategies—especially physical protests.

Embodied Protest

Once the counternarratives started to slowly build up and as more national media outlets picked up McDonald's story, representatives from national queer and trans organizations also began to voice their support. For example, Mara Keisling from the NCTE and the late trans rights activist Leslie Feinberg both traveled to Minneapolis to attend McDonald's pretrial and rallies in May 2012, lending their voices and faces to the protest.[47] Feinberg was even temporarily arrested for spraying "Free CeCe!" on the walls of the Hennepin County Government Center after McDonald's sentencing. In this sense, Feinberg took the hashtag #FreeCeCe from the disembodied space of the Internet and sprayed it into materiality, creating a material hashtag. The materialization of the hashtag through graffiti speaks to the blurring of immaterial and physical spaces, the converging of online and offline worlds. Feinberg's defiant act further illustrates how social media and on-the-ground activism do not and cannot function separately from one another.

The Support Committee's social media work allowed supporters to create alternatives to existing communication infrastructures and to direct people toward specific sites of protest—a "*material precipitation from symbolic assemblages to bodily assembly in public space*"[48]—for example, with rallies in front of the Hennepin County Government Center and the "occupation" of the courtroom itself. While Castells argues that networked social movements are "born on the Internet, diffused by the Internet, and maintain [their] presence on the Internet," the importance of occupying the symbolic space of state-sanctioned violence for the Support Committee's protests and demonstrations cannot be understated.[49] The amorphous and ephemeral interactions of the committee online coalesced with the materiality of bodies on the ground occupying spaces of protest. In other words, disembodied social media activism around transgender rights and social justice converged with material and embodied activism offline: bodies protesting, bodies being surveilled, contained, incarcerated, and marked by the intersecting oppressions of identity categories.

As the history of the committee shows, activism around McDonald could not have taken place solely on the Internet and was not completely leaderless or decentralized, as convergence scholarship suggests.[50] On the contrary, it is important to recognize that mobilization efforts are always inscribed by hierarchies between those who mobilize and those who are mobilized, between those who have the technological know-how to lead and those who follow. Much more accurately, the committee's DIY grassroots activism is indicative of complex choreographing processes that are primarily dependent on the "mediated 'scene setting' and 'scripting' of people's physical assembling in public space."[51] Undoubtedly, social media have drastically changed the way activism takes place; however, social movement theory should not simply laud the Internet for enhancing engagement with issues of social justice but must acknowledge the role of material, physical practices in contemporary activism. For example, Bennett and Segerberg claim that connective action "does not require strong organizational control or the symbolic construction of a united 'we,'" as it thrives mainly on highly flexible and personalized experiences enabled by social media.[52] However, the fusion of online and offline protests in McDonald's case shows that the formation of collective action and identity processes is still highly relevant. The fact that a nucleus of core organizers tirelessly rallied supporters and led marches attests to the importance of individual key actors; moreover, achieving the committee's goals depended on the construction of a collective voice. The materiality of social media activism manifesting in large on-the-ground protests and call-in campaigns created a sense of belonging, common cause, and "shared ideological frame."[53] Fostered by both digital *and* physical collaborations, this sense of collective action was critical for exerting pressure on state institutions. What the CeCe Support Committee demonstrates is that social movements are neither spontaneous nor self-maintaining; instead, they are the product of intensive, unpaid labor and careful planning.

According to Horan, the committee was mindful at all times of not creating backlash through pressure tactics that could have negatively impacted McDonald's case and consulted with her whenever possible. As it became clear, for example, that McDonald would be housed in an all-male facility based on her birth-assigned sex (as are most incarcerated trans people), several petitions began circulating that asked Minnesota governor Mark Dayton for a pardon. These petitions were not authorized by McDonald or the committee. Through these gubernatorial pardon requests, it was easy to infer that the injustice in McDonald's case centered solely around her being placed in a male correctional facility and not from the fact that McDonald should never have been convicted in the first place.

For McDonald and her supporters, discussions about where McDonald would be housed were mechanisms of distraction that cloaked more direct challenges to the actual injustice and violence enacted against her by the state; they failed to ask one essential question: why are there so many trans people in prison in the first place? These petitions failed to account for the fact that prisons are fundamentally racist, sexist, homophobic, and transphobic institutions, rife with sexual violence, and unsafe for *everyone*. In short, as Horan recalled from conversations with McDonald: "A prison is a prison. A prison isn't safe for anybody."[54]

In conjunction with the *City Pages* cover story calling her a "transgender Matthew Shepard," these repeated calls for pardoning only worked to exceptionalize McDonald.[55] Turning to the multiple feedback loops and input channels created by social media, the committee reached out to these groups and individuals and requested that they stop advocating for these well-intended yet ill-conceived pardon requests. Explaining the committee's reasoning, Horan noted, "We really believed that CeCe shouldn't go to prison and we didn't believe that because she was special . . . even though she is incredibly special, but it's because that system is unjust for anybody like CeCe who interacts with it. . . . So that calling for pardon for many of us was just really crossing the line into exceptionalizing her in a particular way." In contrast to what some of the local media outlets had alleged, the committee was very conscious about not exceptionalizing McDonald's case. With these uncritical pardon requests, the Support Committee directly encountered one of the potentially negative side effects and drawbacks of the "mass self-communication" or "many-to-many" communication engendered by social media, where the roles of information recipient/consumer and producer are constantly in flux and increasingly blurred.[56] As some of McDonald's supporters decided independently to produce and spread messages about pardoning requests, they undermined the committee's larger goal of raising awareness about (and McDonald's own approach to) the prison-industrial complex's perpetuation of systemic injustices. The popularity of these unauthorized pardoning petitions (which were advocated for by people who did not experience marginalization and oppression themselves), therefore, illustrates the difficulty of maintaining control and authorship over a particular narrative in the age of convergence media. As cross-media pollination allows for the fast and unlimited dissemination and multiplication of messages, the originally intended meaning of a narrative may get easily modified or go astray. Finally, these pardoning struggles also point to the ongoing tensions and difficulty around doing activist work for an individual prisoner that does not simply exceptionalize or tokenize that particular subject but instead highlights larger systemic inequalities and injustices.

In sum, the committee's social media work effectively allowed for "the construction of an emotional narration" that was able to preserve and orchestrate the (physical) coming together and organization of supporters over a prolonged period of time.[57] Through status updates on

Twitter, Tumblr, and Facebook, supporters from the Bay Area to Berlin could feel an emotional connection to McDonald's case. In addition to traditional activist tools—protests, singing, chanting, creating posters, and fundraising—social media mobilization successfully established a tight-knit community support network for McDonald that far exceeded the local boundaries of the Twin Cities. Unlike the bottleneck structure of local legacy media, social media actively enabled the committee to shape and change the epistemologies surrounding the value of trans lives. These grassroots knowledges slowly but persistently spread and were then taken up by a variety of larger national, alternative media outlets. This increased uptake successfully disrupted the devaluing ideologies perpetuated by local media outlets. And while the committee was fully aware that public outcry and protest would not necessarily topple the white supremacist structures upholding the justice system, they were determined to at least expose these structures and create fissures in a profoundly biased institution.

The Centrality of Whiteness

As my interview with Lex Horan came to a close, I asked him about any shortfalls or failures he had observed in the committee's organizing. Horan, himself transmasculine and white, was self-reflexive and identified a major shortcoming of the campaign in the lack of outreach to civil rights and black organizations that did not necessarily have an LGBT focus in their work. Horan acknowledged that this was mainly due to "white supremacy playing out in organizing." While the committee was a multiracial group, it was still a "majority white-multiracial group." Many strategy conversations at committee meetings were most often attended by white and brown activists without the presence of any local black organizers. In praxis the group was much more familiar and comfortable with organizing around homophobia and transphobia than around racism, which led them to cast their outreach efforts narrowly: "I think that a lot of us . . . weren't sure how to best build relationships with black-led organizations that were doing work around the criminal legal system, around imprisonment, around police brutality; or by women-of-color-led organizations that were not trans focused. . . . Those weren't the first organizations that we thought about on top of our heads, those weren't the ones that would first ring in our networks."[58] While not formally a part of the Support Committee, numerous black queer and trans people did, however, play a crucial role in providing support to McDonald, for example, by giving rides to protests, hosting fundraisers and events, supporting her family members, and visiting her in prison. Horan clearly identified this major dialectic between the committee's media framing, which always emphasized *both* racism and transphobia affecting McDonald's case, and the lack of devotion to the same emphasis in the committee's actual organizing and outreach work:

> We should have done what we did with media, to open the door and keep inviting. And not to say that it would have or wouldn't have become a top priority of local black-led organizations, or national black-led organizations, or national civil rights organizations, but we didn't do enough asking, we didn't do enough reaching out. . . . I think that we played out a mistake that happens a lot with young organizers and young white organizers in particular, . . . we came on with a lot of rage and passion about what was happening and I think we didn't always have enough of the humility around folks that have been doing this for a long time; how do we connect with them and ask questions, and listen if they have push-back for us.[59]

Although the majority-white Support Committee was able to build strong support in left, anarchist, and queer circles, it was not able to build the same bridges with communities of color, which ultimately reinforced a harmful centering of whiteness in the campaign. This centering of whiteness was further reinforced by ageism and the unwillingness of the Support Committee, mainly composed of young activists in their mid-twenties to mid-thirties, to engage in a cross-generational approach to organizing. The community organizing around McDonald, therefore, illustrates several of the problems and stratification processes that have affected other U.S. social movements, including the Civil Rights movement, the Women's Liberation movement, the Occupy Movement with its white, middle-class focus, or concerns of inclusivity in the Black Lives Matter organizing.[60]

The committee's difficulty in organizing support for McDonald across racial boundaries reflects how the collusion of dominant media and state discourses in vilifying trans women and the repeated assertion of the justice system's alleged impartiality also affects the ways in which social movements are able to challenge these realities. The material convergence of the committee's activism not only mirrors Minneapolis's geographic makeup as a deeply gentrified and segregated city, but it also complicates its image as a midwestern bastion of progressive, *white* liberalism. Despite their ability to recognize their white privilege, activists are not immunized against discourses of colorblindness, making it extremely difficult to create sustainable coalitions. Similarly, I recognize how my own positionality as a privileged white cisgender queer scholar influenced my limited outreach to interview other trans committee members of color or their unwillingness to speak to me as an "outsider" to the community.

Jenkins believes in the possibility of convergence media to create "meaningful social change under the conditions of Neoliberal capitalism" and predicts a "new ethic of knowledge sharing that will allow us to deliberate together."[61] In Castells's and Jenkins's narrow vision, the success of new networked social movements may be measured by their ability to reform capitalism and representative democracy—but not to question, replace, or topple these systems through more radical socioeconomic reforms: "They aim to transform the state but not to seize the state." Castells, even more explicitly than Jenkins, makes it quite clear that he considers anticapitalist and socialist reform efforts "ideologies of the past."[62] But as Chandan Reddy and others have demonstrated, current forms of neoliberal capitalism are dependent upon and perpetuate virulent forms of white supremacy.[63] As white supremacy is inextricably linked to modern forms of (racial) capitalism, my analysis of the grassroots organizing work surrounding McDonald shows that Jenkins's and Castells's viewpoint is, at the very least, misguided: white supremacy is not reformable; it must be abolished. More specifically, McDonald's case demonstrates that whiteness continues to permeate online activism just as much as it influences our material realities offline. More recently Jenkins has become more cognizant of the systemic and structural challenges impacting grassroots organizing and has expressed a more cautionary tone about the democratic potential engendered by changes in technology. He has acknowledged that "participatory culture" oftentimes functions as an empty signifier that is used superficially by different groups to induce participation without actually giving up control.[64]

Undoubtedly, the plethora of new communication technologies has allowed for the multiplication of voices from a vastly different set of people, has increased mutual awareness, illuminated alternative epistemologies, and enabled new scales of political organizing across spatial boundaries. However, the proliferation of previously unheard and suppressed voices online alone will not result in meaningful and lasting social change that acknowledges or actually changes the lived experiences of trans people. Social media activism alone cannot and will not change the perception and devaluation of trans women of color within larger society and specifically the legal system—changing such perceptions needs broader reinforcement and a recognition of voices such as McDonald's in mainstream media. As Couldry rightfully observes, "Making voice *matter* is hard; it is even harder, amid a proliferation of new voices, to challenge the hidden forces and dislocations that prevent them mattering when it counts."[65] My ethnographic analysis of the CeCe Support Committee's grassroots activism calls for a more cautionary approach to social media scholarship and demonstrates that the potential for participation through engagement with social media does not automatically lead to greater diversity or to the empowerment of oppressed communities. The mixed results of the social media activism around McDonald echo the limitations other larger social movements have faced in achieving actual political change, for example, in the varying levels of success (and failure) that have characterized Occupy, the Iranian Green Revolution, and the Arab Spring. Despite social media's ability to mobilize significant crowds in Zuccotti Park, Tehran, or Cairo's Tahrir Square, these movements largely failed to replace exploitative capitalism and oppressive authoritarian rule because of lacking material infrastructures.

Conclusion

The politics of convergence media are intricate and contradictory, and most importantly, they are deeply embedded in hierarchies of difference that characterize the material spaces in which convergence takes place. Despite the committee's access to these new media technologies, its members' own sociodemographic backgrounds functioned as stratification factors that resulted in limited intersectional outreach efforts to build support for McDonald. Notwithstanding these shortcomings and the prosecution's unwillingness to drop the charges against her, the committee's grassroots campaign presented significant challenges to local news outlets' derogatory coverage resulting, for example, in the *Star Tribune*'s aforementioned adoption of an official transgender style guide in 2014. The committee's activism also helped to unveil the justice system's institutionalized racism and raised a critical consciousness in the larger public about the rampant violence and discrimination against transgender people, particularly those of color. The committee's work also directly contributed to a plea deal carrying a reduced charge of second-degree manslaughter due to negligence and a forty-one-month prison sentence for McDonald, who originally faced up to forty years.

After her release from prison in January 2014, the media attention surrounding McDonald grew exponentially, and she has since become a prominent figure in LGBT activist circles and beyond. McDonald is a tireless advocate for transgender rights, appearing on national TV, speaking on college campuses across the country, and participating in LGBT galas. She is also the subject of the critically acclaimed and crowdfunded documentary *Free CeCe* (released in 2016, directed by Jac Gares and produced by Laverne Cox), which addresses transmisogyny and the epidemic of violence against trans women of color. In 2018 McDonald was named an activist in residence at the Barnard Center for Research on Women, where she is continuing to work on transformative, abolitionist justice models that do not rely on the prison-industrial complex.

Despite the increased media visibility of McDonald and her work for social justice and prison abolition, the material reality is that she is still stigmatized as a trans woman of color with a felony on her record. Since her release McDonald has been struggling to find employment and pay for her basic living expenses. She has experienced homelessness and had to temporarily sleep on supporters' couches. Two fundraising campaigns via the GoFundMe and YouCaring websites have

 **FreeCeCe McDonald**
@Free_CeCe

Follow ⌄

#cecefree CeCe's Support Committee, friends, family & @Lavernecox stopping for breakfast Mon morning

Fig. 12. The Support Committee (@Free_CeCe) welcomes McDonald after her release, January 14, 2014. Screenshot.

raised more than twenty thousand dollars to help with her precarious financial situation by covering the security deposit for rent and to support her activism by allowing her to buy a computer and cell phone. As Alexander so powerfully chronicles in *The New Jim Crow*, after release from prison, felony records present another means of racialized social control that reinforce a racial caste system and relegate people to the margins of society.[66] With a felony record, people like McDonald are legally denied the ability to secure housing, employment, or public benefits, let alone the right to serve on juries or vote. In Minnesota convicted felons cannot vote while in prison or on probation, and in some states a felony conviction carries a denial of voting rights for the rest of one's life. Whenever McDonald applies for a job, chances are good that she must list prior convictions on her applications, or they may turn up during a background check conducted by a landlord upon applying for housing. If McDonald were to consider continuing her studies toward a degree in fashion design, she is likely to be denied financial aid as a result of her record. In short, felony records marginalize and severely impact the ability of individuals to reintegrate into society long after they have served their sentences. Felony records present such an impediment to economic survival and well-being that they set individuals up for failure and often feed them right back into the vicious cycle of the prison-industrial complex.

Similarly, although TYSN gained some national prominence through its connection to McDonald's case, for the small youth-led trans grassroots organization, which survived mainly on grants, the increased visibility around the struggles of trans people did not translate into the support necessary to keep the organization viable and healthy for the long run. TYSN closed its doors on January 31, 2015, after it had been led entirely by trans people of color, all under the age of thirty, who had come up through the organization since its founding in 2004. In their final newsletter, TYSN's codirectors cited the lack of funding, training, and shared communication between former adult members and future leaders as the main reasons for shutting down the organization as the work, "personally and collectively," had become unsustainable. The codirectors thus decided "to put an end to a harmful cycle—leaders working their hardest, and then burning out and failing to train future leaders, running an organization unsustainably—instead of allowing it to continue."[67]

Transgender visibility and the politics of convergence thus do not automatically equate to improvement in the living conditions of marginalized and oppressed trans communities. As I explicated in chapter 2 with the emergence of transpatriotism, we are in a moment wherein certain able-bodied, transnormative people can access national belonging and citizenship rights through raced, classed, and gendered privileges. At the same time, the surveillance, policing, and violence against trans communities of color are reaching unprecedented heights. What, then, really are the material benefits of this increase in trans visibility? For the future success of trans rights activism and organizing, it is imperative to engage in building alliances across boundaries that are shaped predominantly by racial categories. The members of the CeCe Support Committee were fully cognizant that overcoming the interrelations of oppressive systems as well as building and cultivating stronger and long-lasting relationships between multiracial, queer and trans communities are essential for the transgender movement's future.

Since the activism around McDonald's case in 2012, we have witnessed the proliferation of Twitter hashtags in the United States that demand the recognition of differences across intersecting identity categories. Black Twitter's powerful momentum has successfully brought attention to police brutality and violence committed against communities of color.[68] Hashtags such as #BlackLivesMatter, #GirlsLikeUs, and #SayHerName have generated nationwide debates about social justice and challenge incidents of racial tone-deafness among legacy media. In particular, the hashtag #TransLivesMatter, which was coined in the wake of a transgender teen's suicide in 2014, has become a rallying cry to combat the epidemic of violence that trans people face. These hashtags not only confront the persistent harmful centering of whiteness in activist and feminist organizing, but they also dissect how the seemingly all-inclusive term *women of color* still renders invisible women who are not cisgender or who fall outside the black-white binary.[69] Through bold Twitter commentary, Mikki Kendall (@Karnythia), Raquel Willis (@RaquelWillis), Lauren Chief Elk's Save Wiyabi Project (@SaveWiyabi), Suey Park (@sueypark01), and Bamby Salcedo (@translatinbamby) tirelessly analyze how intersecting oppressions impact the everyday lives of indigenous, Asian, Latinx, trans, and women of color.[70] These previously silenced and marginalized women successfully utilize social media platforms for sharp cultural criticism, which has not only caught the attention of dominant media but has also allowed some of them to publish their works in the *Guardian* and *New York Times*, among other mainstream media outlets.[71] These women's successful appropriation of social media tools demonstrates that social media can function as what Nakamura calls a "feminist countersurveillant media," which produce epistemologies that challenge traditional ideologies perpetuated by mainstream media and subsequently penetrate these institutions to reframe the privileging of certain lives and narratives over others.[72] Despite neoliberal attempts to coopt social justice efforts and the persistent risk of social media's replication if not exacerbation of intersecting oppressions, we are now at a critical juncture where historically excluded and marginalized voices may generate unprecedented movement building by demanding truly intersectional social justice approaches and engagements with the visibility politics produced by mainstream and social media.

5

SEX WORK, SECURITAINMENT, AND
THE TRANSGENDER TERRORIST

"Walking while trans" is a . . . known experience in our community of being routinely and regularly harassed and facing the threat of violence or arrest because we are trans and therefore often assumed to be sex workers.

Monica Jones, interview with the ACLU, April 2, 2014

A U.S. transgender activist who had her visa cancelled at Sydney airport claims Seven Network producers knew details of her case that she had not told them, and that they pressured her into agreeing to be filmed for the TV program *Border Security.*

The Guardian, December 2, 2014

In May 2013 Monica Jones, a trans woman of color, sex work activist, and student in Arizona State University's (ASU) social work program was arrested in Phoenix on a manifesting prostitution charge for accepting a ride to a bar with an undercover cop. The Phoenix Municipal Code stipulates that a person may be guilty of such offense if they are "in a public place, a place open to public view or in a motor vehicle on a public roadway and manifest . . . an intent to commit or solicit an act of prostitution."[1] To determine whether such an intent is manifest, the statute cites everything from repeatedly stopping on a sidewalk, waving at cars, engaging in a conversation with a passerby, to asking whether a potential patron is a police officer as proof of prostitution. Jones is part of Phoenix's Sex Workers Outreach Project (SWOP), which advocates for the rights of those who choose to work within the sex industry. The day before her arrest, Jones had protested against Project ROSE, an antiprostitution collaboration between ASU's School of Social Work, the Phoenix Police Department, and Catholic Charities. Project ROSE deliberately targeted sex workers, offering a "prostitution diversion" program—including emergency housing, detox, counseling, and DIGNITY Diversion, a thirty-six-hour "re-educational" classroom program—for qualifying sex workers in exchange for not filing criminal charges. Despite the police and Project ROSE's insistence that individuals were not officially arrested, according to the Phoenix ACLU, sex workers were handcuffed and brought to Project ROSE's command post at a church to speak with a project volunteer and a city prosecutor. They were not given the option to speak to an attorney, nor were they free to leave.[2] The diversion program could last up to six months. Those who did not qualify for the program (for example, those with outstanding warrants, had completed a prior diversion program, or were in possession of drugs at the time of arrest), declined to participate, or "failed" out of the program were sent court summons in the mail and faced criminal charges. Through massive street sweeps and online sting operations, more than 350 arrests were carried out between Project ROSE's inception in 2011 and its closure in 2014. On the day Jones was arrested in Phoenix, she had posted a warning of an upcoming sting operation on Backpage.com, an advertising service used by sex workers.[3] Many supporters believe that Jones was arrested precisely because of her activism for sex workers' rights and outspokenness against Project ROSE and because she is a trans woman of color.

With help from the ACLU, Jones challenged the charges brought against her, arguing that Phoenix's manifesting prostitution statute infringed on protected free speech rights and was "unconstitutionally vague and overbroad."[4] However, a year later in 2014, a judge found Jones guilty of prostitution charges and she received a mandatory thirty-day jail sentence and five-hundred-dollar fine for repeat offenders under Arizona's prostitution law. During her trial, the prosecutor repeatedly referenced Jones's previous convictions for sex work in efforts to further criminalize her. After growing public outcry over Jones's treatment by the police and state prosecutors—as in McDonald's case mainly fueled by social media activism and on-the-ground grassroots organizing—Project ROSE was disbanded in November 2014; yet Phoenix's "manifesting prostitution" statute still stands. In January 2015 an appeals court declared a mistrial in Jones's case, vacated her conviction, and ordered a new trial, in part because the trial court had used evidence of Jones's prior prostitution convictions to conclude that she was not credible and, therefore, guilty, depriving her of a fair trial.[5] Prosecutors have since dropped all charges against Jones.[6] However, the criminalization and surveillance of Jones neither ended with nor was confined to the events in Phoenix. Her story became international news when a reality TV crew from the Australian hit show *Border Security: Australia's Front Line* wanted to film Jones's encounter with Australian custom officials at the Sydney airport, which led to her subsequent voluntary deportation in late 2014.

In this chapter I first detail the long history of criminalizing sex work in the United States to illustrate that the disproportionate racial profiling of trans women of color, such as Monica Jones, as sex workers for "walking while trans" is intimately connected to the security state's larger bio- and necropolitical efforts to manage certain "at-risk" populations—both inside and outside of its own borders. Even diversion programs that present themselves as benevolent such as Project ROSE become a key tool for the security state to further regulate alleged sexual and gender deviants and to bring them under the purview of the state's surveillant gaze. I then trace how Jones's criminalization by the U.S. security state subsequently impacted her ability to travel to Australia, where she was considered a "possible threat" to national security and thus denied entry. Jones's convictions for prostitution in the United States and her racialized gender identity effectively flagged and marked her as "deviant" in international systems of surveillance and regulation. Even more notably, during Jones's interrogation by Australian immigration officials, she was repeatedly pressured to consent to the filming by the production crew from *Border Security*. Jones's story presents an unprecedented and undisputable example of how the neoliberal security state and media corporations explicitly collude to capitalize on the racialized criminalization of trans- and gender-nonconforming people as terrorists.

Criminalizing Sex Work

The criminalization of sex work in the United States dates back to the early twentieth century and is inextricably tied to racial anxieties and the changing role of women in society. Most prominently, the White Slave Traffic Act, better known as the Mann Act of 1910, made it a crime to transport women across state lines "for the purpose of prostitution or debauchery, or for any other immoral purpose."[7] The early nineteenth-century moral panic about white slavery was fueled by sensationalistic accounts that innocent white women were being kidnapped, forced into prostitution, and shuttled around the country by vast immigrant-controlled networks. While the act was designed to combat forced prostitution, its broad wording was in actuality used to criminalize consensual sexual activities, particularly in interracial relationships.[8] While prior to World War I only a few laws criminalized prostitutes themselves, by the end of the war "the law had recognized a class of prostitutes who would constitute a social group of criminal outcasts."[9] With heightened fears of a looming health crisis due to the widespread presence of venereal diseases among U.S. soldiers, a series of public health policies were enacted that criminalized and stigmatized predominantly poor and working-class women as sexual deviants, while soldiers were merely seen as "victims" of their "immoral" solicitations.[10] The Chamberlain-Kahn Act of 1918, for example, authorized government officials to surveil and arrest any woman under suspicion of having a sexually transmitted disease. Violating their basic civil rights, these women were then quarantined for an unspecified amount of time and forced to undergo medical examination and, if necessary, treatment. By the end of World War I, roughly thirty thousand women had been criminalized and brought under government regulation.[11]

Since the early 2000s a renewed moral crusade, driven by a coalition of religious antiprostitution and antiporn feminist organizations has successfully reshaped government policies at the local, state, and federal levels toward further criminalizing sex work in the United States.[12] Driven by a strict abolitionist orientation and "rescue" mentality strikingly similar to the logic of twentieth-century moral crusaders, this coalition strategically conflates sex trafficking with all forms of commercialized sex in order to end what is now framed as women's oppression.[13] Except for some counties in the state of Nevada, sex work remains illegal in the United States, and statutes similar to Phoenix's prohibition of "manifesting prostitution" exist all across the country, specifically through loitering and vagrancy codes that prohibit engaging in a prostitution offense or intent to commit prostitution.[14] Congress recently also passed two far-reaching anti–sex trafficking bills, FOSTA (Fight Online Sex Trafficking Act) and SESTA (Stop Enabling Sex Trafficking) which amend Section 230 of the Communications Decency Act to hold websites such as Backpage.com and Craigslist liable for hosting "sex trafficking content." While constitutional scholars argue that such legislation sets a dangerous precedent for disregard of the First Amendment, sex work advocates see these trafficking charges only as a pretext to further criminalize and stigmatize sex workers.[15]

Diversion programs in particular have gained popularity across the United States in recent years as an offspring of the problem-solving court movement for drug related offenses in the 1990s. Created with the intention to "divert" offenders from their "criminal behavior," diversion programs want to change such behaviors through therapeutic interventions, thereby constructing consensual commercial sex as a mental health issue. Participants commonly indicate that they are motivated to join programs, such as Project ROSE, in order to avoid jail time and lengthy probation periods, as well as to expunge prostitution charges from their record.[16] However, as Stéphanie Wahab notes, despite the prevalence of diversion programs, there is "limited empirical evidence of recidivism benefits" from them.[17] While carceral feminism advocates for obtaining social justice for women by expanding the state's penal apparatus and reach through these programs, the "sex-positive" activism of Phoenix's SWOP and other sex workers' rights groups vehemently opposes such efforts and advocates for the decriminalization of sex work. The savior mentality of diversion programs such as Project ROSE fails to carefully distinguish between individuals who are subject to human trafficking and forced into prostitution from those who engage in sex work by their own consent for financial support. Chrysanthi Leon and Corey Shdaimah further criticize these programs for subjecting sex workers to various forms of surveillance and supervision, including curfews, drug testing, and mandatory attendance at individual and group therapy sessions if they want to pass the programs and avoid criminal charges.[18] In practice and effect, these diversion programs are, therefore, startlingly similar to early twentieth-century laws such as the Chamberlain-Kahn Act that allowed the government to arrest, examine, quarantine, and treat women without their consent.

Today, these programs constitute a key mechanism of the security state's bio- and necropolitical population management: by making assistance for secure housing, (mental) health care, substance abuse treatment, and educational programs available only in and through the criminal justice system, the security state ensures its ability to manage "deviant" behavior and oversee "at-risk" populations without directly physically containing them. Offering social programs through seemingly less coercive and benign public-private partnerships, such as Project ROSE, is particularly insidious because their availability is still tied to participation in and subjection to intensive state surveillance and regulation. Diversion programs do not make sex workers safer; rather, they further surveil, stigmatize, and funnel marginalized communities, especially those of people of color, poor people, and LGBTQ-identified people who rely on sex work for economic survival, into the criminal justice system.[19]

Monica Jones's case and her arrest are not unique: two-thirds of the roughly fifty-five thousand annual arrests for prostitution involve women, most of them are women of color and trans women.[20] The criminalization of sex work is therefore inextricably tied to racial profiling practices. "Walking while trans"—very similar to the racial profiling of "driving while black"—describes the known and all-too-common experience in trans communities of routine harassment, violent threats, and arrests as a result of being read or "clocked" as trans and concurrently profiled as a sex worker. Trans women of color are disproportionally profiled as being engaged in sex work, public lewdness, or other sexual offenses because they exist at the precarious intersections of multiple sites of oppression.[21] For many trans women, sex work is often the only work available to them due to widespread employment discrimination and economic hardships they face.[22] These factors disproportionally drive trans women into underground economies where they tend to take on more dangerous forms of sex work, such as street-based sex work, that often renders them vulnerable to violence and harassment by both johns and law enforcement. Because stereotypes about race and gender manifest themselves in biased policing practices, trans women of color are not only profiled as prostitutes because of their gender nonconformity but because as black and brown women they are often stereotyped as hypersexual and promiscuous. Hence, trans women are repeatedly criminalized and arrested merely for standing at a bus stop in a tight dress, waving at cars, or possessing condoms. Such stereotypes are also often perpetuated on U.S. television: in a ten-year survey of scripted content featuring transgender characters between 2002 and 2012, GLAAD found that the most common profession trans people were depicted in was sex work.[23] Prominent crime shows such as CSI and Law and Order frequently feature trans characters as deceptive prostitutes and ruthless serial killers. Because media actively (re)produce meaning and not merely reflect it, these problematic visual representations of trans women are instrumental in upholding dominant understandings of trans criminality. Jones's case thus further reflects the frequent criminalization and regulation trans people of color face by the public, mainstream media, and the state.

Securitainment at the Border

As part of her ASU social work studies, Jones had visited Australia several times to conduct HIV/AIDS research and to volunteer with the Scarlet Alliance Sex Workers Association to learn about Australia's sex worker laws. When she tried to reenter the country in late November 2014, she was detained at the Sydney airport because she had allegedly breached her student visa status on an earlier trip. Jones indicated she had not worked in Australia, but the Department of Immigration and Border Protection (DIBP) presented proof that she had advertised sexual services online.[24] Although sex work is not illegal in Australia, this work was a violation of Jones's student visa. Customs officials informed her that she was not entitled to "engage in any activity that included the sale of goods and services to the general public" and that her visa would therefore be canceled.[25]

While Jones was interrogated by DIBP, a television crew from Channel 7's reality TV program Border Security: Australia's Front Line approached her, wanting to film the interview. Border Security, which debuted in 2004, is a popular, internationally syndicated reality TV show that has consistently earned high ratings and is currently in its fourteenth season. The show follows the work of border protection officials as they enforce customs, immigration, and finance laws and "sort out" potential rule-breakers and criminals at ports of entry around Australia. In what would constitute a gross breach of her confidentiality, Jones later claimed that it seemed like DIBP had deliberately shared information with the show's producers about details of her case: "I felt pressured to consent to the filming by both DIBP staff and the producers of the show. . . . Every aspect of the process gave me the impression that the television program was connected to the DIBP and its decision making." Jones said she came to believe that agreeing to appear on the program would help solve her visa issues: "My impression was that everything relied on that interview."[26] After initially agreeing to the interview, she developed second thoughts and told them to stop rolling. "That's when immigration got really strict with me," Jones observed, and although she repeatedly told them that she did not want to be filmed, the television crew kept badgering her.[27] Even after the TV crew finally left the interrogation room, the immigration officer continued to pressure her: "Are you OK if they continue to film or do you want this to stop? This is what it goes like. . . . They come in, they film, they clear out whenever you like. It is up to you completely, it's your will. Whatever you want."[28] The immigration officer's comments reveal not only his familiarity with the presence of a TV crew during what one would assume is a private and confidential interrogation process but his active investment, perhaps more than that of the TV crew, in filming the encounter.

Media scholar Mark Andrejevic has aptly observed that shows such as *Border Security* belong to a constellation of popular culture formats, especially reality TV shows, that have emerged in the wake of 9/11 and function as "securitainment"—a hybrid genre that combines entertainment values with pedagogical lessons by providing instructions in strategies for risk management and security training.[29] These shows provide a tutorial on both the multiple threats to the nation posed by porous borders and on the array of skills and techniques used by "experts," for example, custom officials and border patrol agents, to detect, manage, and contain these risks. Andrejevic points out that these shows present the perfect symbioses of public-private partnerships and synergies between entertainment, information, and public relations that subtly and effectively promote individualization and personal responsibility for securing and protecting the nation. Based on such neoliberal logics, securitainment formats educate and activate what Andrejevic calls the "citizen-soldier" in the domestic space of the nation.[30] Furthermore, as I illustrate below, the security state not only grants free access and resources—"cast members," locations, and dramatic situations—to producers in exchange for promoting the patriotic work of its customs and immigration agencies, but it strategically uses the show to capitalize on the ever-looming specter of terrorism and to disguise the ruthless bio- and necropolitical processes at the heart of its targeted population management.

After being detained and having her student visa revoked, Jones agreed to voluntarily leave Australia. Despite initially alleging that Jones had been denied reentry for breaching her status on an earlier trip by engaging in (sex) work, the DIBP later confirmed that her deportation was due to her classification as a "possible threat" to Australia under the "movement alert list."[31] Australia's movement alert list is a database similar to the Terrorist Screening Database in the United States, which monitors border entries and in 2015 had approximately seven hundred thousand people registered as possible threats.[32] Although it is unclear exactly how Jones went from a visa breach due to alleged work violations to being classified as a national security threat, it is likely that the DIBP targeted Jones because of her existing criminal record in the United States. It is also likely that immigration officials at the airport intentionally flagged Jones because of her high story value for Channel 7's *Border Security* reality TV show.

Because Jones's criminalization as a threat to Australian national security is most likely a product of her prior convictions for prostitution, it is also implicitly rooted in her gendered and racialized identity as a sex worker. Denying Jones entry into Australia based on her criminalization for sex work extends a long history of racist immigration policies in dominant white countries that barred entry to immigrants who threatened the nation's racial and sexual purity.[33] While sex work has been legalized in Australia with varying regulations in different territories, it remains an excluded category on Australian work visas. For example, the 457 visa, which is the only long-term temporary work visa, does not list sex work on its extensive Consolidated Sponsored Occupation List and thus effectively denies sex workers legal employment or entry.[34] Australian immigration policies and visa regulations, therefore, continue to criminalize and penalize sex work.

What happened to Monica Jones upon entering Australia and encountering the TV crew from *Border Security* is an unprecedented example of the explicit cooperation and collusion between the security state and corporate media's framing of transgender people, particularly trans women of color, as deceptive, deviant, and thus threatening. Would *Border Security* have been interested in Jones's case if she were not a trans woman of color involved in a legal challenge over sex work in the United States? As a trans woman of color whose activism had garnered significant attention, Monica Jones knew that she was likely to stand out: "They knew details of what immigration was going to do to me. I think they knew it was great TV, [and] that [they] could sensationalize my story. . . . When you say you've got a very interesting story to a trans woman, I know you're going to sensationalize my story."[35] Given the problematic history of dominant trans representations in Western media, Monica Jones would have undoubtedly made a profitable story for Australian television, which would have likely focused on a stereotypically criminalizing portrayal of a trans woman of color as a sex worker, whose deceptive and promiscuous body threatens Australian national security. Thanks to "juicy" stories similar to Jones's, *Border Security*—which has been running for over a decade—continues to generate high ratings. In conjunction with its low production costs (a result of the DIBP's providing access to all "cast members," storylines, and locales for free), the show has become a guaranteed money maker for its producer, the Seven Network. This illustrates that there is an explicit economic and financial interest that drives the collusion between corporate media and the security state. While high ratings guarantee steady advertising revenue for the Seven Network, the security state also capitalizes on securitainment media because it actively sells and inculcates the citizenry with its conceptions of safety versus (terrorist) threat.

Despite the fact that Seven Network is a commercial corporation and not a government-funded public broadcaster, documents obtained under a freedom of information request filed by the Australian *Guard-*

ian in 2015 demonstrate that the security state exerts complete content control over what is aired on *Border Security* and is free to use the program for its own propagandistic messages. A deed of agreement between Seven Networks and DIBP for the 2013–14 season shows that Seven Network was only allowed to air episodes after it received official approval from DIBP lawyers. The deed outlines that Seven Network "will provide the Commonwealth with a DVD disk of each completed episode for approval" and that "the Commonwealth may require the removal of any footage that, in the Commonwealth's opinion, infringes the law or compromises the Commonwealth's working practice and/ or current investigation, is defamatory, or may prejudice an issue in pending or existing litigation."[36] If the DIPB requires changes, an edited DVD must be provided for final approval. When asked by the *Guardian* how often DIBP requested such changes, a spokesperson indicated that these are occasionally required for operational or security reasons but that both parties "have experienced personnel who work constructively and collaboratively on stories so that it minimises the need for changes."[37] Similarly, a representative of Seven Network commented that the network considered the approval requirement "a fair process" in order "to showcase the hard work of ABF [Australian Border Force] officers" and further asserted that the approval process did not impact the storytelling and was, therefore, "irrelevant to viewers" because "the interest is in the stories, not the mechanics of getting the program to air."[38]

However, Seven Network's claims that the stories being filmed speak for themselves and that the government-controlled editing process does not change an original storyline are not credible. From the first decision to film certain people and their immigration experiences to the framing of shots and to the selection of which scenes are included and which are cut when editing an episode, all of these "mechanics" *do* impact how a story's narrative arc is built and the type of engagement and emotions they elicit from the viewer.[39] Especially because the stories on *Border Security* are functionally lessons about proper citizenship that encourage self-responsibilization and peer-to-peer monitoring and because they actively construct who constitutes a threat to the nation, Seven Network's denial of admitting to the full extent to which the state is directly involved in the show's content creation is concerning, if not disturbing. If viewers were more aware of the state's role in the show, they would probably be more likely to question how "real" and accurate the majority of the depicted cases really are. While the deed states that editorial control of the show lies with Seven Network, it explicitly asserts that "editorial control does not limit the Commonwealth's right to require changes to the Program and ultimate right of refusal."[40] Seven Network also consents to destroying any footage "if required by the Commonwealth in writing."[41] This deed thus illustrates how intertwined and codependent the workings of the security state and private media corporations are. Despite Seven Network's insisting on the alleged integrity of its stories and creative independence, the security state maintains tight content control over the program and has the ultimate authority and final say over what gets aired and what does not. Therefore, the state effectively determines which media stories bolster its bio- and necropolitical population management to shore up patriotic citizen support and vigilance. In short, the show functions as nothing but state-sanctioned propaganda.

The deed also clarifies that in exchange for access, "Seven grants the Commonwealth a permanent, irrevocable, royalty-free, worldwide, non-exclusive licence (including a right to sublicence) to use and reproduce vision from camera and the Program following broadcast of the relevant episode for training and promotional purposes at no cost to the Commonwealth."[42] Demanding the right to reuse and repurpose any of Seven Network's footage for free highlights the DIBP's explicit financial investment in the show to further profit from its content by using it as promotional material for the security state and for training the next cadre of border patrol agents. Jones's encounter with the television producers from *Border Security* highlights both the economic and pedagogical interests driving the collusion between dominant media and the security state. As media play an increasingly crucial role in "educating" and "securitizing" viewers about potential threats, the security state strategically relies on and deploys securitainment to (re)produce its dominant assemblages of risk versus safety, us versus them, and domestic versus foreign rooted in gendered and racialized logics of white supremacy and heteropatriarchy. Shows such as *Border*

Security further demarcate lines between those who are granted access and belong to the nation and those who must remain firmly excluded.

Transgender Terrorism

In my own analysis of the U.S. spin-off of *Border Security*, ABC's *Homeland Security USA* (2009), I demonstrate that the majority of people exhibiting "suspicious behavior" and "deviant acts" depicted on the show were nonwhite and non-U.S. citizens, predominantly individuals from the Global South or the Middle East.[43] Western business travelers or tourists rarely make an appearance. Instead, the *Border Security* franchise further feeds into racialized post-9/11 anxieties that all too often falsely equate brown and Muslim people with terrorist threats and deliberately lumps together various risks such as drug trafficking and illegal immigration under the umbrella of terrorism. The security state and the producers of shows such as *Border Security* understand all too well that terrorism sells.

Australia has been one of the United States' closest allies in the War on Terror and has also experienced surges in nativism and Islamophobia. With the events of 9/11 firmly entrenched in public memory, the criminalization of Jones, initially attributed to an alleged breach of her student visa but then explained by her status as a "possible threat," is inextricably tied to an amorphous terrorist corporeality. In *Terrorist Assemblages*, Puar argues that "queerness is always already installed in the project of naming the terrorist."[44] Characterized by an "unknowable monstrosity," the terrorist is always failed, perverse, and deviant, as "these emasculated bodies always have femininity as their reference point of malfunction" and are further tied to numerous pathologies, including (suppressed) homosexuality, pedophilia, insanity, and disease.[45] Similar to fears circulating after 9/11 that male suicide bombers may "cross-dress" as women in order to avert scrutiny, Jones invokes the specter of the "trickster" terrorist—produced by her racialized gender nonconformity and assumed deviancy as a sex worker—who threatens to silently seep into the Australian homeland. Jones's encounter with officials at the Australian border and the framing of her as a threat to national security are not isolated incidents but show how precarious border-crossing situations are for transgender people—especially those visibly marked as gender nonconforming—and how their monitoring is connected to larger questions about the security state's surveillance of certain minority groups post-9/11.

After the attacks of 9/11, we are witnessing the rise of new identification technologies that reinscribe existing social norms and inequalities, aiming for the "securitization of identity," as sociologist Nikolas Rose explains.[46] Similarly, Rachel Hall has persuasively argued that the domestic security cultures emerging after 9/11 invest incredible amounts of resources "into producing docile global citizen-suspects who willingly become 'transparent' or turn themselves inside out, such that they are readily and visibly distinct from the 'opaque' enemies of the United States in the theatres of the war on terror."[47] Policy changes that have been enacted as part of the War on Terror to administer identity verification systems not only target immigrants and terrorist others but also function as exclusionary mechanisms limiting the movement of and presenting challenges to trans people, particularly through the use of advanced imaging technologies, ambiguous gender (re)classification policies that outline when and how the gender marker on identity documents can be changed, as well as the Transportation Security Administration's (TSA) SPOT program, which is supposed to detect and deter potential terrorist behavior.

In the United States, full-body scanners used by the TSA at airports point to the intersections between racial profiling, the War on Terror, and the (trans)gender surveillance enabled by these technologies. First introduced at U.S. airports in 2010, these scanners initially revealed a passenger's complete anatomy to a TSA agent in a remote location who never saw or met the actual passenger. After privacy advocates raised concerns, the TSA agreed to remove detailed images and replaced them with a software known as Automated-Target-Recognition, which creates a generic outline of a passenger based on two categories: male or female.[48] Before scanning a passenger, the TSA agent selects either a pink (female) or blue (male) button based on the traveler's perceived gender presentation. The scanner then alerts agents to "irregularities," such as genitalia, breasts, or prosthetics that do not match the physical appearance of a traveler. Conducting a "virtual strip search" by singling out bodily anomalies that contradict security expectations, these gendered and racialized surveillance practices function as "disciplining technologies," which essentialize conventional gendered attributes as they target and police those who deviate from normative understandings of biological sex.[49] What the state considers normal and normative is, of course, always dependent on the intersectionalities of race, class, and gender and dominated by hierarchies that typically privilege white, middle-class, heterosexual, and abled bodies. This effectively renders trans and gender-nonconforming people, people wearing religious clothing, and members of disability communities as threats to the security state.

Similarly, the implementation of the U.S. REAL ID Act of 2005, which seeks to standardize the reliability and accuracy of state-issued identification documents, has expanded the regulation and surveillance of legal gender. Some state agencies still require gender-affirmation surgery before they will change the gender classification on identification documents, while others do not.[50] In 2010 the State Department changed its policy for identification requirements for "gender reassignment applicants" on U.S. passports and eliminated the requirement for genital surgery. The Social Security Administration followed suit and eliminated the surgical requirement for changing the gender category on social security records in 2013. The legal regulation of gender not only relies on a flawed belief in a technological determinism, which assumes that through gender markers "visible" on identification documents, verifiable identities can be tracked, but it falsely presumes a fixity and secured link between sex, gender, identity, and identification. Because the legal measures to document trans people's gender status frequently contradict one another, they are particularly susceptible to the policies and practices enacted as a result of the War on Terror.[51]

Since 2007 the TSA has also trained special agents, behavioral detection officers, for the Screening of Passengers by Observation Techniques program, better known as the SPOT program, to identify potential "transportation security risks"—i.e., terrorists—based on suspicious behavior. The ninety-two-point checklist outlined in the SPOT Referral Report is divided into categories, such as "stress," "fear," and "deception." Despite a persistent lack of scientific evidence for the program's reliability and validity, the SPOT report lists anything from "face pale due to recent shaving of beard," "Adam's apple jump," "excessive perspiration inconsistent with the environment," and "hesitation/indecision on entering checkpoint," to "wearing improper attire for location" as evidence of suspicious behavior.[52] Given especially the descriptors targeting nonnormative gender presentation and attributes, such as "appears to be in disguise" and "change in voice, pitch, rate, volume, choice of words, dry mouth," it is easy to see how trans and gender-nonconforming travelers are especially prone to catch the attention of such behavioral detection officers and score high on this checklist. This usually results in additional screening, questioning, and potentially the denial to clear security. As evidenced further with the SPOT program and its detection categories, the security state explicitly links gender nonnormativity with its construction of terrorist behavior.

It is not only through identification documents that trans and gender-nonconforming people are susceptible to be flagged by tightened security measures post-9/11, but it is precisely because their gender identity is not deemed authentic in a larger networked security apparatus that is exclusively coded according to white Western heteronormative binary categories. Trans people often evoke the specter of terrorism because the possible mismatch between their gender presentation, physical characteristics, and identification documents is read as a deliberate attempt to conceal their "true" identity from the security state and fly under its radar. The security state, ever concerned with verifying and tracking identities as a means of terrorism prevention, therefore, considers trans and gender-nonconforming people as fraudsters who trick and cheat administrative systems. In conjunction with hegemonic tropes that (re)inscribe queer as terrorist monstrosity—especially the fear of terrorists using cross-dressing as a tactic to escape security mechanisms at airports, borders, or public spaces—trans people become intimately entangled in the state's ever-expanding antiterrorism programs. As the examples above illustrate, such programs are not only inherently and intentionally racialized but also gendered.

Conclusion

As the neoliberal security state outsources not only its welfare duties but also its responsibilities to "protect" its citizenry, it increasingly relies on surveillance data and mechanisms that do not necessarily emanate from official government sources but depend on private corporations and partnerships to aid in its bio- and necropolitical population management. Whether it is a community diversion program like Project ROSE aiming to "correct" deviant sexual behavior; L3, a leading manufacturer for detection systems that provides airport security around the globe with ProVision 2 full-body scanners; or TV shows such as *Border Security* that help to "securitize" the nation—they all are part of the security state's ever-expanding surveillance network. These surveillance technologies and practices are thoroughly cultural forms that reflect the power relations and ideological conflicts of the societies that produce them.[53] In particular, intersecting logics of race, gender, sexuality and class inform such practices, which disproportionly subject trans and gender-nonconforming communities to frequent policing, discrimination, and incarceration. The criminalization of consensual sex work in the United States generally and the racialized profiling of trans women of color as sex workers specifically illustrate how the security state seeks to further limit and control the economic livelihoods and survival of those already at the margins of society.

David Lyon urges that surveillance practices must be theorized in ways that transcend its local and specific manifestations.[54] Monica Jones's story illustrates that the criminalization of trans people is not limited to but extends beyond the confines of U.S. domestic territory. Jones's classification as a possible threat to Australian national security due to her racialized gender nonconformity highlights that the security state's surveillance practices strategically expose certain "at-risk" populations to further scrutiny by other allied neoliberal Western states, which work in tandem to prohibit trans people from traversing borders. Moreover, the unprecedented cooperation between the Australian DIBP and Channel 7's *Border Security* demonstrates that the security state strategically uses seemingly independent corporate entities to further infuse citizens with its framing of risk and safety, of who belongs to the nation and who does not. What makes this collusion particularly insidious is that both dominant media organizations and the security state frame and deploy trans people as a racialized terrorist threat to maintain and advance support for larger imperial projects, specifically the

War on Terror. Fundamental to this collusion is thereby an economic interest: while the media benefits from high viewership, the security state constantly (re)deploys tropes of terrorism to maintain and justify its vast military-industrial-surveillance complex, which requires large numbers of immigration agents, militarized borders, and extensive surveillance technology.

The simultaneous production of normative patriot corporealities (e.g., the vigilant customs agent or the citizen-soldier who takes it upon himself to monitor and defend the border, or in George Zimmerman's case, the gated neighborhood) and terrorist corporealities (e.g., the black trans woman advocating for sex workers' rights, the hijab-wearing Muslim woman, or the amputee "abnormally" marked by prostheses) thereby cohere through and against each other. These bio- and necropolitical processes thus exert their power to let live or make die as they expose various marginalized and vulnerable groups living at the intersections of oppressive systems to a constant state of precarity, disposability, and death.

Transgender visibility did not improve Monica Jones's livelihood but instead rendered her more vulnerable and exposed to state-sanctioned violence. Jones's criminalization for "walking while trans" made her the subject of numerous local and national news reports, which consequently generated a widespread social media following to support her; thus, her visibility was a double-edged sword. In spite of successfully fighting the manifesting prostitution charge leveled against her, the state's far-reaching security systems ensured her continued surveillance, even beyond the nation's borders. Jones's visibility as a black trans woman—produced by the media coverage surrounding her case and her existing legal record for prior sex work convictions— activated a transnational security apparatus that selectively targets, monitors, and restricts certain bodies and their movement. Despite *Border Security*'s producers insisting they had no knowledge of her history, Jones's visibility made her a prime candidate for exploitative storytelling in Australia. Jones herself did not benefit from this visibility—rather she was unable to complete her ASU research project and faced increased state surveillance and criminalization. In short, visibility for Jones produced more harm, vulnerability, and exposure to brutal and degrading state and media agendas, not the security, safety, and protection that proponents of visibility politics so often proclaim. Unfortunately—as illustrated throughout this book—Jones's experiences with trans visibility are not the exception but mirror broad and systemic patterns of violence, discrimination, and harassment against trans and gender-nonconforming people that are all too often engendered by such visibility.

I have lost count of how many times in the past year I've stood on stage and said that trans women of color and gender non-conforming people of color—some I've known, others not—continue to be murdered or die from structural abandonment, despite the fact that there are trans people on television, in movies, and on the cover of magazines, trans friendly jails, trans friendly military. Again and again, I say that visibility and representation within institutions doesn't get to the root causes of these harms, doesn't bring employment, nor does it bring housing; it doesn't end prisons, and it doesn't end police. Just because we're being seen, doesn't mean we're any safer. Hypervisibility endangers us, representation is a trap.

Tourmaline, commencement address at Hampshire College in 2016

Through *Terrorizing Gender* I have tried to make explicit precisely how the media's framing of transgender people as inauthentic, deceiving, deviant, and threatening not only reproduces and sanctions but reinforces and colludes with state interests and surveillance practices in violating, discriminating against, and criminalizing trans communities. Bringing surveillance studies and queer methodologies, specifically an ethnographic on-the-ground approach, into conversation with critical media studies highlights the complex relations between cultural representations, modern governance, and the everyday lived experiences of trans people. This allows us to better understand how political and legal systems interpellate trans and gender-nonconforming subjects. Additionally, the book also highlights the importance of intersectionality as an essential analytical tool for critical media and legal studies to address the means by which oppressive systems interlock. In short, I have sought to expose, following the lead of trans activists' long-standing critique of visibility, how dominant media and legal discourses of trans visibility often negatively impact the material, lived realities of transgender communities. Because the increased visibility of trans people in popular discourse is accompanied by heightened exposure to state surveillance practices, *Terrorizing Gender* cautions against the trap of visibility, arguing that it does not suffice to focus on representational politics alone or even primarily if we are to account for the multifaceted operations of state power and its dispersal of violence. As an integral component of the security state's larger bio- and necropolitical aims, the law's alleged impartiality and colorblindness continue to protect and advance white supremacy. Within prevailing public discourse, trans people, especially those of color, are recognizable only as threats to the security of the state and are, therefore, marked for disposability, unable to claim legal protections and abandoned as *homi sacer*. The experiences of Manning, McDonald, and Jones vividly illustrate how the surveillance practices enacted against trans people function to normalize and reinforce the gender binary, heteronormativity, able-bodiedness, white supremacy, and capitalism in the service of U.S. hegemony and empire. The emergence and popularity of transgender as an identity category in public discourse and the increased media visibility of trans people, therefore, must be understood as a *contingent* cultural belonging within the historic context of the state's racialized and gendered violence enacted against these communities.

Nothing has illustrated the persistent paradoxes of trans visibility and trans death more starkly than the media hype surrounding Caitlyn Jenner's coming out on the cover of *Vanity Fair* in June 2015.[1] Titled "Call Me Caitlyn," the *Vanity Fair* cover depicted Jenner, a former Olympic gold medalist and part of the Kardashian-Jenner clan, after her transition into a conventionally beautiful woman. For the cover, Jenner was shot against the luxurious setting of her Beverly Hills mansion in feminine, suggestive poses flaunting various dresses and outfits. After several facial feminization surgeries as well as breast augmentations, Jenner's body had been molded to reflect white cisnormative female beauty standards. Later that summer, Jenner also starred in her own

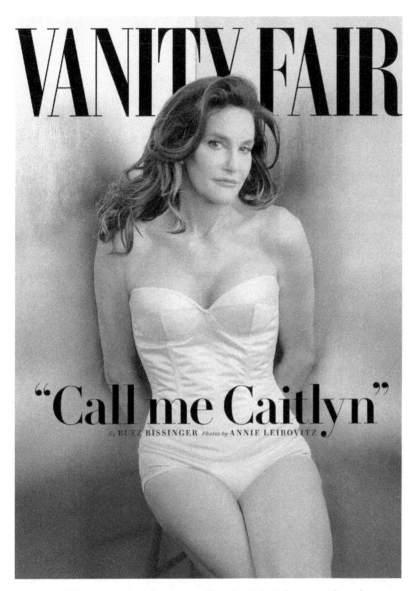

Fig. 13. Caitlyn Jenner on the cover of *Vanity Fair*, July 2015. Photo by
Annie Leibovitz. Courtesy of Condé Nast.

reality TV show, *I Am Cait* (2015–16), on E!, which documented her experience as a newly out trans woman.

Although mainstream media outlets applauded Jenner's "bravery" and labeled her a "prominent role model for the trans community," it is important to recognize that Jenner's visibility is inherently privileged: she is wealthy, able bodied, and white.[2] Jenner has unrestricted access to health care, housing, employment, and a secure income—resources that are unattainable not only for many trans people but for most people in general. Jenner's feminization surgeries, for example, are typically excluded from health coverage and are therefore unaffordable for the majority of trans people. It is precisely this set of privileges, in conjunction with the public's long-standing fascination with celebrity makeovers, that has allowed Jenner to garner media attention unlike any other trans person before her. Author Janet Mock recalled that within an hour after the release of the *Vanity Fair* cover, she was inundated with media requests to comment on Jenner's transition. "That one hour resulted in more requests than I have received from the release of my book, the release of Laverne Cox's *Time* cover, my infamous CNN debate and the consistent deaths of trans women of color—combined," Mock noted.[3] Jenner's success as a former athlete, her affiliation with the Republican Party and support of Donald Trump, and her public discomfort with same-sex marriage exemplify the narrow inclusion and recognition of certain privileged, white transnormative and transpatriotic bodies into assimilationist frameworks of neoliberal equality.

In contrast to Jenner's celebrity, it is important to repeat and remember that this alleged "transgender tipping point" has been reached through social movements and decades of transgender rights activism, spearheaded particularly by trans women and gender-nonconforming people of color who have been systematically erased from LGBT history.[4] The 1969 Stonewall riots, often hailed as the origin of the gay rights movement in the United States, were led by drag queens and trans women of color, including Marsha P. Johnson, Sylvia Rivera, and Miss Major Griffin-Gracy, not by white, cisgender, gay men as is so often claimed and represented.[5] Without the decades-long struggle, resistance, labor, and love of these queens and trans women, not only would the present moment of transgender visibility be unthinkable, but the modern gay rights movement as we know it would not exist. As trans activist and filmmaker Tourmaline, herself a black trans woman, observes: the "historical erasure of black trans life means so many of us are disconnected from the legacies of trans women before us, denied access to stories about ourselves, in our own voices."[6]

Tourmaline spent years digging through archives, libraries, and living rooms to gather whatever she could find on Marsha P. Johnson to help reverse that erasure. Johnson was HIV positive, a sex worker, performer, and organizer who had cofounded the Street Transvestite Action Revolutionaries (STAR) together with Sylvia Rivera to provide community care and housing for poor queer and trans people. Yet when Netflix introduced Johnson's remarkable life to a wider audience with the documentary *The Death and Life of Marsha P. Johnson* in the fall of 2017, it was a white cisgender gay man with an extensive filmography, David France, who got to direct and claim credit for the project. In an Instagram post shortly after the movie's release, Tourmaline accused France of not only "finding inspiration" for his movie from a grant application she had submitted for a short film project on Johnson but of stealing her archival footage for use in his film.[7] France had resources at his disposal that allowed him, like so many other white cis male authors, producers, directors, and actors, to tell, appropriate, and extract value from the story of a black trans woman without crediting or acknowledging Tourmaline for the years of unpaid labor she had spent researching, archiving, and digitizing this previously inaccessible content. What Tourmaline's experience illuminates are the insidious connections between the historic erasure of trans women of color from the LGBT movement in the 1960s and 1970s and the transphobic violence and disposability that continues to haunt them today despite increased trans visibility.

How can we reconcile the "truth seeking" of white trans reality TV stardom à la Jenner and the tokenizing hypervisibility of Janet Mock and Laverne Cox, who are automatically expected to represent and speak for an entire group of people, given the continued devaluation and disposability of trans women of color? The number of trans people, predominantly those of color, being murdered in the United States has seen a steady increase in recent years. In February 2017 alone, three young black trans women from Louisiana—Ciara McElveen, Chyna Doll Dupree, and Jaquarrius Holland—were murdered just within days of each other.[8] As Tourmaline reminds us in the epigraph to this coda, there remains a stark disparity between trans representation and lived trans experiences: "Just because we're being seen, doesn't mean we're any safer."[9] Even if the representation of trans people in popular discourse would more accurately reflect their lived experiences and realities, those representations alone will not be able to transform the systemic nature of intersecting oppressions and the widespread institutionalized violence enacted against trans communities.

Even in movements with powerful, nationwide organizing and public outcry against state-sanctioned and state-enforced violence against black and brown people, the deaths of trans women of color have not prompted the same response and remain largely unnoticed. Because trans people, especially trans women of color, exist at vulnerable intersections of gender, race, class, and sexuality, they continue to be placed at the margins of society as well as at the margins of social and civil rights movements for racial, economic, and gender justice. The few organizations that have centered their advocacy on the lives and experiences of trans communities are often struggling to survive because they are severely underfunded and are largely volunteer run, as TYSN's abrupt closing, detailed in chapter 4, illustrates. Eric A. Stanley alludes to the dubious role of visibility politics in the limited life chances of trans people by posing the crucial question, "if we are to understand the visual itself as technologies of anti-black and anti-trans optics, then how might we continue the important project of representation in a visual regime hostile to black trans life?"[10] In other words, the tipping point in trans visibility has not equated to a tipping point around care for or value of transgender lives, trans women's lives in particular. In fact, the hypervisibility of trans people may even contribute to and exacerbate the violence targeting trans communities.

The current political climate in the United States illustrates that since 2014's purported "transgender tipping point" there has also been a stark increase in efforts to pass anti-transgender legislation, which further demonstrates not only the complexity of visibility politics but also its attending detrimental impact on the livelihoods of the very communities it claims to represent. Even though the Obama administration enacted unprecedented legal protections for trans people, including coverage for transition-related care under the Affordable Care Act as well as the extension of Title IX protections to transgender students barring discrimination on the basis of gender identity, during his first year in office President Trump rolled back many of those policies.[11] In February 2017 Trump rescinded Obama's federal protections for trans students and issued a series of tweets announcing the re-institution of the trans military ban (as I have discussed at length in chapter 2). Since then the Department of Justice has also repeatedly taken the position that Title VII does not protect employees from discrimination based on sexual orientation and gender identity, because, as the department alleges, "sex" only refers to binary, biological sex, the "'physiological distinction . . .' between 'male and female.'"[12] Similarly, a leaked memo from the Department of Health and Human Services in the fall of 2018 proposes a strict legal definition of gender as a biological, immutable condition determined by genitalia at birth, whereby "the sex listed on a person's birth certificate, as originally issued, shall constitute definitive proof of a person's sex unless rebutted by reliable genetic evidence."[13]

Not only are the drastic and far-reaching reversals and reinterpretations of these federal policies effectively attempting to legislate and erase queer, trans, and intersex people out of existence, but they also reflect a broader legal landscape at the local and state levels in which religious freedom and anti-transgender bathroom bills have emerged as the latest contentious battleground between religious, mainly Christian, conservatives and LGBT rights activists in the aftermath of the Supreme Court's nationwide legalization of same-sex marriage in 2015. In the 2017 legislative session, sixteen states, including Illinois, Kentucky, Minnesota, New York, Texas, and Wyoming, introduced so-called bathroom laws.[14] Advanced by Republican lawmakers, these bills make it illegal for trans people to use the restroom aligned with their gender identity. In 2016 North Carolina became the first and, so far, only state to pass such anti-trans bathroom legislation.[15] Similarly, numerous school districts are witnessing heated debates and panics over athletic policies allowing trans students to play for the team consistent with their gender identity. In November 2014 Minneapolis's *Star Tribune* published full-page ads on the back of its sports section by the Minnesota Child Protection League, a conservative anti-LGBT organization. The ads deployed pseudofeminist rhetoric with implicit references to Title IX and sexual assault, casting trans students as patriarchal threats to women's hard-won rights: "The end of girls' sports? Her dreams of a scholarship shattered, your 14-year-old daughter just lost her position on an all-girl team to a male . . . and now she may have to shower with him. Are you willing to let that happen?"[16] Echoing the rhetoric of trans-exclusionary radical feminists who argue that trans women are really men who infiltrate, invade, and "rape" the sanctity of cis women's spaces, the Minnesota Child Protection League similarly alleges that trans women are also really men who masquerade as women in order to prey on innocent girls. The ad thus also feeds into popular anxieties about child abuse as it casts specifically queer and trans people as child molesters and pedophiles. Furthermore, these transphobic anxieties cannot be separated from historically racialized scripts that cast white women as in need of protection from nonwhite males, especially black men. At the heart of these kinds of transphobic bills and ads is therefore a redeployment of age-old virulent stereotypes and mythologies that characterize trans women as "perverted predators" who threaten the safety and purity of white cis women.

The surge in anti-LGBT political and legislative campaigns must be understood as a direct reaction to the civil rights gains for gays, lesbians, and transgender people under (neo)liberalism generally and the Obama administration specifically. Moreover, the rise of and debate about legal definitions of sex and gender, discriminatory athletic policies, and bathroom bills must concurrently be seen as a reaction to the heightened visibility of transgender people in mainstream media and national discourse. While proposed bathroom laws, for example, already circulated in Colorado and Vermont in 2008 and 2009, tracking by the National Conference of State Legislatures shows that such bills dramatically increased between 2013 and 2016, during which at least twenty-four states considered legislation that aimed to restrict access to public restrooms and locker rooms based on biological sex.[17] As I have illustrated throughout this book, these years were also marked by a heightened sense of cultural awareness of transgender identities, albeit one that has been problematically influenced by dominant media's reductive and demeaning coverage of trans communities and issues.

Furthermore, the stark acceleration in transphobic and discriminatory legislation since the election of President Trump illustrates that the pendulum's swing back on transgender rights is not unconnected from the larger workings of the security state, specifically its continued investment in nativist nationalism, imperialism, and capitalist exploitation. The transphobia at the heart of the trans military ban, for example, must be put in the larger context of Trump's "Make America Great Again" rhetoric and policies that seek to curb both documented and undocumented immigration to the United States, most prominently through an Islamophobic travel ban against citizens from six Muslim-majority countries as well as the proposed erection of a wall along the U.S.-Mexican border. On the same day he officially announced the trans military ban in a memo, Trump also issued his first presidential pardon to notorious Arizona Sheriff Joe Arpaio, who illegally targeted and terrorized Latinx immigrants for decades.[18] Only a few days later, Trump declared the end of the Deferred Action for Childhood Arrivals program, commonly known as DACA, which has protected nearly eight hundred thousand young undocumented immigrants brought to the United States as children from deportation. The trans military ban, in conjunction with anti-immigration policies and requests for increased defense funding, caters to Trump's voter base, which wants to see a strengthened military and impenetrable borders. These policies at the core of the Trump administration's (and most of the Republican establishment's) political agenda reflect the (re)assertion of white nationalism wherein marginalized populations are denied a right to exist. At a moment when white supremacists feel emboldened—most prominently on display with the events unfolding during the Unite the Right rally in Charlottesville, Virginia, in 2017—by a president who actively courts them by feeding into economic protectionism and nativism, marginalized groups are further criminalized and disposed of, especially those who are racialized, classed, and gender nonconforming.

For example, in the same way that trans and gender-nonconforming people are represented as a risk and threat to white heteronormative nationalism and militarism, so too are undocumented immigrants portrayed as thieves stealing jobs from hardworking Americans, rapists menacing American women, and violent drug traffickers seeping through porous borders. Evident in the stereotypes and myths deployed against them, the criminalization of both trans and immigrant communities is intimately tied to fears about the sanctity of white cis womanhood—whether it is a so-called perverted man passing himself off as a trans woman to prey on women in public restrooms or alleged members of the Salvadorian gang MS-13 kidnapping and killing U.S. girls on Long Island.[19] The security state's surveillance of trans people and its surveillance and deportation of immigrants is intimately connected to larger bio- and necropolitical population management processes.

The links between the state's regulation of trans, gender-nonconforming, and immigrant populations require us to ask whether trans military service or selective immigration and naturalization rights are the kinds of goals that will achieve true liberation. How does the security state pit marginalized communities against one another? Popular acceptance of the dominant narrative that claims a need for intensive national security measures encourages political trade-offs in which, for example, LGBT activists argue for the inclusion of trans people in the military in the name of national security, while simultaneously supporting immigration restrictions that take away the rights of (undocumented) immigrants. Conceding to ramped-up border security in exchange for a DACA deal further cements a class system where some immigrants are more deserving than others. What makes the workings of neoliberalism and its politics of colorblindness so insidious is that the security state's claim to provide social emancipation and legal protections for certain marginalized groups depends on its systematic deployment of violence against those people who are already at the margins of the marginalized. A critical queer and trans politics must attend to these intricate intersectionalities if it wants to pose an effective challenge to the security state's insatiable appetite for more surveillance, border monitoring, and population disposal.

When LGBT organizations and thinkers continue to tout institutional representation as the primary site through which social progress, legal reform, and the full incorporation of queer and trans people into U.S. citizenship may be achieved, they not only fail to recognize the increased surveillance and harm produced by such visibility but ignore how these strivings for equality render queer and trans people themselves complicit in the bio- and necropolitical management of the security state. Communication studies scholar Isaac West, for example, argues that it is necessary to recuperate citizenship as a useful category, rejecting some theorists' dismissal of it as inherently normative and therefore problematic. Instead, West argues we should engage dominant formations, such as citizenship and the law as opportunities because, he maintains, by inhabiting them they will ultimately be transformed: "When trans people . . . articulate themselves as transgender citizens entitled to equal treatment before the law, they transform the law as they work within and stretch its limits. Concurrently, the law transforms, which is not the same as normalizes, individuals in ways great and small, in both constraining and enabling ways."[20] This conceptualization of what West calls "impure politics," which contends transformative articulations of citizenship are possible within current dominant, normative structures, does not fully acknowledge or problematize the law as a key site of normalization, nor as a persistent site of state-generated and state-sanctioned violence.[21] Even though the law may seem "transformable" or "stretchable," to use West's terms, history has demonstrated that the law only stretches to the extent that it needs to, contingently including some subjects in order to maintain its dominance as the arbiter of rights and manager of populations.[22]

How can trans lives be seen and recognized as deserving of protection with the ability to live fully but without subjection to violent state intervention processes? How do we conceive of different modes of recognition and collectivity without falling into the traps of the visual, of bio- and necropolitical systems of valuation and economic extraction? What role should visibility play in the future of a critical queer and trans politics? A critical queer and trans politics can help us formulate modes of resistance and alternative collectivities beyond the racialized, classed, and gendered politics of visibility through what Tourmaline calls "nobodiness."[23] While a somebody is an individual who is not only recognized but given value by the market, the state, and mainstream society, a nobody is neglected, ignored, or actively exploited for value and targeted for disposal by those same entities. Nobodiness is therefore a strategic use of one's marginalization to subvert the logics and institutions of heteronormative white supremacist capitalist patriarchy.

As Tourmaline explains in relation to her own experience with the commodification and exploitation of her recently acquired fame as an activist and filmmaker, "some of us somebodies need to remember the joy and the power of that less visible place that is actually *so deeply* visible to those in it and so violently hyper-visible to those that seek to destroy it."[24] The power and possibility of nobodiness then lies in its paradoxically invisible/hypervisible status. Even as nobodies are always subject to violent forms of surveillance, criminalization, and elimination, by engaging in everyday, local, and collective forms of care, organization, resistance, and action nobodies not only imagine, but "model... the worlds we want to actually live in."[25] In other words,

> We all know the damage that it can be to be called nobody and yet there is power in that word and in that world of no-bodies. It's a power Denise Ferreira da Silva cites when she asks 'Do we want to be *somebody* under the state or *nobody* against it?' ... do we want to be visible subjects of... inhospitable institutions earning good credit by doing actions it deems of consequence and important or do we want to go undercover, be fugitives to the institution and its morals, unruly to its attempts at incorporation and assimilation. *Maybe, and this is one of the hardest lessons I've learned, sometimes we want or need to do both.*[26]

Thus, nobodiness does not equate to invisibility, but rather, is a tactical navigation and subversion of the constraints of visibility and the dominant institutions that exploit those constraints for profit and power.

A political shift to a perspective of nobodiness recognizes the importance of truly coalitional and intersectional social justice work, which often starts in the unglamorous "muck of local systems" as Dean Spade notes.[27] Nobodies are the ones that do the work of caring for and organizing their own communities or neighborhoods: nobodies arrange rides to the doctor's office for elderly neighbors; nobodies volunteer at their local needle exchange program; nobodies protest against prison expansionism in their state, set up bail funds for National Bail Out Day, and take the time to write their incarcerated pen pals; nobodies arrange informal safety networks to accompany their friends and acquaintances in threatening situations; and nobodies join rapid response teams for Immigration and Customs Enforcement raids in their neighborhoods.

Nobodies are also the ones working and driving grassroots organizations such as the Sylvia Rivera Law Project or the Trans Women of Color Collective, who tirelessly work for trans and queer liberation outside of the LGBT mainstream, who recognize that trans issues cannot be treated separately from issues of racism, (cis)sexism, classism, and ableism and serve as inspiration for and lead us to a different kind of queer and trans politics. Jennicet Gutiérrez, a founding member of Familia: Trans Queer Liberation Movement, which was established to advocate for LGBTQ immigrants who are often excluded in immigration debates, is such a nobody. Recognizing that "the queer migrant [i]s an inherently coalitional subject, one whose identities and relationships to power mandate managing multiplicity," Gutiérrez audaciously interrupted President Obama at a White House gathering celebrating LGBT Pride Month in 2015 to call for the release of all LGBTQ immigrants from detention centers, stopping the abuse of detained trans women, and ending deportations.[28] Similarly, Bamby Salcedo and activists from the TransLatin@ Coalition, a Los Angeles–based advocacy organization for Latinx trans people, unfurled a giant transgender flag during the final 2018 World Series game between the LA Dodgers and the Boston Red Sox, asserting "Trans People Deserve To Live" in response to the Trump administration's latest attacks on trans rights.[29] In these moments, both Gutiérrez and the activists of the TransLatin@ Coalition utilized their hypervisibility under the security state as (undocumented) trans women of color to speak truth to power. As Gutiérrez and the TransLatin@ Coalition show, nobodies do not totally eschew visibility but use it strategically, for instance in the #TransLivesMatter, #SayHerName, and #WontBeErased campaigns, to highlight and demand accountability for the countless cis, trans, queer, and disabled women of color—the nobodies—who continue to be neglected, abused, assaulted, and killed without spurring mass mobilization or evoking mass media empathy.

Nobodiness as a means of political resistance and alternative world-making functions not as a position of total abdication—as if that were ever totally possible—but as a tactic of interruption and direct-action movement building.[30] For nobodies, the primary goal is neither to work toward reforming existing institutions, such as the prison-industrial complex, nor is it to further invest in the contingent belonging offered by the assimilatory logics of visibility politics. Yet nobodiness is not a politics of purity.[31] As Tourmaline stresses, "it's ok to be a somebody in your nobod[iness] when you need to. It's ok to move contradictor[il]y" because we do not live in a pure world.[32] And sometimes it is necessary to be a somebody, to use one's clout or get on stage to manipulate the state's resources, ideologies, and practices for one's own purposes. At its root then, nobodiness turns the trap of visibility into a trapdoor and makes it function as a secret passageway to places yet unknown to imagine a queer and trans futurity beyond the harrowing death worlds of the here and now.[33] In so doing, nobodiness evades and exceeds current systems of valuation by aspiring to alternative epistemologies and modes of belonging and care—ones that, indeed, make trans and black lives *matter*. Nobodies "are not just valuable" according to the metrics of capitalism but are "*invaluable*, as in non-disposable and of *incalculable* worth, a value that exceeds even the measure of value itself."[34]

With the systemic antiblack racism, Islamophobia, (cis)sexism, homophobia, and transphobia at the heart of the current conservative sociopolitical backlash, neither academic nor activist spaces committed to a critical queer politics can afford to exclude transgender voices from formulating strategies for resistance. The voices of trans women especially need to be front and center of cross-coalitional movement building not because they are "just like" cis women but because of their own unique experiences *as* women. It is also on us within the academy to reflect more critically on our research and subject positionalities and to question our own complicity and investments in exploitative knowledge production practices to ensure that critical queer and trans scholarship does not only accrue "diversity" capital for neoliberal universities but actually benefits the communities from which it emanates. Because universities privilege individualistic tenure requirements, which often incentivize predatory and exploitative academic behavior, over community engagement and collaborative or activist scholarship, it is imperative that those of us with institutional privileges leverage our advantages to amplify marginalized trans voices and perspectives. This approach includes properly acknowledging trans people's intellectual labor in our citational practices, listing our trans research informants as coauthors in publications, and adequately compensating those informants for interviews and talks.[35] In the current political climate, we also need to make social justice part and parcel of our critical pedagogy in the classroom. It is my hope that this book contributes to cross-community and multidimensional coalition-building between queer, trans, poor, and people of color communities that enables trans women of color to have their brilliant voices heard loud and clear.

NOTES

Introduction

1. While I often use simplified language to refer to various dominant, corporate, mainstream media organizations simply as "the media," I want to emphasize that media institutions and the representations produced by them are not monolithic. In this book I specifically use phrases such as *dominant discourse* or *hegemonic discourse* and *dominant representations* to point to the powerful and often preeminent role mainstream media occupy in meaning-making processes because such discourses tend to have greater influence and reach in our society than smaller, independent, and minority-owned and -operated media organizations.

2. Samantha Allen and Nico Lang, "11 Ways 2014 Was the Biggest Year in Transgender History," *Rolling Stone*, December 23, 2014, rollingstone.com/culture/features/11-ways-2014-was-the-biggest -year-in-transgender-history-20141223; Katy Steinmetz, "The Transgender Tipping Point: America's Next Civil Rights Frontier," *Time* 183, no. 22.

3. Steinmetz, 44.

4. Video clips of the segments available at Chris Geidner, "Transgender Advocate Janet Mock: Piers Morgan 'Sensationalized' My Story," *BuzzFeed*, February 4, 2014, buzzfeed.com/chrisgeidner /transgender-advocate-janet-mock-piers-morgan-sensationalized# .gwejo4p8dw.

5. Parker Marie Molloy, "Op-Ed: Janet Mock Slams Piers Morgan for Transphobic Questions, Tweets," *Huffington Post*, February 5, 2014, advocate.com/commentary/2014/02/05/op-ed-janet-mock-slams -piers-morgan-transphobic-questions-tweets.

6. "Carmen Carrera's Quest to become a Victoria's Secret Angel," *Katie*, season 2, episode 76, ABC, January 6, 2014, katiecouric

.com/videos/carmen-carreras-quest-to-become-a-victorias
-secret-angel.

7. "*Orange Is the New Black* Laverne Cox," *Katie*, season 2, episode 76, ABC, January 6, 2014, katiecouric.com/videos/orange-is-the-new -black-laverne-cox.

8. James et al., *Executive Summary*, 2–4, 12–13.

9. The exact number of murdered trans people is difficult to track because police often release incorrect birth names and gender identities of the victims. Law enforcement are also not required to report these murders to a central database. See Maggie Astor, "Violence against Transgender People Is on the Rise, Advocates Say," *New York Times*, November 9, 2017, nytimes.com/2017/11/09/us /transgender-women-killed.html.

10. I recite these statistics above not to reduce trans people to dehumanizing statistics of horror and violence. Rather, I seek to provide a holistic view of trans people and their everyday experiences by providing insight into the larger sociopolitical context surrounding their increased media visibility.

11. Such cultural and national belonging can manifest itself in numerous and intersecting ways, i.e., legally, politically, socially, and economically. I consciously use this phrasing to include issues as broad as trans people's (circumscribed) access to citizenship rights and public space, their cultural representation and visibility, and their opportunities for housing and employment, to name just a few.

12. See for, example, the anthologies *Media / Queered* by Barnhurst and *Queer TV* by Davis and Needham, as well as Ahn, Himberg, and Young, "Introduction to In Focus."

13. With origins in black feminist thought, intersectionality, a term originally coined by legal theorist Kimberlé Crenshaw, is an interpretive framework that rejects additive models of identity and oppression and instead highlights how they interlock. In other words, neither identities nor oppressive institutions function separately, one layered on top of the other, but are mutually constitutive; for example, racism does not function separately from, or on top of, sexism. While not using the term *intersectionality* explicitly, the 1977 Combahee River Collective Statement had already identified that for black women, "we . . . often find it difficult to separate race from class from sex oppression because in our lives they are most often experienced

simultaneously" (cited in Taylor, *How We Get Free*, 19). In her analyses, Crenshaw specifically dissects how women of color are impacted by structural, political, and representational intersectionality. See Crenshaw, "Demarginalizing the Intersection"; Crenshaw, "Mapping the Margins." Patricia Hill Collins specifically linked intersectionality to the "matrix of domination"—the organization of systems of oppression—to show how black women are differently positioned in society based on race, ethnicity, gender, sexuality, class, nation, and age. See Hill Collins, *Black Feminist Thought*, 221–38.

14. See for example, Cloud, "Private Manning and the Chamber of Secrets"; or Bean, "U.S. National Security Culture."

15. Puar, *Terrorist Assemblages*.

16. West, *Transforming Citizenships*, 9.

17. I follow Susan Stryker here, whose definition particularly emphasizes the performativity and social construction of identity by referring to transgender as "people who move away from the gender they were assigned at birth, people who cross-over (*trans-*) the boundaries constructed by their culture to define and contain that gender" (*Transgender History*, 1, emphasis in original). *Cisgender* refers to those whose gender identity matches their biological sex. Biologist Dana Leland Defosse is widely credited for putting the neologism *cisgender* into public circulation in the mid-1990s. *Cis-*, based on the Latin root, references things that are "on the side of" or do not change property. Many find the introduction of the term *cisgender* useful because it consciously marks gender identities that usually go unnoticed and are considered normal, i.e., the unstated assumption of non-transgender status contained in the words *man* or *woman*.

18. Moreover, transgender and queer are both products of Western theorizing that tend to leave unaccounted or override other non-Western and nonbinary understandings of gender, sexual desire and practice. As Tom Boellstorff notes, the tendency to project Euro-American theoretical frameworks of race, gender, and sexuality onto other non-Western contexts presents persistent barriers to theorizing queerness, particularly in a global context ("Queer Studies under Ethnography's Sign," 627).

19. I use quotations around these self-identifications to indicate they reflect individuals' own labels. See Valentine, *Imagining Transgender*.

20. See Love, "Queer."

21. Cohen, "Punks, Bulldaggers, and Welfare Queens," 463.

22. While beyond the scope of this book, the continued erasure of bisexuality from queer spaces also demands renewed scholarly attention. For a good introduction on bisexuality as an alternative formation that challenges dominant understandings of gender and sexuality see Hemmings, *Bisexual Spaces*.

23. Gray, *Out in the Country*, 12.

24. Duggan, *The Twilight of Equality?*, 50.

25. Puar, *Terrorist Assemblages*.

26. See, for example, Cohen, "Punks, Bulldaggers, and Welfare Queens"; Ferguson, "Racing Homonormativity."

27. ENDA, which seeks to extend federal protections to LGBT people, became controversial and caused rifts among transgender and gay rights activists in 2007 when legislators sought to add federal discrimination protections for sexual orientation but not for gender identity or expression. For ENDA's contentious place in the LGBT movement, see Stryker, *Transgender History*, 150–53; and West, *Transforming Citizenship*, 129–62.

28. In a similar vein, the Michigan Womyn's Music Festival, which was founded in 1976 and billed itself as an event for "womyn-born womyn" only, faced boycotts and controversy for years for its persistent exclusion of trans women. The festival closed its doors in 2015.

29. Raymond, *The Transsexual Empire*, 104.

30. Jeffreys, *Gender Hurts*.

31. Stryker and Currah, "Introduction," 6.

32. Foucault, *Discipline and Punish*, 200.

33. Hall, "What Is This 'Black,'" 24.

34. Gray, "Subject(ed) to Recognition."

35. Aizura, "Unrecognizable," 609.

36. Armstrong, "Certificates of Live Birth," 624.

37. Gross, *Up from Invisibility*, xvi.

38. Crimp, "Mario Montez, for Shame," 72.

39. See Barnhurst, "Visibility as Paradox."

40. Teena, who identified as a trans man, was brutally raped and then killed by two of his girlfriend's acquaintances in Humboldt, Nebraska, in 1993.

41. See, for example, Halberstam, *In a Queer Time*; Henderson, *Love and Money*; Sloop, "Disciplining the Transgendered"; Squires and Brouwer, "In/discernible Bodies."

42. Sloop, *Disciplining Gender*, 2.

43. Hale, "Consuming the Living," 337.

44. See, e.g., Davis and Needham, *Queer TV*; Sender, *Business, Not Politics*; Becker, *Gay TV*.

45. See C. Riley Snorton, *Black on Both Sides*, 177–98.

46. See e.g., Roderick Ferguson, who defines queer of color analysis as an "interrogat[ion] of social formations as the intersections of race, gender, sexuality, and class, with particular interest in how those formations correspond with and diverge from nationalist ideals and practices. Queer of color analysis is a heterogeneous enterprise made up of women of color feminism, materialist analysis, poststructuralist theory, and queer critique" (*Aberrations in Black*, 149n1). I build on important works calling for and engaging with an intersectional approach to communication and media studies, such as Chávez and Griffin, *Standing in the Intersection*; Johnson, "Cisgender Privilege"; and Lünenborg and Fürsich, "Media and the Intersectional Other."

47. Spencer and Capuzza, *Transgender Communication Studies*. "Deadnaming" describes the practice of referring to trans people by their birth names instead of their chosen names.

48. For current trends see Billard, "Writing in the Margins"; and Capuzza, "Improvements Still Needed."

49. Capuzza, "Who Defines Gender Diversity?"; Barker-Plummer, "Fixing Gwen"; Lovelock, "Call Me Caitlyn," 1.

50. See, for example, Miller, "Becoming One of the Girls/Guys"; Patterson and Spencer, "What's So Funny"; Booth, "Queering *Queer Eye*."

51. Cavalcante, "Centering Transgender Identity"; Cavalcante, "Breaking into Transgender Life."

52. Lester, "From Abomination to Indifference."

53. Capuzza and Spencer, "Regressing, Progressing, or Transgressing."

54. Dame, "Making a Name for Yourself"; Fink and Miller, "Trans Media Moments"; Jackson, Bailey, and Foucault Welles, "#GirlsLikeUs."

55. Reina Gossett, Grace Dunham, and Constantina Zavitsanos, "Commencement Address at Hampshire College," ReinaGosset

.com, May 17, 2016, reinagossett.com/commencement-address
-hampshire-college/.

56. Grewal, *Saving the Security State*, 12.

57. See Grewal, *Saving the Security State*, 11ff.

58. See Hay and Andrejevic, "Introduction"; and Ouellette and Hay, "Makeover Television."

59. Mark Andrejevic explores the emergence of certain reality TV securitainment formats after 9/11 that combine entertainment values with precise risk management instructions. See "'Securitainment' in the post-9/11 Era."

60. Foucault, *"Society Must Be Defended,"* 241. He further states, "Killing or the imperative to kill is acceptable only if it results not in a victory over political adversaries, but in the elimination of the biological threat to and the improvement of the species or race" (256).

61. Mbembe, "Necropolitics," 40, emphasis in original.

62. See Puar, *Terrorist Assemblages*, 32–36; Snorton and Haritaworn, "Trans Necropolitics."

63. See, for example, Gates, *Our Biometric Future*.

64. Lyon, *Surveillance Studies*, 14.

65. See, for example, Dubrofsky and Magnet, *Feminist Surveillance Studies*; Conrad, "Surveillance, Gender"; Foucault, *The History of Sexuality*.

66. Gray, *Out in the Country*, xiv; Halberstam, *Female Masculinity*, 13.

67. Boellstorff, "Queer Studies under Ethnography's Sign," 628. See Puar, *Terrorist Assemblages*, xv.

68. According to Foucault, it is discourse that produces knowledge, not the things-in-themselves: subjects like madness, punishment, and (homo)sexuality exist meaningfully only within the moral, legal, medical, and psychiatric discourses, practices, and institutional apparatuses about them. See Hall, "The Work of Representation," 45–46.

69. Hall, "The Work of Representation," 50.

70. Althusser, "Ideology and Ideological State Apparatuses."

71. Hall, "Culture, the Media," 346.

72. Hall, "Culture, the Media," 341, emphasis in original.

73. Engaging in what Clifford Geertz terms "thick description" in an eponymous chapter, I began to closely study the field sites of McDonald's neighborhood in south Minneapolis. In order to gain a

better understanding of the complicated legal procedures, I spoke with McDonald's legal representatives. I also talked to reporters and editors at local newspapers covering her case to gain insights into reporting and editorial decisions that were made in the newsroom. Most importantly, I was able to connect with members of McDonald's support committee, whose perspectives were essential to this project. After her release from prison 2014, I was also able to listen to and speak with McDonald herself during several public events in Minneapolis and Denver.

74. Weiss, "The Epistemology of Ethnography," 650.

75. Lugones and Spelman, "Have We Got a Theory," 579–80.

76. Because this book is comprised mostly of the stories of trans women of color, I will donate all personal proceeds to trans of color organizations that were founded and are operated by trans people themselves.

77. As Lugones and Spelman aptly point out feminist and queer scholars should be concerned not only by the male monopoly over accounts of women's lives but also the hierarchical privileging of some women's voices over others, particularly as white middle-class women in the United States "have in the main developed 'feminist theory'" (see "Have We Got a Theory," 575).

78. See Weiss, "The Epistemology of Ethnography."

79. Serano, "Skirt Chasers."

80. Of course, the sensationalism around the "World's First Pregnant Man," Thomas Beatie in 2007, presents a notable exception here and so does the attention given to Chaz Bono's appearance on ABC's *Dancing with the Stars* in 2011.

81. The critique of casting cis actors to play transgender characters is not new. Fictional trans people are predominantly played by cis actors, whether it is Felicity Huffman in *Transamerica* (2005), Hilary Swank in *Boys Don't Cry* (1999), Jared Leto in *Dallas Buyer's Club* (2013), or more recently Eddie Redmayne in *The Danish Girl* (2015). Amazon recently announced that Tambor would not return for *Transparent*'s fifth season after sexual harassment allegations by two trans actresses against him became public in the wake of #MeToo in late 2017. For critiques of *Transparent*, see, for example, Leela Ginelle, "*Transparent* Producers Say They 'Welcome the Debate' on Casting Jeffrey Tambor," *Bitch Magazine*,

October 6, 2014, bitchmedia.org/post/transparent-producers
-say-they-"welcome-the-debate"-on-casting-jeffrey-tambor-as
-a-transgender-; Cael Keegan, "Op-Ed: How *Transparent* Tried
and Failed to Represent Trans Men," *Advocate*, October 22, 2014,
advocate.com/commentary/2014/10/22/op-ed-how-transparent
-tried-and-failed-represent-trans-men.

82. For one of the few in-depth studies of the self-identification, perception, and representation of transmasculine people, see matthew heinz, *Entering Transmasculinity*. Heinz complicates dominant
images of transmen as white, middle-class, educated, able bodied,
and gender conforming by pointing to the liberating yet also constraining and homogenizing implications of transmasculinity.

83. Serano, "Skirt Chasers," 226.

84. It is commonly assumed that trans men are not the targets of violence to the same extent as trans women are (and this is true when
only looking at hate crime statistics), but data shows that transmasculine people are more likely to be victims of sexual assault, domestic violence, and stalking than transfeminine individuals. See Loree
Cook-Daniels, "Op-Ed: Trans Men Experience Far More Violence
Than Most People Assume," *Advocate*, July 23, 2015, advocate.com
/commentary/2015/07/23/op-ed-trans-men-experience-far-more
-violence-most-people-assume.

85. Snorton and Haritaworn, "Trans Necropolitics," 67.

1. A (Gender) Traitor

1. I avoid deadnaming Manning whenever possible except when
using direct quotes from secondary sources that still referred to her
as "Bradley" and with male pronouns. While I disapprove of and
would prefer to highlight each instance of the violent misgendering
that is occurring in these quotes by inserting a [*sic*], especially after
Manning officially announced her transition, I choose not to do so in
order to maintain better reading flow.

2. Kevin Poulsen and Kim Zetter, "U.S. Intelligence Analyst Arrested
in Wikileaks Video Probe," *Wired*, June 6, 2010, wired.com/2010
/06/leak/.

3. Robert Mackey, "U.S. Soldier Arrested in Wikileaks Inquiry after
Tip from Former Hacker," *New York Times*, June 7, 2010, LexisNexis
Academic.

4. See Leigh and Harding, *WikiLeaks*.

5. Lamo was found dead at age thirty-seven in March 2018. The circumstances of his death are still unknown.

6. Janet Reitman, "The Trials of Bradley Manning," *Rolling Stone*, March 14, 2013, rollingstone.com/politics/news/the-trials-of -bradley-manning-20130314.

7. Ginger Thompson, "Last Witness for Military Takes Stand in Leak Case," *New York Times*, December 20, 2011, nytimes.com/2011/12 /21/us/governments-last-witness-takes-stand-at-bradley-manning -hearing.html.

8. Stryker and Currah, "Introduction," 2.

9. Smith, "Dismantling Hierarchy, Queering Society," 60.

10. I use the term *alien enemy* throughout this chapter to point to the ways in which intersecting discourses of sexuality, gender, and race were constitutive of one another in othering Chelsea Manning. I also consciously employ the term in reference to a specific legal category in the United States that differentiates between aliens as individuals who are not U.S. citizens, mainly for tax and immigration purposes. In the wake of Pearl Harbor, the Roosevelt administration, for example, had used the Alien Enemies Act of 1798 to incarcerate enemy aliens and confiscate their property during World War II. As a result, thousands of Japanese, Germans, and Italians were arrested and interned for the duration of the war and were later deported to their nations of origin. Today, the Alien Enemies Act is still in effect in modified form and authorizes the president to apprehend, restrain, secure, and remove alien enemies in times of war (see 50 U.S. Code Chapter 3: Alien Enemies). As I elaborate later in this and the next chapter, I explicitly use the term in response to the government's leveling the aiding the enemy charge against Manning to illustrate how modes of national belonging and access to U.S. citizenship are always contingent and precarious at best.

11. Stryker and Aizura, "Introduction: Transgender Studies 2.0," 3.

12. Stryker, *Transgender History*, 48.

13. Of particular interest for a qualitative media analysis of Manning's news coverage were prominent, large-circulation newspapers, news broadcasts on national network television, and cable news channels. To target stories about Manning, I searched the LexisNexis database and the Vanderbilt Television News Archive for stories about "Bradley

Manning" and "Chelsea Manning" during the time period between May 2010 and March 2014 across multiple media outlets, including the *New York Times*, the *Washington Post*, and the *Guardian*; ABC, CBS, and NBC network television news; CNN, Fox News, and MSNBC cable news channels; and NPR. The programs and publications I selected for analysis were prominent; appealed to large-scale, mainstream news audiences; and substantially and centrally concerned Manning. I eliminated stories that were either duplicates or only marginally concerned with her. For example, if a story covered the Afghan and Iraq War logs, focused on Edward Snowden's National Security Agency leaks, or portrayed Julian Assange or WikiLeaks but only briefly referenced Manning, it was eliminated because the article was not *substantially* about Chelsea Manning. However, if a story was *centrally* concerned with Manning—specifically, her (pre)trial proceedings, her upbringing and family life, treatment in the army and detention, her alleged sexual orientation and gender identity, or her motivations for disclosing classified documents—then I included that story. I also eliminated very short pieces, anything under about twenty seconds for television news or fewer than four hundred words for print. For this time period, the total sum of news stories that fit the criteria and that I scrutinized for my in-depth discursive analysis was approximately 236 articles.

14. Article 32 hearings are a required proceeding under the United States Uniform Code of Military Justice to determine whether there is enough evidence to merit a general court-martial.

15. Margaret Sullivan, "An Empty Seat in the Courtroom," *New York Times*, December 9, 2012, LexisNexis Academic.

16. David Leonhardt, the *New York Times*'s Washington bureau chief, cited in Margaret Sullivan, "The Times Should Have a Reporter at the Bradley Manning Hearing," *New York Times*, December 5, 2012. LexisNexis Academic.

17. Editorial Board, "Snowden's Disclosures Do Not Amount to Treason," *New York Times*, June 12, 2013, LexisNexis Academic; David Carr, "Whistle-Blowers in Limbo, Neither Hero nor Traitor," *New York Times*, August 1, 2013, LexisNexis Academic; Haroon Siddique and Matthew Weaver, "US Embassy Cables Culprit Should Be Executed, Says Mike Huckabee," *Guardian*, December 1, 2010, theguardian.com/world/2010/dec/01/us-embassy-cables-executed-mike-huckabee.

18. *The O'Reilly Factor*, "Soldier Pleads Guilty in WikiLeaks Case," Fox News, March 1, 2013, video.foxnews.com/v/2198349268001 /soldier-pleads-guilty-in-wikileaks-case.

19. Greg Jaffe and Joshua Partlow, "Mullen Says Leak Put Troops and Afghans in Danger," *Washington Post*, July 30, 2010, LexisNexis Academic.

20. Eyder Peralta, "Bradley Manning Says He Leaked Classified Info to 'Spark a Domestic Debate,'" NPR, February 27, 2013, npr.org /sections/thetwo-way/2013/02/27/173095114/bradley-manning -says-he-leaked-classified-info-to-spark-a-domestic-debate.

21. Alexa O'Brien, "Bradley Manning's Full Statement," Salon, March 1, 2013, salon.com/2013/03/01/bradley_mannings_full_statement/.

22. The title of this section comes from the headline of NPR's *Morning Edition* from March 19, 2011, LexisNexis Academic. I explore the purpose of the military's DADT policy and its repeal in 2011 more closely in the following chapter. For information on Manning's background, see Ginger Thompson, "Early Struggles of Soldier Charged in Leak Case," *New York Times*, August 8, 2010, nytimes .com/2010/08/09/us/09manning.html.

23. Barbara Starr, "Who Is Bradley Manning?" CNN, August 5, 2010, cnn.com/video/#/video/us/2010/08/05/starr.pvt.manning .message.cnn.

24. Ellen Nakashima, "Despondent Words from an Alleged Leaker," *Washington Post*, June 10, 2010, LexisNexis Academic; Rachel Martin cited in "Leaks Probe Focuses On Low-Level Army Analyst," *Morning Edition*, NPR, November 30, 2010, LexisNexis Academic; Thompson, "Last Witness"; Thompson, "Early Struggles."

25. Associated Press, "Pvt. Bradley Manning Says He Thought He'd Die in Custody after Being Arrested for Allegedly Sending Info to Wikileaks," Fox News, November 29, 2012, foxnews.com/us /2012/11/29/judge-accepts-terms-pvt-bradley-mannings-plea-in -wikileaks-trial-likely-to-face.

26. Ed Pilkington, "Naive Idealist or Notoriety Seeker? Manning Trial Begins," *Guardian*, June 4, 2013, LexisNexis Academic; Bill Keller, "Private Manning's Confidant," *New York Times*, March 10, 2013, nytimes.com/2013/03/11/opinion/keller-private-mannings -confidant.html.

27. Bill Keller, "Private Manning's Confidant."

28. Maggie O'Kane, Chavala Madlena, and Guy Grandjean, "Special Investigation: The Beaten, Bullied Outsider Who Knew US Military's Inner Secrets," *Guardian*, May 28, 2011, LexisNexis Academic.

29. Paul Lewis, "Bradley Manning Sentenced: Trial Shows Young Man Scarred by Childhood Neglect and Loneliness; The Army Offered Escape from Early Years Blighted by Parental Alcoholism," *Guardian*, August 22, 2013, LexisNexis Academic.

30. John M. Broder and Ginger Thompson, "Loner Sought a Refuge, and Ended Up in War," *New York Times*, July 31, 2013, LexisNexis Academic.

31. DeFoster, *Terrorizing the Masses*.

32. Cited in Thom Shanker, "Loophole May Have Aided Theft of Classified Data," *New York Times*, July 8, 2010, nytimes.com/2010/07 /09/world/09breach.html.

33. For details see, e.g., Bean, "U.S. National Security Culture"; or Stein, *Rethinking the Gay and Lesbian Movement*, 41ff.

34. Alexander and Mohanty, "Introduction," xxvi.

35. Cited in Chris Johnson, "Gay Soldier Accused of Leaking Classified Files," *Bay Windows*, August 12, 2010, 3–16.

36. Cited in Adam Gabbatt, "'I Am Chelsea Manning,' Says Jailed Soldier Formerly Known as Bradley," *Guardian*, August 22, 2013, theguardian.com/world/2013/aug/22/bradley-manning-woman -chelsea-gender-reassignment.

37. Cited in *Evening News*, CBS, August 22, 2013, LexisNexis Academic.

38. Evan Hansen, "Manning-Lamo Chat Logs Revealed," *Wired*, July 3, 2011, wired.com/2011/07/manning-lamo-logs.

39. Charlie Savage, "Manning Played Vital Role in Iraq Despite Erratic Behavior, Supervisor Says," *New York Times*, August 14, 2013, LexisNexis Academic.

40. Hansen, "Manning-Lamo Chat Logs."

41. Hansen, "Manning-Lamo Chat Logs."

42. Forwarded email from MSG Adkins to CPT Lim, titled "My Problem," June 3, 2010, photocopy retrieved from *Firedoglake*, documentcloud .org/documents/757463-de-qqq-from-lim-to-kerns.html.

43. *In the Matter of: United States vs. PFC Bradley E. Manning*, vol. 34, Morning Session, August 13, 2013, unofficial transcript, Freedom of the Press Foundation, 70, pressfreedomfoundation.org/sites /default/files/08-13-13-am-session.pdf.

44. PFC *Bradley E. Manning*, 34:82.
45. For a detailed analysis of meta-reporting practices surrounding Manning's name and pronoun change, see Capuzza, "What's in a Name?"
46. Margaret Sullivan, "The Soldier Formerly Known as Bradley Manning," *New York Times*, August 22, 2013, LexisNexis Academic.
47. Christine Haughney, "'He'? 'She'? News Media Are Encouraged to Change," *New York Times*, August 23, 2013, LexisNexis Academic.
48. Haughney, "'He'? 'She'?"
49. Carlos Maza, "CNN Has No Excuse for Continuing to Call Chelsea Manning a Man," Media Matters, August 28, 2013, mediamatters.org/blog/2013/08/28/cnn-has-no-excuse-for-continuing-to-call-chelse/195647.
50. "Fox & Friends Teases Segment on Chelsea Manning with Aerosmith's 'Dude (Looks like a Lady),'" Media Matters, August 27, 2013, mediamatters.org/video/2013/08/27/fox-amp-friends-teases-segment-on-chelsea-manni/195615.
51. *The Legal View with Ashleigh Banfield*, CNN, August 15, 2013, LexisNexis Academic.
52. *Here And Now*, "'I Am Chelsea': Bradley Manning Wants to Live as a Woman," NPR, August 22, 2013, LexisNexis Academic.
53. *Today Show*, NBC, August 22, 2013, LexisNexis Academic; *Legal View with Ashleigh Banfield*, CNN, August 22, 2013, LexisNexis Academic; Danny Cevallos, "Is Bradley Manning Entitled to Gender Change in Prison?," CNN, August 23, 2013, cnn.com/2013/08/23/opinion/cevallos-bradley-manning-gender-identity/; *The Lead with Jake Tapper*, CNN, August 22, 2013, LexisNexis Academic.
54. "Is It Legal?," *The O'Reilly Factor*, Fox News Network, August 27, 2013, LexisNexis Academic.
55. See Serano, *Excluded*.
56. See, for example, Ruth Tam, "He or She Might Actually Favor 'Ze,'" *Washington Post*, September 6, 2013, LexisNexis Academic; or "The Manning Moment," *Washington Post*, September 2, 2013, LexisNexis Academic. I elaborate on the disproportionate criminalization and incarceration of transgender people and people of color in more detail in chapter 3.
57. Cited in *Good Morning America*, ABC, August 15, 2013, LexisNexis Academic.
58. Cited in *Newsroom*, CNN, August 24, 2013, LexisNexis Academic.

59. *In the Matter of: United States vs.* PFC *Bradley E. Manning*, vol. 37, August 19, 2013, Afternoon Session, unofficial transcript, Freedom of the Press Foundation, 11, pressfreedomfoundation.org/sites /default/files/08-19-13-PM-session.pdf.

60. PFC *Bradley E. Manning*, 37:46.

61. Chase Madar, "Review: My Hero Bradley Manning," *Guardian*, August 3, 2013, LexisNexis Academic.

62. *In the Matter of: United States vs.* PFC *Bradley E. Manning*, vol. 33, August 12, 2013 Morning Session, unofficial transcript, Freedom of the Press Foundation, 22, pressfreedomfoundation.org/sites/default/files /08-12-13-AM-session.pdf. See also PFC *Bradley E. Manning*, 37:61.

63. Chelsea Manning, "Bradley Manning Statement: 'Unfortunately, I Can't Go Back and Change Things,'" *Guardian*, August 14, 2013, theguardian.com/world/2013/aug/14/bradley-manning-statement -sentencing-trial, my emphasis.

64. See Puar and Rai, "Monster, Terrorist, Fag," 122–23.

65. Chelsea Manning, "Appeal for Presidential Pardon," Global Research News, August 21, 2013, globalresearch.ca/text-of-bradley -mannings-letter-to-president-obama/5346626.

66. JAG stands for Judge Advocate General's Corps and refers to the legal branch within the military that deals with military jus-tice and law. See "Judge: Bin Laden Raid Member Can Testify in WikiLeaks Case," Fox News, April 11, 2013, video.foxnews.com/v /2293646359001/judge-bin-laden-raid-member-can-testify-in -wikileaks-case.

67. David Carr, "In Leak Case, State Secrecy in Plain Sight," *New York Times*, March 25, 2013, LexisNexis Academic.

68. Cited in Rothe and Steinmetz, "The Case of Bradley Manning," 286.

69. Chelsea Manning, "Additional Information in Support of Manning's Application for Clemency," Clemency Application for Ms. Chelsea Manning to Office of the Pardon Attorney, November 10, 2016, 5.

70. Nathan Fuller, "Quantico Psychiatrist Says Bradley Treated Worse than Death Row," Chelsea Manning Support Network, November 28, 2012, chelseamanning.org/news/quantico-psychiatrist-bradley -manning-treated-worse-than-death-row-inmates.

71. Ed Pilkington, "Clinton Spokesman Quits over Manning: Crow-ley Called Handling of WikiLeaks Suspect 'Stupid;' Remarks Force Obama to Address Issue Directly," *Guardian*, March 14, 2011, Lex-

isNexis Academic. See also *Live with Cenk Uygur*, MSNBC, April 14, 2011, LexisNexis Academic.

72. Cited in Mary Beth Sheridan, "State Department Spokesman Quits," *Washington Post*, March 14, 2011, LexisNexis Academic.

73. Ellen Nakashima, "U.N. 'frustrated' over Manning," *Washington Post*, April 12, 2011, LexisNexis Academic.

74. Ed Pilkington, "Bradley Manning's Treatment Was Cruel and Inhuman, UN Torture Chief Rules," *Guardian*, March 12, 2012, theguardian.com/world/2012/mar/12/bradley-manning-cruel-inhuman-treatment-un. See Yochai Benkler, "The Dangerous Logic of the Bradley Manning Case," *New Republic*, March 1, 2013, newrepublic.com/article/112554.

75. Editorial, "Abu Ghraib in America," *Nation*, March 28, 2013, EBSCO-host; Elisabeth Bumiller, "WikiLeaks Defendant to Be Moved," *New York Times*, April 19, 2011, nytimes.com/2011/04/20/us/20manning.html; Reitman, "The Trials."

76. Cited in Esther Addley, "Bradley Manning Moved to 'More Open' Military Prison," *Guardian*, April 21, 2011, LexisNexis Academic.

77. Nathan Fuller, "Judge Limits Manning's Whistle-Blower Defense, Pretrial Confinement Nears 1,000 Days," Chelsea Manning Support Network, January 16, 2013, chelseamanning.org/news/judge-limits-bradley-mannings-whistle-blower-defense-pretrial-confinement-nears-1000-days.

78. Hansen, "Manning-Lamo Chat Logs."

79. *In the Matter of: United States vs. PFC Bradley E. Manning*, vol. 21, July 25, 2013, Morning Session, unofficial transcript, Freedom of the Press Foundation, 166–67, pressfreedomfoundation.org/sites/default/files/07-25-13-am-session.pdf.

80. See Benkler, "A Free Irresponsible Press." In recent years, WikiLeaks and its founder Julian Assange, have faced intense scrutiny for purportedly aiding Russia in interfering with the 2016 U.S. elections, specifically by publishing emails from John Podesta, a Hillary Clinton aide, and by hacking information from the Democratic National Committee. Assange himself has become an increasingly contested figure. Since 2012, Assange was hiding out at the Ecuadorian Embassy in London, which had granted him asylum, to avoid extradition to Sweden for charges of sexual assault. In the most recent turn of events, Assange was arrested by British police in

April 2019 after Ecuador ejected him from their London embassy. The U.S. Justice Department is currently requesting his extradition and has charged him with "conspiracy to commit computer intrusion" for assisting Manning in 2010 with cracking a password stored on U.S. Department of Defense computers. Assange's arrest has reignited debates over whether WikiLeaks counts as a journalistic publishing platform with First Amendment protections and whether his arrest sets a dangerous precedent for criminal investigations of other news organizations. See Sasha Ingber, "Julian Assange Arrested, Faces U.S. Charges Related to 2010 WikiLeaks Releases Assange," NPR, April 11, 2019, npr.org/2019/04/11/712128612 /julian-assange-arrested-in-london.

81. *PFC Bradley E. Manning*, 37:45.

82. Ed Pilkington, "US Whistleblowers: Manning Sentencing; No Record of Deaths Caused by WikiLeaks Revelations, Court Told," *Guardian*, August 1, 2013, LexisNexis Academic.

83. Puar, *Terrorist Assemblages*, 3. I elaborate on this concept in detail in the next chapter.

84. Butler, *Precarious Life*, 94, emphasis in original.

85. Agamben, *Homo Sacer*, 8.

86. Agamben, 28.

87. Mbembe, "Necropolitics."

88. Manning, "Appeal for Presidential Pardon."

89. Grossberg, *We Gotta Get Out*, 99.

2. Transpatriotism

1. Manning did not come out as trans until August 2013. Some of the statements and news articles cited in this chapter, therefore, still refer to her by male pronouns or her deadname. As outlined in the previous chapter, I maintain these original quotes to specifically highlight the violent misgendering and deadnaming that Manning was and continues to be subject to. Linda Williams, "SF Pride Statement about Bradley Manning," Facebook, April 26, 2013, facebook .com/SanFranciscoPride/posts/622822351079480.

2. Sean Sala, "Press Statement for Gay Military to Boycott San Francisco Pride," Facebook, April 26, 2013, facebook.com/permalink .php?story_fbid=562622293778040&id=298749953498610 (content has since been deleted).

3. Cited in Associated Press, "San Francisco Gay Pride Rescinds Honour for Bradley Manning," *Guardian*, April 27, 2013, guardian.co.uk /world/2013/apr/27/san-francisco-gay-pride-bradley-manning.

4. Cited in Kevin Gosztola, "sf Pride Capitulates, Drops Manning," Salon, April 27, 2013, salon.com/2013/04/27/sf_pride_capitulates _drops_manning.

5. Puar, *Terrorist Assemblages*, 3ff.

6. See Gosztola, "How the LGBT Community Helped"; Douglas-Bowers, "The Politics of Abandonment"; Queer Strike and Payday, "Chelsea Manning"; or Brownworth, "Bradley Manning," for activist and journalistic accounts of the retraction.

7. Puar, *Terrorist Assemblages*, 39; in addition see Puar, "Mapping U.S. Homonormativities," 71–73.

8. Puar, *Terrorist Assemblages*, 230n9. In her latest book, *The Right to Maim*, Puar wonders whether the recent ascent of transgender rights "signal[s] the uptake of a new variant of homonationalism—a 'trans(homo)nationalism'? Or is transgender identity a variation of processes of citizenship and nationalism through disciplinary normativization rather than a variation of homonationalism?" (34). According to Puar, either occasion produces new figures of citizenship and biopolitical abjection.

9. Susan Stryker specifically points to the 1966 riot in San Francisco's Tenderloin District, in which drag queens and gay hustlers banded together against police harassment and social oppression to locate transgender action as a means to unsettle hetero-and homonormative categories and subjectivities. See Stryker, "Transgender History, Homonormativity."

10. Williams, "sf Pride Statement."

11. The Personal Responsibility and Work Opportunity Reconciliation Act of 1996 presented a significant overhaul to the United States' welfare system and has been widely considered a hallmark of neoliberal governing principles that strive to further privatize and reduce welfare programs for citizens. The Welfare Reform Act not only redistributed the primary responsibility for administering welfare from the federal government to the individual states but also requires recipients to work in exchange for time-limited assistance.

12. Reddy, *Freedom with Violence*, 8; Eng, *The Feeling of Kinship*.

13. Bill Clinton campaigned in 1992 on the promise that he would overturn the ban on gays', lesbians', and bisexuals' serving in the military. However, Clinton severely underestimated the fierce opposition and resistance he would face from the military service chiefs (among them Colin Powell and Norman Schwarzkopf) as well as social conservatives and the religious right. After five months of hearings and mounting congressional resistance, Clinton agreed to a compromise, 10 United States Code §654—colloquially known as the Don't Ask, Don't Tell policy—which for the first time sanctioned that admitting to being gay in the military was against the law. The arguments repeatedly voiced at the time stressed that DADT was mainly necessary in order maintain "unit cohesion": "(6) success in combat requires military units that are characterized by high morale, good order and discipline, and unit cohesion"; whereby "unit cohesion" is defined as "(7) . . . the bonds of trust among individual service members that make the combat effectiveness of a military unit greater than the sum of the combat effectiveness of individual unit members" (107 stat. 1671, Public Law 103-160, Nov. 30, 1993, Subtitle G—Other Matters). Hence, DADT held that "the presence in the armed forces of persons who demonstrate propensity or intent to engage in same-sex acts would create an unacceptable risk to the high standards of morale, good order and discipline, and unit cohesion which are the essence of military capability." See Burrelli, "'Don't Ask, Don't Tell,'" 1.

14. See "HRC Statement on the End of 'Don't Ask, Don't Tell,'" Human Rights Campaign, September 19, 2011, hrc.org/press-releases/entry /hrc-statement-on-the-end-of-dont-ask-dont-tell; Department of Defense, "Report of the Comprehensive Review of the Issues Associated with a Repeal of 'Don't Ask, Don't Tell'" November 30, 2010, archive.defense.gov/home/features/2010/0610_dadt.

15. Lymari Morales, "In U.S., 67% Support Repealing 'Don't Ask, Don't Tell': The Most Opposition Comes from Conservative Republicans," Gallup Politics, December 9, 2010, gallup.com/poll/145130 /support-repealing-dont-ask-dont-tell.aspx.

16. The story of Lt. Col. Victor Fehrenbach, for example, generated much publicity. Fehrenbach had served in the U.S. Air Force for nineteen years, flew almost ninety combat missions in Iraq, Afghanistan, and Kosovo, and was eligible for retirement in September

2011. Under military regulations, however, he would lose his retirement benefits if he was discharged before reaching twenty years of service. Fehrenbach, with support from the Servicemembers Legal Defense Network, tried to block the air force from discharging him, arguing that a discharge would cause irreparable harm. The legal basis for his argument was established by a 2008 ruling of the U.S. Court of Appeals for the Ninth Circuit, which stated that the government had to prove homosexual conduct was affecting morale, discipline, and unit cohesion before a service member could be discharged. In August 2010 an agreement was reached that allowed Fehrenbach to successfully retire on September 30, 2011. See Chris Johnson, "Fehrenbach Assured Retirement from Air Force with Pension," *Washington Blade*, February 16, 2011, washingtonblade .com/2011/02/16/fehrenback-assured-retirement-from-air-force -with-pension.

17. See Farrow, "A Military Job"; Nopper, "Why I Oppose Repealing DADT," 34. Lisa Cacho, for example, points toward "differential inclusion" mechanisms offered to those living with few or no rights: the increased Latino incorporation in the U.S. military after 9/11 was framed as a benign "opportunity for legal recognition" that effectively glossed over the gruesomeness of war and the fact that these "cheap" foot soldiers serve(d) as cannon fodder on the front lines. Former president G.W. Bush had issued an executive order in 2002 that not only expedited the process of attaining naturalized citizenship for active-duty soldiers but also waived the residence requirement and naturalization fees for soldiers serving during military hostilities. See Cacho, *Social Death*, 108. Similarly, the DREAM (Development, Relief, and Education for Alien Minors) Act, which has been introduced to Congress in several variations since 2001 but has yet to pass, also lures undocumented students with the promise of citizenship through military service. Carolina Bank Muñoz notes that the option of participating in military service not only gives military recruiters further ammunition to prey on communities of color but also incentivizes states to encourage military service since it relieves them of granting in-state tuition and saves federal Pell Grant money. See Muñoz, "A Dream Deferred," 14.

18. Barack Obama, "Statement by the President on the Repeal of 'Don't Ask, Don't Tell,'" White House, Office of the Press Secretary, Sep-

tember 20, 2011, whitehouse.gov/the-press-office/2011/09/20
/statement-president-repeal-dont-ask-dont-tell.

19. Brownworth, "Bradley Manning," 108.

20. See Puar, *Terrorist Assemblages*.

21. Robert Mackey, "American Uses Kremlin-Financed Network to
Denounce Russia's Anti-Gay Legislation," *New York Times*, August
21, 2013, LexisNexis Academic.

22. Davis, *Are Prisons Obsolete?*, 16. Also see Alexander, *The New Jim
Crow*; and Wacquant, "Deadly Symbiosis," for detailed analyses of
the prison-industrial complex.

23. See Agathangelou, Bassichis, and Spira, "Intimate Investments," 123.

24. *Rachel Maddow Show*, MSNBC, Friday March 20, 2009, nbcnews
.com/id/29836340/ns/msnbc-rachel_maddow_show/t/rachel
-maddow-showfor-friday-march/-.u9z2bqggamE.

25. Cited in Amy Goodman, "Does Opposing 'Don't Ask, Don't Tell'
Bolster US Militarism? A Debate with Lt. Dan Choi and Queer
Activist Mattilda Bernstein Sycamore," *Democracy Now!*, October
22, 2010, democracynow.org/2010/10/22/does_opposing_dont_ask
_dont_tell.

26. Cited in Nair, "Rage," 21.

27. Cited in Meredith Bennett-Smith, "Lt. Dan Choi, Gay Military
Activist on Trial for Protesting DADT policy, Facing 6 Months in
Jail," *Huffington Post*, March 28, 2013, huffingtonpost.com/2013/03
/28/dan-choi-trial_n_2963990.html.

28. Cited in Gabriel Arana, "The Passion of Dan Choi," *American Prospect*, December 2, 2013, prospect.org/article/passion-dan-choi.

29. Cited in Amy Goodman, "Iraq Combat Veteran Dan Choi Forci-
bly Ousted, Barred from Bradley Manning Hearing at Ft. Meade,"
Democracy Now!, December 21, 2011, democracynow.org/2011/12
/21/iraq_combat_veteran_dan_choi_forcibly.

30. Arana, "The Passion of Dan Choi."

31. Cited in Goodman, "Iraq Combat Veteran."

32. Goodman, "Iraq Combat Veteran."

33. Cited in Goodman, "Iraq Combat Veteran," my emphases.

34. John Pilger, "Never Forget That Bradley Manning, Not Gay Marriage, Is the Issue," *New Statesman*, May 21, 2012, EBSCOhost.

35. Cited in Jeff Krehely, "Pvt. Chelsea E. Manning Comes Out,
Deserves Respectful Treatment by Media and Officials," *HRC Blog*,

August 22, 2013, hrc.org/blog/pvt.-chelsea-e.-manning-comes-out
-deserves-respectful-treatment-by-media-an, my emphasis.

36. Haritaworn, *Queer Lovers and Hateful Others*, 109.

37. Cited in Lou Chibbaro Jr., "Will Manning Case Harm Effort to
Lift Trans Military Ban?," *Washington Blade*, August 22, 2013,
washingtonblade.com/2013/08/22/will-chelsea-manning-bradley
-harm-effort-to-lift-trans-military-ban-transgender-lgbt-news-army
-wikileaks.

38. Autumn Sandeen, "Thoughts on Chelsea Manning's Coming Out,"
TransAdvocate, August 24, 2013, transadvocate.com/thoughts-on
-chelsea-mannings-coming-out_n_10072.htm-sthash.shqouzfl.dpuf.

39. Kristin Beck, "The 'Manning Debacle,'" Facebook, August 22, 2013,
facebook.com/kristin.hills.125/posts/496798800413582 (post has
since been deleted).

40. Charlie Savage, "Manning, Facing Prison for Leaks, Apologizes at
Court-Martial Trial," *New York Times*, August 15, 2013, LexisNexis
Academic.

41. Beck and Speckhard, *Warrior Princess*, 155–56, 143, emphasis in original.

42. Beck, "The 'Manning Debacle,'" emphasis in original.

43. See Hanssens et al., "A Roadmap for Change," 25ff.

44. Beck, "The 'Manning Debacle.'"

45. Agathangelou, Bassichis, and Spira, "Intimate Investments," 3.

46. Editorial, "Bradley Manning: A Sentence Both Unjust and Unfair,"
Guardian, August 21, 2013, theguardian.com/commentisfree/2013
/aug/21/bradley-manning-sentence-unjust.

47. Chase Strangio, staff attorney with the ACLU's LGBT Project, said,
"The official policy of the Federal Bureau of Prisons and most state
agencies is to provide medically necessary care for the treatment
of gender dysphoria, and courts have consistently found that denying such care to prisoners based on blanket exclusions violates the
Eighth Amendment of the Constitution" (cited in Sunnivie Brydum,
"WikiLeaks Source Comes Out as Transgender," *Advocate*, August
22, 2013, advocate.com/politics/transgender/2013/08/22/watch
-wikileaks-source-comes-out-transgender).

48. See Tom Vanden Brook, "Military Approves Hormone Therapy
for Chelsea Manning," *USA Today*, February 13, 2015, usatoday
.com/story/news/nation/2015/02/12/chelsea-manning-hormone
-therapy/23311813/.

49. See Ryan Grim and Matt Sledge, "Court Orders Army to Stop Referring to Chelsea Manning as a Man," *Huffington Post*, March 5, 2015, huffingtonpost.com/2015/03/05/chelsea-manning_n_6811352.html.

50. Chelsea Manning, "Additional Information in Support of Manning's Application for Clemency," Clemency Application for Ms. Chelsea Manning to Office of the Pardon Attorney, November 10, 2016, 6.

51. Manning, "Additional Information in Support."

52. Chelsea Manning, "The Fog Machine of War," *New York Times*, June 14, 2014. nytimes.com/2014/06/15/opinion/sunday/chelsea -manning-the-us-militarys-campaign-against-media-freedom.html.

53. Hill et al., "Fit to Serve?," 9. For an insightful discussion on the difficulties and political implications of doing "covert operations" research on trans service members, see Barnett and Hill, "Covert Operation."

54. Kerri Ryer, "Former Surgeon General Faults Military's Transgender Ban," Palm Center, March 13, 2014, palmcenter.org/press/trans /releases/commissionreport.

55. Lisa Leff, "Panel Urges End to U.S. Ban on Transgender Troops," *AirForce Times*, March 13, 2014, airforcetimes.com/article/20140313 /CAREERS/303130023/Transgender-troop-ban-faces-scrutiny.

56. Sunnivie Brydum, "Pentagon on Trans Troops: 'These Are the Kind of People We Want,'" *Advocate*, June 30, 2016, advocate .com/transgender/2016/6/30/breaking-pentagon-ends-ban -transgender-service-members.

57. Donald Trump (@realDonaldTrump), Twitter, July 26, 2017, my emphasis.

58. Office of the Press Secretary, "Presidential Memorandum for the Secretary of Defense and the Secretary of Homeland Security," White House, August 25, 2017, whitehouse.gov/the-press-office /2017/08/25/presidential-memorandum-secretary-defense-and -secretary-homeland.

59. White House, "Presidential Memorandum."

60. RAND is a nonpartisan public policy think tank. See Gereben et al.'s report, *Assessing the Implications of Allowing Transgender Personnel to Serve Openly*.

61. Brynn Tannehill, "We're Not Astroturf: Why Open Trans Military Service Is a Worthy Fight," *Huffington Post*, September 16, 2013, huffingtonpost.com/brynn-tannehill/were-not-astroturf_b _3903502.html.

62. Dean Spade cited in *Democracy Now!*, "What Role Should the Military Play in the Fight for Transgender Rights?," July 27, 2017, democracynow.org/2017/7/27/what_role_should_the_military_play.

63. Cited in Toshio Meronek, "Transgender Activists Speak Out Against Campaign to End Trans Military Ban," Truthout, July 21, 2015, truth-out.org/news/item/25015-transgender-activists-speak -out-against-campaign-to-end-trans-military-ban.

64. Much of my thinking about a queer politics that is untethered from the mainstream gay rights movement is informed by the writers and artists of Against Equality, a collective that poses "queer challenges to the politics of inclusion." See againstequality.org/.

65. Chelsea Manning, "Additional Information in Support of Manning's Application for Clemency," Clemency Application for Ms. Chelsea Manning to Office of the Pardon Attorney, November 10, 2016, 1, 7.

66. Barack Obama's comments on the commutation of Chelsea Manning, We the People Team email, January 19, 2017, petitions .whitehouse.gov/petition/commute-chelsea-mannings-sentence -time-served-1 (site discontinued).

67. Eric A. Stanley (@Eric_A_Stanley), Twitter, January 17, 2017.

68. Matthew Shaer, "The Long, Lonely Road of Chelsea Manning," *New York Times Magazine*, June 12, 2017, nytimes.com/2017/06/12 /magazine/the-long-lonely-road-of-chelsea-manning.html; ABC *Nightline*, "Declassified: The Chelsea Manning Story," June 15, 2017, abc.go.com/shows/nightline/episode-guide/2017-06/15-061517 -declassified-the-chelsea-manning-story; Nathan Heller, "Chelsea Manning Changed the Course of History; Now She's Focusing on Herself," *Vogue*, August 10, 2017, vogue.com/article/chelsea -manning-vogue-interview-september-issue-2017.

69. Donald Trump (@realDonaldTrump), Twitter, January 26, 2017.

70. James Kirchick, "When Transgender Trumps Treachery," *New York Times*, August 29, 2017, nyti.ms/2wgdm2r.

71. Kirchick, "When Transgender Trumps Treachery."

72. Report under Subsection 44 (1) of the Canadian Immigration and Refugee Protection Act; screenshot of letter tweeted by Manning (@xychelsea) on September 25, 2017.

73. Harvard Kennedy School, "Statement from Douglas W. Elmendorf, Dean of Harvard Kennedy School, regarding the School's Invitation to Chelsea Manning to Be a Visiting Fellow," September 15,

2017, hks.harvard.edu/announcements/statement-dean-elmendorf
-regarding-invitation-chelsea-manning-be-visiting-fellow.

74. Morell's letter is available in Stefan Becket, "Ex-CIA Chief Michael Morell Resigns Harvard Post over Chelsea Manning," *CBS News*, September 14, 2017, cbsnews.com/news/michael-morell-ex-cia-chief -resigns-harvard-post-over-chelsea-manning/.

75. Manning (@xychelsea), Twitter, September 15, 2017.

76. Cited in Chase Strangio, "Instead of Certain Death, Chelsea Manning Now Has a Chance at Life," ACLU, January 18, 2017, aclu.org/blog/speak -freely/instead-certain-death-chelsea-manning-now-has-chance-life.

77. Manning's bid for a senate seat failed in June 2018. She was unable to unseat incumbent senator Ben Cardin during Maryland's Democratic primary.

78 The Sparrow Project, "Statement from Chelsea Manning's Support Team Regarding Assange Indictment and Punitive Nature of Chelsea's Continued Detention," April 11, 2019, sparrowmedia.net/2019/04/statement-from -chelsea-mannings-support-team-regarding-todays-unsealed-indictment -and-the-purely-punitive-nature-of-chelseas-continued-detention/.

79. Manning (@xychelsea), Twitter, October 21, 2017.

3. Blind(ing) (In)justice

1. Andy Mannix, "CeCe McDonald Murder Trial: Behind the Scenes of the Transgender Woman's Case," *City Pages*, May 9, 2012, citypages .com/news/cece-mcdonald-murder-trial-6757078.

2. Home page, Schooner Tavern, accessed October 16, 2018, schoonertavern.com.

3. Larry Tyaries Thomas, one of McDonald's friends, recalling those slurs cited in Mannix, "CeCe McDonald Murder Trial." I chose to maintain the full spelling of the derogatory and offensive language deployed here to fully capture the vicious bigotry directed at McDonald and her friends.

4. Cited in Sabrina Rubin Erdely, "The Transgender Crucible," *Rolling Stone*, July 30, 2014, rollingstone.com/culture/news/the-transgender -crucible-20140730.

5. CeCe McDonald interviewed by Michelangelo Signorile, host of Sirius XM's *Progress Show*. Transcript retrieved from "CeCe McDonald, Transgender Activist, Recalls Hate Attack, Manslaughter Case," *Huffington Post*, February 22, 2014, huffingtonpost.com/2014/02/22 /cece-mcdonald-manslaughter-case_n_4831677.html.

6. Cited in Signorile, "CeCe McDonald, Transgender Activist."

7. Security guard Gary Gilbert cited in Mannix, "CeCe McDonald Murder Trial."

8. Scales Transcript, *State of Minnesota v. Chrishaun Reed McDonald*, Hennepin County, Fourth Judicial District, June 5, 2011, Court File No. 27-CR-11-16485, 24.

9. Johnson, "Cisgender Privilege."

10. Using search terms such as *CeCe McDonald, Chrishaun McDonald,* and *Dean Schmitz,* I conducted a search of prominent Minneapolis and Saint Paul news outlets, such as the *Star Tribune,* the *Pioneer Press,* the *Minnesota Daily,* Minnesota Public Radio, the *MinnPost,* and *Lavender Magazine* for the time frame between McDonald's arrest on June 5, 2011, until September 2014. I also searched for transcripts from the local affiliates of ABC, NBC, CBS, and Fox using the same keywords. After I eliminated duplicates and articles only peripherally addressing the case, my search resulted in sixty-four articles and broadcasts about McDonald.

11. While I disapprove of and would prefer to highlight each instance of the violent misgendering that is occurring in these and some of the following quotes by inserting a [*sic*], as in the Manning chapters I choose not to do so in order to maintain better reading flow. "Charges Filed in Minneapolis Stabbing," WCCO: CBS Minnesota, June 7, 2011, minnesota.cbslocal.com/2011/06/07/charges-filed-in-minneapolis-stabbing; "Murder Charges Filed in Mpls. Weekend Stabbing," KARE 11 News, June 7, 2011, archive.kare11.com/rss/article/925977/391/Murder-charges-filed-in-Mpls-weekend-stabbing; Paul Walsh, "Minneapolis Stabbing Victim Ran into Scissors, Suspect Says," *Star Tribune,* June 8, 2011, startribune.com/local/west/123370453.html.

12. "Man Faces Murder Charge in Minneapolis Bar Stabbing," myfox9.com, June 7, 2011.

13. Jeremy Williams, Schmitz's son, cited in "Man Faces Murder Charge."

14. Tammy Williams cited in "Man Faces Murder Charge."

15. Abby Simons, "Transgender Defendant Gets 3 Years in Fatal Bar Fight," *Star Tribune,* June 5, 2012, 1B.

16. Cram, "'Angie Was Our Sister,'" 419.

17. Mannix, "CeCe McDonald Murder Trial." *City Pages* is the only alternative weekly remaining in the Twin Cities. Founded in 1979 as

a music- and entertainment-oriented publication, it was originally called *Sweet Potato* before being renamed *City Pages* in 1981. Similar to other print publications, which are experiencing declining revenue streams and readership numbers, alternative weeklies are also struggling with declining advertising sales while trying to expand their digital publishing platforms. In May 2015 the *Star Tribune* bought the paper for an undisclosed amount from the Denver-based Voice Media Group. *City Pages* currently reaches approximately 360,000 readers a month in print and records around 1.3 million visits a month to its website. See Evan Ramstad, "Star Tribune Makes Deal to Buy Alt-Weekly City Pages," *Star Tribune*, May 6, 2015, startribune.com/star-tribune-buys-city-pages/302763201/.

18. Mannix, "CeCe McDonald Murder Trial."

19. Abby Simons, "2nd Weapon Raises Questions," *Star Tribune*, 4B, July 12, 2011; Simons, "Transgender Defendant Gets 3 Years"; Brian Lambert, "Local CEO Prods Peers to Oppose Marriage Amendment," *MinnPost*, June 18, 2012.

20. Eric Best, "Transgender in the Prison System," *Minnesota Daily*, June 27, 2012, 7; Editorial Board, "Transgender in a Binary System," *Minnesota Daily*, January 21, 2014, 14A.

21. "Torture: The Use of Solitary Confinement in U.S. Prisons," Center for Constitutional Rights, May 2012, updated March 2017, ccrjustice .org/solitary-factsheet.

22. See Hanssens et al., *A Roadmap for Change*, 25ff.

23. Campbell and Holding, "The Trans-Exclusive Archive," 202.

24. After several ownership changes in the early 2000s and filing for bankruptcy in 2009, the *Star Tribune* was sold to local businessman and former Republican state senator Glen Taylor for $100 million in 2014. Taylor also owns professional Minnesota sports teams, including the Minnesota Timberwolves and the Minnesota Lynx. After a decade of declining revenue, Star Tribune Media has seen marginal revenue growth and operating profits over the past few years. The *Tribune*'s weekday circulation reaches about 300,000 readers, and its website gets more than seven million unique visits a month. See Ramstad, "Star Tribune Makes Deal." In April 2014 Taylor indicated that the *Tribune*, which Republicans consider too liberal, will "have better balance" in its reporting aided by veteran reporters retiring. Taylor's comments on the political changes at Minnesota's largest

daily newspaper are characteristic of ongoing concerns about private ownership influencing editorial decisions. See Britt Robson, "New Owner Glen Taylor: Less Liberal *Star Tribune* Ahead," *MinnPost*, April 16, 2014, minnpost.com/business/2014/04/new-owner-glen-taylor-less-liberal-star-tribune-ahead.

25. Simons, "2nd Weapon"; Abby Simons, "Woman Charged with Starting Fatal Melee," *Star Tribune*, May 23, 2012, 4B, LexisNexis Academic.

26. See Barker-Plummer, "Fixing Gwen."

27. "Transgender Woman Gets 41 Months after Accepting Plea Deal," WCCO: CBS Minnesota, June 4, 2012; Laura Yuen, "Transgender Woman Gave Up Self-Defense Claim in Plea Deal," Minnesota Public Radio, May 3, 2012, mprnews.org/display/web/2012/05/03/cece-plea/.

28. See, for example, Ghandnoosh, "Race and Punishment."

29. Simons, "2nd Weapon"; Abby Simons, "Attorney for Mpls. Transgender Murder Suspect Says New Charge Is 'Retaliation,'" *Star Tribune*, October 7, 2011; Simons, "Transgender Defendant Gets 3 Years."

30. Paul Walsh, "'CeCe' McDonald Freed after 19 Months in Prison for Killing Mpls. Bar Patron," *Star Tribune*, January 13, 2014.

31. See Crenshaw's groundbreaking work on intersectionality, "Mapping the Margins."

32. Collins, *Black Feminist Thought*, 18, 227–28.

33. The Minnesota Free Flow of Information Act protects journalists from compelled disclosure of the identity of their sources to the disclosure of "any unpublished information procured by the person in the course of work or any of the person's notes, memoranda, recording tapes, film or other reportorial data whether or not it would tend to identify the person or means through which the information was obtained" (Minnesota Statue § 595.023).

34. Minnesota Free Flow of Information Act, Memorandum in Support of Application for Disclosure, *State of Minnesota v. McDonald*, November 3, 2011, 1; Order and Memorandum of Law Granting the State's Application for Disclosure, *State of Minnesota v. McDonald*, December 9, 2011, 6, 13.

35. Paul Walsh, personal correspondence with author, October 11, 2014.

36. Abby Simons, personal correspondence with author, October 1, 2014.

37. Lex Horan, interview by author, September 27, 2014.

38. See "GLAAD Media Reference Guide—In Focus: Covering the Transgender Community," GLAAD, August 2014, glaad.org/reference/transgender.

39. Duchesne Drew, personal correspondence with author, November 3, 2014.

40. Drew, personal correspondence with author, October 20, 2014.

41. Horan, interview.

42. Melamed, "The Spirit of Neoliberalism," 1.

43. Alexander, *The New Jim Crow*, 2.

44. Support CeCe, "Prosecutors Retaliate for Plea Refusal, Raise Charge against McDonald," Support CeCe, October 8, 2011, supportcece .wordpress.com/2011/10/08/prosecutors-retaliate-for-plea-refusal -raise-charge-against-mcdonald/.

45. Simons, "Attorney for Mpls. Transgender Murder Suspect."

46. Alexander, *The New Jim Crow*, 87.

47. McDonald was represented by the Legal Rights Center in Minneapolis, which specializes in pro-bono representation of low-income and poor people of color.

48. Leo J. Sioris in a letter to Hersch Izek, "Re: State of Minnesota v. Chrishaun Reed McDonald," March 13, 2012.

49. Notice of Motion and Motion to Exclude Expert Testimony, *State of Minnesota v. McDonald*, April 16, 2012.

50. Offer of Proof in Support of Motion to Admit Evidence under MINN.R.EVID.Rule 404(b), *State of Minnesota v. McDonald*, April 19, 2012, 1, 3.

51. Offer of Proof in Support of Motion to Admit Evidence, 8.

52. Notice of Motion and Motion to Suppress Defendant's Statements, *State of Minnesota v. McDonald*, November 11, 2011.

53. Scales Transcript, *State of Minnesota v. McDonald*, June 5, 2011, 24.

54. Scales Transcript, 13, 19, 34.

55. State's Memorandum in Opposition to Defendant's Motion to Suppress Evidence, *State of Minnesota v. McDonald*, November 29, 2011, n.p.; Order and Memorandum of Law Denying Defendant's Motion to Suppress Evidence, *State of Minnesota v. McDonald*, April 23, 2012, emphasis in original.

56. Freeman interviewed by Andy Mannix, "Michael Freeman Talks Prosecution of CeCe McDonald," *City Pages*, May 11, 2012, citypages .com/news/michael-freeman-talks-prosecution-of-cece-mcdonald -video-6539787. The Minnesota Practice Series outlines the general

rules for self-defense cases as follows: "(1) An absence of aggression or provocation by the defendant; (2) Good faith; that is, an actual and honest belief; (3) Belief of imminent or immediate danger; (4) The danger must be of death, great bodily harm, or a felony crime; (5) The action taken must appear to be 'necessary' or unavoidable; (6) That is, the defendant must have been unable to retreat or otherwise reasonably avoid the danger (except when the incident occurs in the defendant's own dwelling); and (7) The belief must be based upon 'reasonable grounds.'" See Westlaw, § 47.19 "Self Defense: Defense of Dwelling; Defense of Others; Imperfect Self-Defense," Minnesota Practice Series, November 2011, 1.

57. I am drawing here from Judith Butler's *Precarious Life*, in which she explores how certain forms of grief become nationally recognized and amplified, whereas other losses become unthinkable and ungrievable, particularly through the construction of the Arab as the terrorist other post-9/11.

58. Cited in Mannix, "Michael Freeman Talks Prosecution."

59. See, for example, Alexander, *The New Jim Crow*; Williams, *The Alchemy of Race*; Spade, *Normal Life*.

60. Williams, *The Alchemy of Race*, 121; Crenshaw, "Demarginalizing the Intersection."

61. Crenshaw, "Demarginalizing the Intersection," 151. Title VII of the Civil Rights Act of 1964 prohibits employment discrimination based on race, color, religion, sex, and national origin. The Civil Rights Act of 1991 and the Lily Ledbetter Fair Pay Act of 2009 have amended several sections of Title VII (see U.S. Equal Employment Opportunity Commission, "Title VII of the Civil Rights Act of 1964," n.d., eeoc.gov/laws/statutes/titlevii.cfm). Similarly, Crenshaw points out that the singular focus of rape statutes on white male power over white female sexuality conceals the use of rape as a weapon of racial terror and does not account for the multidimensionality of the lives of women of color: "When Black women were raped by white males, they were being raped not as women generally, but as Black women specifically: Their femaleness made them sexually vulnerable to racist domination, while their Blackness effectively denied them any protection. This white male power was reinforced by a judicial system in which the successful conviction of a white man for raping a Black woman

was virtually unthinkable" (Crenshaw, "Demarginalizing the Intersection," 158–59).

62. Harris, "Whiteness as Property," 1713–14, 1753.

63. Offer of Proof to Limit the Publication of Photographs of the Deceased, *State of Minnesota v. McDonald*, n.d., 2.

64. Order and Memorandum of Law Granting the State's Motion to Exclude Tattoo Evidence, *State of Minnesota v. McDonald*, April 30, 2012, 6–7.

65. Granting the State's Motion to Exclude Tattoo Evidence, *State of Minnesota v. McDonald*, April 30, 2012, 7.

66. State's Memorandum in Support of Motion to Impeach, *State of Minnesota v. McDonald*, April 19, 2012.

67. See also Cacho, *Social Death*.

68. State's Memorandum in Support of Motion to Restrict Spectator's Case-Related Buttons, Clothing, and Signs, *State of Minnesota v. McDonald*, March 30, 2012, 3.

69. Harris, "Whiteness as Property," 1777.

70. Cited in Simons, "Transgender Defendant Gets 3 Years."

71. CeCe McDonald, "Injury and Insult: Trayvon Martin, Racism in the System, and a Revolution amongst Us," Support CeCe, August 4, 2013, supportcece.wordpress.com/2013/08/04/injury-and-insult-trayon-martin-racism-in-the-system-and-a-revolution-amongst-us.

72. Yamiche Alcindor, "Trayvon Martin Shooting: A Timeline," USA *Today*, April 12, 2012, Opposing Viewpoints in Context database.

73. For a good summary of the case read Lizette Alvarez and Cara Buckley, "Zimmerman Is Acquitted in Trayvon Martin Killing," *New York Times*, July 13, 2013, nytimes.com/2013/07/14/us/george-zimmerman-verdict-trayvon-martin.html.

74. Attorney General Eric Holder cited in Curt Anderson, "Without Hate Crime, US Limited in Prosecuting Zimmerman," ABC News, February 25, 2015, news.yahoo.com/without-hate-crime-us-limited-prosecuting-zimmerman-094657012.html (site discontinued).

75. Marissa Alexander cited in Victoria Law, "Trapped in the Dark: Marissa Alexander and How Our Twisted Legal System Re-victimizes Domestic Violence Survivors," Salon, May 16, 2014, salon.com/2014/05/16/trapped_in_the_dark_marissa_alexander_and_how_our_twisted_legal_system_re_victimizes_domestic_violence_suvivors.

76. An appeals court later reversed Alexander's conviction, and she accepted a plea deal to a three-year prison sentence in November

2014. She was able to serve two of those years under house arrest with electronic monitoring. Alexander officially completed her sentence in February 2017 and is now a free woman again.

77. The New Jersey Four consisted of Venice Brown, Terrain Dandridge, Patreese Johnson, and Renata Hill. A surveillance camera showed that Dwayne Buckle instigated the attack and was choking one of the women. Patreese Johnson pulled a small steak knife out of her purse, aiming for Buckle's arm to prevent him from choking her friend. See Henry, "Lesbians Sentenced for Self-Defense," for a detailed account of the events.

78. Laura Italiano, "Attack of the Killer Lesbians," *New York Post*, April 12, 2007, nypost.com/2007/04/12/attack-of-the-killer-lesbians.

79. See Jose Martinez, "'I'm a Man!' Lesbian Growled during Fight," *Daily News*, April 13, 2007, nydailynews.com/news/crime/man -lesbian-growled-fight-article-1.212761; and "Lesbian Wolf Pack Guilty: Jersey Girl Gang Gets Lockup in Beatdown," *Daily News*, April 19, 2007, nydailynews.com/news/crime/lesbian-wolf-pack -guilty-article-1.209128.

80. Buckle, for example, had initially responded to investigators that two men who had come to help the women had attacked him. Neither was found or charged. Furthermore, Johnson's knife never underwent forensic testing, and no evidence was found that her knife was actually the weapon that penetrated Buckle's abdomen (see Henry, "Lesbians Sentenced for Self-Defense.")

81. See "The Murder of Sakia Gunn and LGBT Anti-Violence Mobilization," OutHistory, 2013, outhistory.org/exhibits/show/queer -newark/murder-of-sakia-gunn.

82. It is noteworthy that Alexander was prosecuted by Angela Corey, the same prosecutor as in Zimmerman's trial. Critics believe that Corey failed to convict Zimmerman because she overcharged him with second-degree murder, which requires proof of intent rather than a lesser charge like manslaughter. However, in Alexander's case the jury found her guilty of aggravated assault in just a little over ten minutes. See Jessica Pishko, "Is Angela Corey the Cruelest Prosecutor in America?," *Nation*, August 16, 2016, thenation .com/article/is-angela-corey-the-cruelest-prosecutor-in-america/.

83. The media's attempt to mitigate charges of racism by explicitly emphasizing Zimmerman's Latino heritage strategically functioned

to mask the ongoing investment of an allegedly colorblind society in whiteness. This also points to the ways in which debates about racism are no longer simply about white versus black or white versus brown. By emphasizing Zimmerman's Latino heritage, the media implied that a brown man cannot possibly be driven by racist motives toward a black teenager. What the Zimmerman case attests to is the fact that the assigning of privilege and value to one group, while devaluing, racializing, and criminalizing another, has become much more complex and flexible in an age of multicultural neoliberalism and that racism today occurs beyond and in between different color lines.

84. See Grewal, *Saving the Security State*, 185ff.

85. The title of this section comes from Dean Spade's article "Their Laws Will Never Make Us Safer." The bill was titled in reference to two brutal deaths in 1998: Matthew Shepard was tortured, tied to a fence, and left to die in Laramie, Wyoming, because he was perceived to be gay. James Byrd Jr., an African American disabled man, was tied to a truck and dragged along county roads by white supremacists until he was decapitated in Jasper, Texas.

86. See Reddy, *Freedom with Violence*, 1–3.

87. See also Lamble, "Queer Necropolitics and the Expanding Carceral State."

88. The act has expanded the authority of the U.S. Department of Justice to prosecute hate-motivated crimes instead of, or in collaboration with, local authorities and provided $10 million to prosecute these crimes—specifically the prosecution of youth for hate crimes. De facto, the Hate Crimes Act allocates more funding for the militarization of police forces and the administrative surveillance and harassment of people of color, especially youth of color, who are already profiled as being more homophobic than their white counterparts. Therefore, it drains resources away from preventive programs that could actually help to build stronger and healthier communities. Additionally, if convicted of a hate crime, an alleged perpetrator is automatically subject to a higher mandatory minimum sentence. At one point during the process, a Republican amendment even proposed to add the death penalty as one of the available sanctions.

89. See, e.g., Spade and Willse, "Confronting the Limits."

90. The Tyler Clementi Higher Education Anti-Harassment Act would require colleges and universities that receive federal fund-

ing to enact an antiharassment policy that prohibits harassment of enrolled students by other students, faculty, and staff based on actual or perceived race, color, national origin, sex, disability, sexual orientation, gender identity, or religion. It would also explicitly prohibit cyberbullying. The bill was originally introduced in 2013 and was most recently reintroduced to Congress in April 2017, but it has yet to pass as of March 2019.

91. U.S. attorney Ripley Rand cited in NBC's *Nightly News*, February 12, 2015. The FBI has launched an official investigation into whether the alleged shooter has violated federal hate crime statues.

92. Amy Goodman, "#MuslimLivesMatter: Loved Ones Honor NC Shooting Victims and Reject Police Dismissal of a Hate Crime," *Democracy Now!*, February 12, 2015, democracynow.org/2015/2/12 /muslimlivesmatter_loved_ones_honor_nc_shooting.

93. Cacho, *Social Death*, 5.

94. See, for example, Smith, "Unmasking the State"; Spade, "Under the Cover"; and Whitlock, *In a Time*.

95. In the summer of 2014, the deaths of Eric Garner and Michael Brown at the hands of law enforcement reignited debates and protests about police brutality against African American men. Garner, a forty-three-year-old father, was put into a chokehold by a New York police officer for allegedly illegally selling single cigarettes. A cell phone video taken by a bystander, which documents Garner gasping for air and saying "I can't breathe" before he turned limp, went viral. The phrase became a key part of the Black Lives Matter movement. Similarly, the fatal shooting of Michael Brown, an unarmed black teenager, by a white police officer, in Ferguson, a suburb outside of Saint Louis, brought simmering racial tensions to the fore. Wilson initially followed Brown because he fit the description of a suspect in a convenience store theft. An altercation ensued in which Wilson claimed that Brown was charging after him and his weapon. Wilson shot at Brown twelve times. The chant "Hands up, don't shoot" became a rallying cry during week-long protests and unrest in Ferguson. A study conducted by the Department of Justice later revealed disturbing patterns of racial bias in Ferguson's police department. In both cases, the involved police officers were acquitted of all charges.

4. #FreeCeCe

1. The Trans Youth Support Network was the only completely youth-led organization in the Midwest until its abrupt closing at the end of January 2015 due to a lack of resources and funding. TYSN was founded as a community response to a series of incidents of violence targeting young trans women of color in the Minneapolis–Saint Paul area in the fall of 2004. TYSN was dedicated to working for racial, social, and economic justice and the freedom to determine gender identity and expression for trans youth. The organization specifically sought to improve the accessibility of social service providers for trans youth.
2. I am indebted to Lex Horan for providing me with an in-depth account of the workings of the Support Committee and sharing his experiences. Most of the information on the committee's work in this chapter is drawn from an hour-long interview conducted with Horan on September 27, 2014.
3. Horan, interview by author, September 27, 2014.
4. Horan, interview. The Support Committee comprised Jude Ortiz, Katie Burgess, Kris Gebhard, Luce Guillen-Givens, Billy Navarro Jr., David Tomlinson, Jess Annabelle, Garrett Fitzgerald, Lex Horan, tj o'connor, Fen Jeffries, Josina Manu, and Abby Beasley. This group did most of the organizing work surrounding McDonald's case between the fall of 2011 and the summer of 2012.
5. Horan, interview.
6. For utopic responses see, e.g., Benkler, *The Wealth of Networks*; Castells, *Communication Power*; and Shirky, *Cognitive Surplus*. For dystopic positions see Dean, *Democracy and Other Neoliberal Fantasies*; Keen, *The Cult of the Amateur*; Morozov, *The Net Delusion*; and Young, *The Rise of Hoaxes*.
7. Jenkins, *Convergence Culture*, 259.
8. Castells, *Networks of Outrage*, 15.
9. Castells, 10.
10. Bennett and Segerberg, "The Logic of Connective Action."
11. Gerbaudo and Treré, "In Search of the 'We,'" 867.
12. See, for example, Bratich, "User-Generated Discontent"; Andrejevic, "The Work."
13. Couldry, "More Sociology, More Culture."

14. See, for example, Driscoll and Gregg, "Convergence Culture"; Ouellette and Wilson, "Women's Work."

15. Darmon, "Framing SlutWalk London," 701.

16. Higgs, "#JusticeforLiz."

17. See, e.g., Cole, "'It's Like She's Eager"; Nakamura, "Blaming, Shaming"; Rentschler, "#Safetytipsforladies"; Rodino-Colocino, "Me Too, #MeToo"; Williams, "Digital Defense."

18. Mann, "What Can Feminism Learn," 293.

19. See Jenkins, *Convergence Culture*; Castells, *Networks of Outrage*.

20. The RNC Welcoming Committee was a local, anarchist, anti-authoritarian group that coordinated and organized protests against the 2008 Republican National Convention in Saint Paul. The so-called RNC 8 were members of the RNC Welcoming Committee who were the first to be charged under the Minnesota statute of the "furtherance of terrorism." Among them were Jude Ortiz, Luce Guillen-Givens, and Garrett Fitzgerald. The terrorism charges against the group were later dropped.

21. Gerbaudo, *Tweets and the Streets*, 5.

22. See Gerbaudo and Treré, "In Search of the 'We.'"

23. Horan, personal correspondence with author, October 11, 2014, emphasis in original.

24. Horan, interview.

25. Hashtags (once more commonly referred to as the pound sign) are metadata tags that were first used in Internet Relay Chats in the late 1990s to categorize content. Since 2007 hashtags have become popular for microblogging and social media platforms to easily group and find conversations with similar themes and content.

26. FreeCeCe McDonald (@Free_CeCe), Twitter, May 7, 2012.

27. Mock created the hashtag #GirlsLikeUs in March 2012 as a means to empower and "to connect all willing trans women across colors, generations, sexual identities and class." The hashtag has since gained a significant following and popularity enabling trans women to tell their stories and highlighting the injustices many trans women are facing. See Janet Mock, "My Journey (So Far) with #GirlsLikeUs: Hoping for Sisterhood, Solidarity, and Empowerment," JanetMock.com, May 28, 2012, janetmock.com/2012/05/28/twitter-girlslikeus-campaign-for-trans-women/.

28. See Marc Lamont Hill, "Why Aren't We Fighting for CeCe McDonald?" *Ebony*, June 11, 2012, ebony.com/news-views/why-arent-we-fighting-for-cece-mcdonald.

29. See Jenkins et al., *If It Doesn't Spread*, 45.

30. Williams and Carpini, *After Broadcast News*, 16.

31. People of color are far more likely to access the Internet from a mobile device, effectively creating "two Internets"—one for privileged high-speed broadband users and another for mobile users who have to deal with the limitations of small keyboards and screens, subpar interfaces, and less interactivity. See Jesse Washington, "For Minorities, New 'Digital Divide' Seen," *USA Today*, January 10, 2011, usatoday30.usatoday.com/tech/news/2011-01-10-minorities-online_N.htm.

32. The #BlackLivesMatter hashtag not only seeks to forcefully affirm the value of black lives and to challenge the historic and systematic dispossession of and the state-sanctioned violence enacted against people of color, but it allows "for contesting and reimagining the materiality of racialized bodies" (Bonilla and Rosa, "#Ferguson," 4). Hashtags such as #IfTheyGunnedMeDown, #NoAngel, and #ICantBreathe have specifically been used to document and challenge the media's perpetuation and stereotyping of racialized bodies as inherently threatening.

33. See Nakamura, "Blaming, Shaming," 223.

34. See Abby Phillip, "Online 'Authenticity' and How Facebook's 'Real Name' Policy Hurts Native Americans," *Washington Post*, February 10, 2015, washingtonpost.com/news/morning-mix/wp/2015/02/10/online-authenticity-and-how-facebooks-real-name-policy-hurts-native-americans.

35. Bivens, "The Gender Binary."

36. Lee Fang, "Why Was an FBI Joint Terrorism Task Force Tracking a Black Lives Matter Protest?," The Intercept, March 12, 2015, firstlook.org/theintercept/2015/03/12/fbi-appeared-use-informant-track-black-lives-matter-protest/.

37. Free CeCe McDonald, Facebook post, December 19, 2011, facebook.com/freecece.mcdonald.

38. Order and Memorandum of Law Granting in Part and Denying in Part Defendant's Motion to Exclude Electronic Materials Allegedly Attributed to Defendant, *State of Minnesota v. Chrishaun Reed McDonald*, November 30, 2012, Court File No. 27-CR-11-16485, 7.

39. FreeCeCe McDonald (@Free_CeCe), Twitter, May 10, 2012.

40. Mannix, "CeCe McDonald Murder Trial."

41. "Drop the Charges against CeCe McDonald," Change.org, change
.org/p/free-cece-we-re-looking-at-you-michael-freeman-drop-the
-charges-against-cece-mcdonald.

42. "Demand that Chrishaun CeCe McDonald be administered the
20 milligrams of hormones that she is prescribed and allowed by
court order!" Free CeCe McDonald Tumblr, accessed April 3, 2015,
freececemcdonald.tumblr.com/post/26836053684/demand-that
-chrishaun-cece-mcdonald-be (site discontinued).

43. Horan, interview.

44. Butler, *Giving an Account*.

45. Benkler, *The Wealth of Networks*, 31.

46. Couldry, *Why Voice Matters*, 144.

47. Leslie Feinberg, author and activist, was well known for the underground classic coming-of-age novel *Stone Butch Blues* (1993) as well
as nonfiction works about transgender history and rights, including *Transgender Warriors: Making History from Joan of Arc to Dennis
Rodman* (1996) and *Trans Liberation: Beyond Pink or Blue* (1998).
Feinberg self-identified as an "anti-racist white, working-class, sec-
ular Jewish, transgender, lesbian, female revolutionary communist"
whose activism around LGBT, civil, and workers' rights reflected a
deep commitment to intersectional social justice. Feinberg died of
complications related to Lyme disease in November 2014. Hir obit-
uary, cowritten with hir partner Minnie Bruce Pratt can be accessed
at "Transgender Pioneer and Stone Butch Blues Author Leslie Feinberg Has Died," *Advocate*, November 17, 2014, advocate.com/arts
-entertainment/books/2014/11/17/transgender-pioneer-leslie
-feinberg-stone-butch-blues-has-died.

48. Gerbaudo, *Tweets and the Streets*, 42, emphasis in original.

49. Castells, *Networks of Outrage*, 168.

50. Castells, 221–28.

51. Gerbaudo, *Tweets and the Streets*, 40.

52. Bennett and Segerberg, "The Logic of Connective Action," 748.

53. Bennett and Segerberg, 753.

54. As recalled by Horan, interview.

55. Mannix, "CeCe McDonald Murder Trial."

56. See Castells, *Networks of Outrage*, 6–7.

57. Gerbaudo, *Tweets and the Streets*, 12.

58. Horan, interview.

59. Horan, interview.

60. Many activists critiqued the Occupy Movement during its early stages of the Zuccotti Park occupation in New York City in 2011 for failing to reach out to communities of color and to articulate a transformative racial justice agenda. Instead, Occupy initially seemed to promote an agenda that was crafted by white, left, middle-class male organizers who did not acknowledge that the 2008 recession and economic crisis had disproportionally affected communities of color and that those communities have been enduring economic and political disenfranchisement for centuries. Later on, the development of other local Occupy chapters in Oakland and Los Angeles, for example, was much more conscious about creating an inclusive movement for indigenous, queer, undocumented, poor, and of-color people. For articles about diversity within Occupy see, e.g., Rinku Sen, "Race and Occupy Wall Street," *Nation*, October 26, 2011, thenation.com/article/164212/race-and-occupy-wall-street.

    While mainstream media has been saturated with the killings of black boys and men in recent years leading to renewed racial justice efforts with the Black Lives Matter movement, this ubiquity has simultaneously erased the very specificity of these gendered deaths. See the policy report by Crenshaw et al., "Say Her Name."

61. Jenkins, "Rethinking 'Rethinking Convergence/Culture,'" 290; Jenkins, *Convergence Culture*, 259.

62. Castells, *Networks of Outrage*, 227, 197.

63. See Reddy, *Freedom with Violence*.

64. See Jenkins's afterword to the paperback reissue of *Convergence Culture*; Jenkins and Carpenter, "Theorizing Participatory Intensities," 266.

65. Couldry, *Why Voice Matters*, 150, emphasis in original.

66. See Alexander, *The New Jim Crow*.

67. "TYSN Will Be Closing," TYSN Newsletter, January 20, 2015, transyouthsupportnetwork.org. In *Gay, Inc.*, Myrl Beam provides a detailed account of TYSN's place within the nonprofit industrial complex. Beam argues that for LGBT nonprofits, the techniques of hailing and mobilizing queer community rely on the policing of racialized others, especially poor queer and gender-nonconforming people of color.

68. In recent years the term *Black Twitter* has emerged to describe a large network of black Twitter users and their loosely coordinated interactions. Minorities are disproportionally represented on Twitter. Around 25 percent of its users are black, which is roughly double the percentage of black people in the U.S. population. See Jesse Washington, "For Minorities, New 'Digital Divide.'" As a result, many of Twitter's trending topics are fueled by black tweets, providing cultural commentary and criticism from black perspectives. Scholars researching the Black Twitter phenomenon have pointed out that participation in its conversations, replete with inside jokes, slang, and rules, requires a certain level of black cultural competency about African American vernacular and African American history. See Meredith Clark interviewed in Donovan X. Ramsey, "The Truth about Black Twitter," *Atlantic*, April 10, 2015, theatlantic.com/technology/archive/2015/04/the-truth-about-black-twitter/390120.

69. For the continued prevalence of universalizing white women's experiences and the reliance on a symbolic multiculturalism that is seemingly welcoming of women of color yet unwilling to change or reform the organizing models of contemporary digital feminism, see Loza, "Hashtag Feminism."

70. The Save Wįyąbi Project is an advocacy group that uses an online database and mapping project to track the disappearances and murders of indigenous women in Canada and the United States.

71. See, for example, Mia McKenzie, "America Only Gets Outraged about Gun Violence in White Neighbourhoods," *Guardian*, April 29, 2013, theguardian.com/commentisfree/2013/apr/29/us-gun-crime-race-disparity; Lauren Wolfe and Lauren Chief Elk, "Sexual Violence Is Tearing Native American Communities Apart," *Guardian*, September 8, 2012, theguardian.com/commentisfree/2012/sep/08/sexual-violence-native-american-communities; Raquel Willis, "Transgender Lives: Your Stories," *New York Times*, January 5, 2018, nytimes.com/interactive/2015/opinion/transgender-today/stories/raquel-willis.

72. Nakamura, "Blaming, Shaming," 225.

5. Transgender Terrorist

1. See Phoenix Municipal Code, Article IV: Offenses Involving Morals, accessed March 2, 2018, codepublishing.com/AZ/Phoenix/frameless/index.pl?path=../html/Phoenix23/Phoenix2352.html.

2. See Reggie Dixon, "Support Monica Jones," SWOP Phoenix, May 18, 2017, swopphoenix.org/uncategorized/support-monica-jones. For a detailed background on Project ROSE and Jones's case, see also Chase Strangio, "Arrested for Walking While Trans: An Interview with Monica Jones," ACLU, April 2, 2014, aclu.org/blog/speakeasy /arrested-walking-while-trans-interview-monica-jones.

3. Backpage.com had to shut down its adult section in January 2018 after increased pressure from members of Congress alleging that it facilitated child sex trafficking. In October 2017 authorities had raided Backpage's headquarters in Dallas and arrested its executives on charges of pimping a minor, conspiracy to commit pimping, and money laundering. Derek Hawkins, "Backpage.com Shuts Down Adult Services Ads after Relentless Pressure from Authorities," *Washington Post*, January 10, 2017, washingtonpost.com/news /morning-mix/wp/2017/01/10/backpage-com-shuts-down-adult -services-ads-after-relentless-pressure-from-authorities.

4. "ACLU of Arizona to Challenge Phoenix's Unconstitutional Manifesting Prostitution Law in Court," ACLU, April 10, 2014, acluaz.org/en/press-releases/aclu-arizona-challenge-phoenixs -unconstitutional-manifesting-prostitution-law-court.

5. Zack Ford, "Court Tosses Out Prostitution Conviction for Woman Who Was Just Walking down the Street," Thinkprogress, January 26, 2015, thinkprogress.org/lgbt/2015/01/26/3615711/arizona-monica -jones-transgender-justice/.

6. See Mitch Kellaway, "Phoenix Drops 'Walking While Trans' Charges against Monica Jones," *Advocate*, February 27, 2015, advocate.com/politics/transgender/2015/02/27/phoenix-drops -walking-while-trans-charges-against-monica-jones.

7. A product of its time the law, named after its author, Representative James R. Mann from Illinois, reflected widespread social anxieties about the rapid changes accompanying the Industrial Revolution, including urbanization, immigration, the changing role of women, and evolving social mores. See Langum, *Crossing over the Line*.

8. For example, Jack Johnson, the first African American heavyweight boxing champion, was charged and convicted under the act in 1913 for allegedly transporting a "prostitute"—who was actually his white girlfriend—from Pittsburgh to Chicago.

9. Rosen, *The Lost Sisterhood*, 36.

10. Sorrell, "Patient-Prisons."

11. See Sorrell, 74.

12. Debates around the (de)criminalization of sex work in the United States mark a longtime battleground between feminists who condemn prostitution as a virulent source of women's oppression on the one hand and "sex-positive" feminists who see the decriminalization of prostitution itself as a feminist act. The antiporn and antiprostitution position was most prominently presented by figures such as Andrea Dworkin and Catharine MacKinnon in the 1980s. For a basic overview of this continued debate see Emily Bazelon, "Should Prostitution Be a Crime?," *New York Times*, May 5, 2016, nytimes.com/2016/05/08/magazine/should-prostitution-be-a -crime.html.

13. Weitzer, "The Movement."

14. Elizabeth Nolan Brown, "Prostitution Precrime? Monica Jones and 'Manifesting an Intent' to Prostitute in America," Reason, April 16, 2014, reason.com/archives/2014/04/16/prostitution-thought -crimes-monica-jones. Furthermore, before the *Lawrence v. Texas* ruling (which invalidated sodomy laws that criminalized sexual acts between two consenting adults of the same sex), these kinds of statues were frequently used to regulate same-sex sex specifically and are still used to police queer and trans people if the sexual conduct is not in private, not within marriage, or in the commercial realm.

15. Those in support of Backpage.com and similar sites argue that they actually create a safer space for sex workers as they enable workers to screen clients, share "bad date lists," and choose whether to work on the streets or not. Closing these sites is unlikely to end child trafficking but may only push traffickers further underground, making it more difficult to track them. See Amy Zimmerman, "Backpage Is Bad; Banning It Would Be Worse," *Daily Beast*, January 15, 2017, thedailybeast.com/backpage-is-bad-banning-it-would-be-worse.

16. Shdaimah and Bailey-Kloch, "'Can You Help?'"

17. Wahab, "Evaluating the Usefulness," 68.

18. See Leon and Shdaimah, "JUSTifying Scrutiny."

19. See SWOP's statement cited in Dixon, "Support Monica Jones."

20. See Alliance for a Safe and Diverse DC, *Move Along*; and Bazelon, "Should Prostitution Be a Crime?"

21. Hanssens et al., *A Roadmap for Change*, 5.

22. See James et al., *Executive Summary*, 12.

23. "Victims or Villains: Examining Ten Years of Transgender Images on Television," GLAAD, 2012, accessed March 1, 2018, glaad.org /publications/victims-or-villains-examining-ten-years-transgender -images-television.

24. The Department of Immigration and Border Protection has since been subsumed into the Department of Home Affairs, which shares various responsibilities, including national security, federal law enforcement, emergency management, immigration, and border control, among other areas.

25. Jason Om, "Deported US Transgender Woman Monica Jones Allegedly Advertised Sexual Services, Court Documents Show," ABC *Lateline News*, December 9, 2014, abc.net.au/news/2014-12 -09/deported-us-transgender-woman-advertised-sexual-services /5955806.

26. Om, "Deported US Transgender Woman."

27. Cited in Michael Safi, "U.S. Transgender Activist 'Pressured to Appear on Airport Reality TV Show,'" *Guardian*, December 2, 2014, theguardian.com/world/2014/dec/02/us-transgender-activist -monica-jones-pressured-to-appear-on-airport-reality-tv-show.

28. Cited in Om, "Deported US Transgender Woman."

29. Andrejevic outlines three common themes of securitainment: the combination of entertainment and risk "tutorial"; the mobilization of risk as an incitement to responsibilization; and the de-differentiation of categories of potential threat (e.g., to oneself, the economy, the environment, or the state). See "'Securitainment'" and "Managing the Borders."

30. See Andrejevic, "'Securitainment.'"

31. See Eloise Brook, "Monica Jones: From Transgender Social Worker to National Threat," *Guardian*, December 2, 2014, theguardian.com /commentisfree/2014/dec/03/monica-jones-from-transgender -social-worker-to-visa-breach-to-national-threat.

32. See "Fact Sheet 77—The Movement Alert List (MAL)," Australian Department of Immigration and Border Protection, accessed April 22, 2015, immi.gov.au/media/fact-sheets/77mal.htm (site discontinued).

33. For example, the Page Act of 1875, which became the first act of federal immigration regulation in the United States, created categories of

exclusion for "any subject of China, Japan or any Oriental Country"
and prohibited the entry of "undesirable immigrants," including prostitutes and those who had been convicted of "felonious crimes." See
Keyes, "Race and Immigration," 904–5. Similarly, Australia passed the
Immigration Restriction Act of 1901, often referred to as the "White
Australia policy," which ended all non-European immigration by
requiring entrance examinations in European languages. The act effectively banned Asian migration to the continent for the next fifty years.

34. Scarlet Alliance, "Migrant Workers in Australia," Scarlet Alliance,
2014, accessed April 3, 2018, scarletalliance.org.au/issues/migrant
-workers.

35. Cited in Safi, "U.S. Transgender Activist 'Pressured.'"

36. Deed of Agreement between the Commonwealth of Australia and
Seven Network (Operations) Limited, November 2012, 4, scribd
.com/document/282223403/Border-Security-Deed-of-Agreement.

37. Paul Farrell, "Border Force and Immigration Officials Have
Final Say on Reality TV Show," *Guardian*, September 21, 2015,
theguardian.com/australia-news/2015/sep/22/border-force-and
-immigration-officials-have-final-say-on-reality-tv-show.

38. Farrell, "Border Force."

39. For the role of editing specifically in reality TV see, for example, Dominguez, "'I'm Very Rich, Bitch!'"; and Mast, "Negotiating the 'Real.'"

40. Deed of Agreement, 4.

41. Deed of Agreement, 5.

42. Deed of Agreement, 6.

43. ABC's *Homeland Security USA* was canceled after its first season in
2009, presumably due to its low ratings. The show's different reception in the United States is interesting and may speak to a particular sociohistorical context: with the election of Barack Obama as
the first black president, frameworks of neoliberal multiculturalism
had gained popularity at the time. The show's overt nationalist and
nativist sentiments may have simply failed to connect with a larger
audience. One can certainly speculate whether the show's focus
on undocumented immigrants would fare better under the current
political climate, which is characterized by a renewed investment
in border security and the criminalization of nonwhite immigrants,
as well as curbing both legal and undocumented immigration. For a
detailed analysis of the show see Fischer, "*Homeland Security USA*."

44. Puar, *Terrorist Assemblages*, xxiv.

45. Puar, xxiii.

46. Rose, *Powers of Freedom*, 240.

47. Hall, "Terror and the Female Grotesque," 128.

48. Mike M. Ahlers, "TSA Removing 'Virtual Strip Search' Body Scanners," CNN, January 19, 2013, cnn.com/2013/01/18/travel/tsa-body -scanners.

49. For insightful scholarship engaging particularly the surveillance of transgender people at airports, see Currah and Mulqueen, "Securitizing Gender"; Magnet and Rodgers, "Stripping for the State"; Spalding, "Airport Outings."

50. Several states first require amended birth certificates in order to change the gender marker on a driver's license. Some states will amend birth certificates only with documentation of surgery, while others, such as Idaho, Ohio, and Tennessee, outright deny the change of gender classification on birth certificates in any case. See "Changing Birth Certificate Sex Designations: State-By-State Guidelines," Lambda Legal, September 17, 2018, lambdalegal.org /know-your-rights/transgender/changing-birth-certificate-sex -designations.

51. For more scholarship on the increased surveillance of trans people through administrative legal systems, see Beauchamp, "Artful Concealment and Strategic Visibility"; Davis, *Beyond Trans*; and Fischer, "Under the Ban-Optic Gaze."

52. SPOT Referral Report, Version 4.0, revised February 23, 2009, documentcloud.org/documents/1697887-spot-referral.html. For the controversy surrounding this program, see Jana Winter and Cora Currier, "Exclusive: TSA's Secret Behavior Checklist to Spot Terrorists," The Intercept, March 27, 2015, theintercept.com /2015/03/27/revealed-tsas-closely-held-behavior-checklist-spot -terrorists.

53. Gates, *Our Biometric Future*.

54. Lyon, *Surveillance Studies*, 47.

Coda

1. See Buzz Bissinger, "Caitlyn Jenner: The Full Story," *Vanity Fair*, July 2015, vanityfair.com/hollywood/2015/06/caitlyn-jenner-bruce -cover-annie-leibovitz.

2. Thessaly La Force, "Bruce Jenner and the Modern American Family," *New Yorker*, April 26, 2015, newyorker.com/culture/culture-desk/bruce-jenner-and-the-modern-american-family.

3. Janet Mock, "Revealing Caitlyn Jenner: My Thoughts on Media, Privilege, Health Care Access and Glamour," JanetMock.com, June 3, 2015, janetmock.com/2015/06/03/caitlyn-jenner-vanity-fair-transgender/.

4. While it has not been the focus of this book, it is important to note that this current moment of heightened trans visibility is not without historic precedent. Abram J. Lewis, for example, demonstrates how numerous developments in the 1970s around cultural representation, significant legal gains, and growing activism regarding transgender issues present an important precursor to this current tipping point. See Lewis, "Trans History"; and Page, "One from the Vaults."

5. Emphasizing that Stonewall was a riot is important because more recent protests against police brutality and racial injustice are frequently criminalized in the media as "riots." Further, the white- and cis-washing of LGBTQ history is exemplified by Roland Emmerich's 2015 *Stonewall* movie. After drawing widespread criticism and calls for boycott, the movie ended up flopping at the box office.

6. Reina Gossett, "Reina Gossett on Transgender Storytelling, David France, and the Netflix Marsha P. Johnson Documentary," *Teen Vogue*, October 11, 2017, teenvogue.com/story/reina-gossett-marsha-p-johnson-op-ed.

7. See Suzannah Weiss, "'The Death and Life of Marsha P. Johnson' Creator Accused of Stealing Work from Filmmaker Reina Gossett," *Teen Vogue*, October 8, 2017, teenvogue.com/story/marsha-p-johnson-documentary-david-france-reina-gossett-stealing-accusations.

8. Nick Adams, "Honoring Known Cases of Deadly Anti-trans Violence in 2017," GLAAD, December 14, 2017, glaad.org/blog/honoring-known-cases-deadly-anti-trans-violence-2017.

9. Reina Gossett, Grace Dunham, and Constantina Zavitsanos, "Commencement Address at Hampshire College," ReinaGossett.com, May 17, 2016, reinagossett.com/commencement-address-hampshire-college.

10. Stanley, "Anti-Trans Optics," 617.

11. It is worth noting that despite Obama's progressive record on LGBTQ rights, his administration also deported more immigrants than any other administration. Between 2009 and 2015, the Obama administration removed more than 2.5 million people through immigration orders, focusing particularly on "criminals, not families." This number does not include the people who were voluntarily deported, were turned away, or returned to their home countries at various border crossings. See Serena Marshall, "Obama Has Deported More People than Any Other President," ABC News, August 29, 2016, abcnews.go.com /Politics/obamas-deportation-policy-numbers/story?id=41715661.

12. Part of the 1964 Civil Rights Act, Title VII "prohibits employment discrimination based on race, color, religion, sex and national origin." The Department of Justice's current position cited in Julie Moreau, "Transgender Workers Not Protected by Civil Rights Law, DOJ Tells Supreme Court," NBC News, October 25, 2018, nbcnews .com/feature/nbc-out/transgender-workers-not-protected-civil -rights-law-doj-tells-supreme-n924491.

13. Erica L. Green, Katie Benner, and Robert Pear, "'Transgender' Could Be Defined out of Existence under Trump Administration," New York Times, October 21, 2018, nytimes.com/2018/10/21/us /politics/transgender-trump-administration-sex-definition.html.

14. Joellen Kralik and Jennifer Palmer, "'Bathroom Bill' Legislative Tracking," National Conference of State Legislatures, July 28, 2017, ncsl.org/research/education/-bathroom-bill-legislative -tracking635951130.aspx.

15. Amid fierce backlash to the notorious House Bill 2 from businesses and entertainers and the NBA's decision to move the 2017 All-Star Game from Charlotte, North Carolina, HB2 was repealed in April 2017 and replaced with a "compromise bill" that still contains a three-year ban on local nondiscrimination ordinances. For more on the bill's repeal see Mark Joseph Stern, "The HB2 'Repeal' Bill Is an Unmitigated Disaster for LGBTQ Rights and North Carolina," Slate, March 30, 2017, slate.com/blogs/outward/2017/03/30/hb2_repeal _bill_is_a_disaster_for_north_carolina_and_lgbtq_rights.html.

16. Joe Strupp, "Misleading Anti-Transgender Newspaper Ads Spark Outrage in Minnesota," Media Matters, December 1, 2014, mediamatters.org/blog/2014/12/01/misleading-anti-transgender -newspaper-ads-spark/201724.

17. See Kralik and Palmer, "'Bathroom Bill' Legislative Tracking."

18. See Matt Ford, "President Trump Pardons Former Sheriff Joe Arpaio," *Atlantic*, August 25, 2017, theatlantic.com/politics/archive /2017/08/trump-pardon-arpaio/537729.

19. Jonathan Blitzer, "The Teens Trapped between a Gang and the Law," *New Yorker*, January 1, 2018, newyorker.com/magazine/2018 /01/01/the-teens-trapped-between-a-gang-and-the-law.

20. West, *Transforming Citizenships*, 179.

21. West is building on Lawrence Grossberg's understanding of "impure politics," which sought to articulate resistance to the hegemony of popular conservative thought and policies in the early 1990s. West describes them "as a tactical navigation of norms and normativities never free from power relations that authorize them but [are] also not subservient to them." See *Transforming Citizenships*, 35.

22. See, for example, Franke, *Wedlocked*; and Spade, *Normal Life*.

23. Gossett, Dunham, and Zavitsanos, "Commencement Address."

24. Gossett, Dunham, and Zavitsanos, emphasis in original.

25. Gossett, Dunham, and Zavitsanos.

26. Gossett, Dunham, and Zavitsanos, first emphases in original; latter emphases my own.

27. Spade cited in Sarah Lazare, "Now Is the Time for 'Nobodies': Dean Spade on Mutual Aid and Resistance in the Trump Era," AlterNet, January 9, 2017, alternet.org/activism/now-time-nobodies-dean -spade-mutual-aid-and-resistance-trump-era.

28. Chávez, *Queer Migration Politics*, 9; "Undocumented Trans Activist Jennicet Gutiérrez Challenges Obama on Deportations at White House Event," *Democracy Now!*, June 25, 2015, democracynow.org /2015/6/25/undocumented_trans_activist_jennicet_gutierrez _challenges.

29. Jessa Powers, "'Trans People Deserve to Live' Flag Flies High at World Series," *Advocate*, October 29, 2018, advocate.com /transgender/2018/10/29/trans-people-deserve-live-flag-flies -high-world-series.

30. Stanley, "Anti-Trans Optics."

31. While Tourmaline also articulates nobodiness as impure, it is important to differentiate her formulation of such a politics from West's aforementioned conceptualization of "impure politics." Unlike the assimilatory and reformatory framework proposed by

West, nobodiness works toward radical, abolitionist transformation. While scholars like West often criticize radical queer politics for taking impossibly pure, i.e., politically transcendent, positions, such critiques about the impossibility to exist outside of dominant structures actually miss the point. Critical trans activists and scholars such as Dean Spade and Tourmaline acknowledge that abolishing the prison-industrial complex, for example, is not an immediately attainable goal. Yet working toward the abolition of oppressive systems is a process—one full of impurities—and it is the process itself that actually matters most. If we continue, however, to invest in these systems, which is what West and the like suggest, and not divest from them as Tourmaline and Spade argue, we cannot realize true transformation and alternative worldmaking practices.

32. Gossett, Dunham, and Zavitsanos, "Commencement Address."
33. See Gossett, Stanley, and Burton, "Known Unknowns"; and Muñoz, *Cruising Utopia.*
34. Gossett, Dunham, and Zavitsanos, "Commencement Address," emphasis in original.
35. See, for example, Patterson, "Entertaining a Healthy Cispicion"; and Fischer, "The Cistakes of Allyship."

BIBLIOGRAPHY

Agamben, Giorgio. *Homo Sacer: Sovereign Power and Bare Life*. Stanford
  CA: Stanford University Press, 1998.
Agathangelou, Anna, Daniel Bassichis, and Tamara Spira. "Intimate
  Investments: Homonormativity, Global Lockdown, and the Seduc-
  tions of Empire." *Radical History Review* 100 (2008): 120–43.
Ahn, Patty, Julia Himberg, and Damon R. Young. "Introduction to In
  Focus: Queer Approaches to Film, Television, and Digital Media."
  Cinema Journal 53, no. 2 (2014): 117–22.
Aizura, Aren Z. "Unrecognizable: On Trans Recognition in 2017." *South
  Atlantic Quarterly* 116, no. 3 (2017): 606–11.
Alexander, Michelle. *The New Jim Crow: Mass Incarceration in the Age of
  Colorblindness*. New York: The New Press, 2012.
Alexander, M. Jacqui, and Chandra Mohanty. "Introduction: Genealo-
  gies, Legacies, Movements." In *Feminist Genealogies, Colonial Lega-
  cies, Democratic Futures*, edited by M. Jacqui Alexander and Chandra
  Mohanty, xiii–xlii. New York: Routledge, 1997.
Alliance for a Safe and Diverse DC. *Move Along: Policing Sex Work in
  Washington, D.C.* Report. Washington DC: Different Avenues, 2008.
Althusser, Louis. "Ideology and Ideological State Apparatuses (Notes
  towards an Investigation)." In *Media and Cultural Studies: Keyworks*,
  revised ed., edited by Meenakshi Gigi Durham and Douglas M. Kell-
  ner, 79–87. Malden MA: Blackwell, 2006.
Andrejevic, Mark. "Managing the Borders: Classed Mobility on Security-
  Themed Reality TV." In *Reality TV and Class*, edited by Beverley
  Skeggs and Helen Wood, 60–72. New York: Palgrave Macmillan, 2011.
———. "'Securitainment' in the Post-9/11 Era." *Continuum: Journal of
  Media & Cultural Studies* 25, no. 2 (2011): 165–75.
———. "The Work that Affective Economics Does." *Cultural Studies* 25,
  nos. 4–5 (2011): 604–20.

Armstrong, Amanda. "Certificates of Live Birth and Dead Names: On the Subject of Recent Anti-Trans Legislation." *South Atlantic Quarterly* 116, no. 3 (2017): 621–31.

Barker-Plummer, Bernadette. "Fixing Gwen: News and the Mediation of (Trans)gender Challenges." *Feminist Media Studies* 13, no. 4 (2013): 710–24.

Barnett, Joshua Trey, and Brandon J. Hill. "Covert Operation: Archiving the Experiences of Transgender Service Members in the US Military." *TSQ: Transgender Studies Quarterly* 2, no. 4 (2015): 584–94.

Barnhurst, Kevin G., ed. *Media / Queered: Visibility and Its Discontents*. New York: Peter Lang, 2007.

———. "Visibility as Paradox: Representation and Simultaneous Contrast." In *Media / Queered: Visibility and Its Discontents*, edited by Kevin G. Barnhurst, 1–20. New York: Peter Lang, 2007.

Beam, Myrl. *Gay, Inc.: The Nonprofitization of Queer Politics*. Minneapolis: University of Minnesota Press, 2018.

Bean, Hamilton. "U.S. National Security Culture: From Queer Psychopathology to Queer Citizenship." *QED: A Journal in GLBTQ Worldmaking* 1, no. 1 (2014): 52–79.

Beauchamp, Toby. "Artful Concealment and Strategic Visibility: Transgender Bodies and U.S. State Surveillance after 9/11." *Surveillance and Society* 6, no. 4 (2009): 356–66.

Beck, Kristin, and Anne Speckhard. *Warrior Princess: A U.S. Navy SEAL's Journey to Coming Out Transgender*. McLean VA: Advances Press, 2013.

Becker, Ron. *Gay TV and Straight America*. New Brunswick NJ: Rutgers University Press, 2006.

Benkler, Yochai. "A Free Irresponsible Press: Wikileaks and the Battle over the Soul of the Networked Fourth Estate." *Harvard Civil Rights-Civil Liberties Law Review* 46 (2011): 311–97.

———. *The Wealth of Networks*. New Haven CT: Yale University Press, 2007.

Bennett, Lance W., and Alexandra Segerberg. "The Logic of Connective Action." *Information, Communication & Society* 15, no. 5 (2012): 739–68.

Billard, Thomas J. "Writing in the Margins: Mainstream News Media Representations of Transgenderism." *International Journal of Communication* 10 (2016): 4193–218.

Bivens, Rena. "The Gender Binary Will Not Be Deprogrammed: Ten Years of Coding Gender on Facebook." *New Media & Society* 19, no. 6 (2017): 880–98.

Boellstorff, Tom. "Queer Studies Under Ethnography's Sign." GLQ: *A Journal of Lesbian and Gay Studies* 12, no. 4 (2006): 627–39.

Bonilla, Yarimar, and Jonathan Rosa. "#Ferguson: Digital Protest, Hashtag Ethnography, and the Racial Politics of Social Media in the United States." *American Ethnologist* 42, no. 1 (2015): 4–17.

Booth, Tristan E. "Queering Queer Eye: The Stability of Gay Identity Confronts the Liminality of Trans Embodiment." *Western Journal of Communication* 75, no. 2 (2011): 185–204.

Bratich, Jack. "User-Generated Discontent." *Cultural Studies* 25, nos. 4–5 (2011): 621–40.

Brownworth, Victoria. "Bradley Manning, Chelsea Manning, and Queer Collaboration." *QED: A Journal in GLBTQ Worldmaking* 1, no. 1 (2014): 105–117.

Burrelli, David. "'Don't Ask, Don't Tell': The Law and Military Policy on Same-Sex Behavior." Congressional Research Service, 7-5700 (2010). https://www.fas.org/sgp/crs/misc/R40782.pdf.

Butler, Judith. *Bodies That Matter: On the Discursive Limits of "Sex."* New York: Routledge, 1993.

———. *Giving an Account of Oneself.* New York: Fordham University Press, 2005.

———. *Precarious Life: The Powers of Mourning and Violence.* New York: Verso, 2004.

Cacho, Lisa. *Social Death: Racialized Rightlessness and the Criminalization of the Unprotected.* New York: New York University Press, 2012.

Campbell, Peter Odell, and Cory Holding. "The Trans-Exclusive Archive of U.S. Capital Punishment Rhetoric." In *Transgender Communication Studies: Histories, Trends, and Trajectories*, edited by Leland G. Spencer and Jamie C. Capuzza, 199–216. Lanham MD: Lexington Books, 2015.

Capuzza, Jamie C. "Improvements Still Needed for Transgender Coverage." *Newspaper Research Journal* 37, no. 1 (2016): 82–94.

———. "What's in a Name? Transgender Identity, Metareporting, and the Misgendering of Chelsea Manning." In *Transgender Communication Studies: Histories, Trends, and Trajectories*, edited by Leland

G. Spencer and Jamie Capuzza, 93–110. Lanham, MD: Lexington Books, 2015.

Capuzza, Jamie C., and Leland G. Spencer. "Regressing, Progressing, or Transgressing on the Small Screen? Transgender Characters on U.S. Scripted Television Series." *Communication Quarterly* 65, no. 2 (2017): 214–30.

Castells, Manuel. *Communication Power.* New York: Oxford University Press, 2009.

———. *Networks of Outrage and Hope: Social Movements in the Internet Age.* Malden MA: Polity Press, 2012.

Cavalcante, Andre. "Breaking into Transgender Life: Transgender Audiences' Experiences with 'First of Its Kind' Visibility in Popular Media." *Communication, Culture & Critique* 10, no. 3 (2017): 538–55.

———. "Centering Transgender Identity via the Textual Periphery: TransAmerica and the 'Double Work' of Paratexts." *Critical Studies in Media Communication* 30, no. 2 (2013): 85–101.

Chávez, Karma. *Queer Migration Politics: Activist Rhetoric and Coalitional Possibilities.* Chicago: University of Illinois Press, 2013.

Chávez, Karma, and Cindy L. Griffin, eds. *Standing in the Intersection: Feminist Voices, Feminist Practices in Communication Studies.* Albany NY: SUNY Press, 2012.

Cloud, Dana. "Private Manning and the Chamber of Secrets." *QED: A Journal in GLBTQ Worldmaking* 1, no. 1 (2014): 80–104.

Cohen, Cathy. "Punks, Bulldaggers, and Welfare Queens: The Radical Potential of Queer Politics?" *GLQ: A Journal of Lesbian and Gay Studies* 3 (1997): 437–65.

Cole, Kristi K. "'It's Like She's Eager to Be Verbally Abused': Twitter, Trolls, and (En)Gendering Disciplinary Rhetoric." *Feminist Media Studies* 15, no. 2 (2015): 356–58.

Collins, Patricia Hill. *Black Feminist Thought: Knowledge, Consciousness and the Politics of Empowerment.* New York: Routledge, 1990.

Conrad, Kathryn. "Surveillance, Gender, and the Virtual Body in the Information Age." *Surveillance & Society* 6, no. 4 (2009): 380–87.

Couldry, Nick. "More Sociology, More Culture, More Politics, or, a Modest Proposal for 'Convergence' Studies." *Cultural Studies* 25, nos. 4–5 (2011): 487–501.

———. *Why Voice Matters: Culture and Politics after Neoliberalism.* London: Sage, 2010.

Cram, Emily Dianne. "'Angie Was Our Sister': Witnessing the Trans-Formation of Disgust in the Citizenry of Photography." *Quarterly Journal of Speech* 98, no. 4 (2012): 411–38.

Crenshaw, Kimberlé. "Demarginalizing the Intersection of Race and Sex: A Black Feminist Critique of Antidiscrimination Doctrine, Feminist Theory and Antiracist Politics." *University of Chicago Legal Forum* 140, no. 1 (1989): 139–67.

———. "Mapping the Margins: Intersectionality, Identity Politics, and Violence against Women of Color." *Stanford Law Review* 43, no. 6 (1991): 1241–99.

Crenshaw, Kimberlé Williams, Andrea J. Ritchie, Rachel Anspach, and Rachel Gilmer. *Say Her Name: Resisting Police Brutality against Black Women. Report.* African American Policy Forum. May 20, 2015. New York: Columbia Law School.

Crimp, Douglas. "Mario Montez, for Shame." In *Gay Shame*, edited by David M. Halperin and Valerie Traub, 63–75. Chicago: University of Chicago Press, 2009.

Currah, Paisley, and Tara Mulqueen. "Securitizing Gender: Identity, Biometrics, and Transgender Bodies at the Airport." *Social Research* 78, no. 2 (2011): 557–82.

Dame, Avery. "Making a Name for Yourself: Tagging as Transgender Ontological Practice on Tumblr." *Critical Studies in Media Communication* 33, no. 1 (2016): 23–37.

Darmon, Keren. "Framing SlutWalk London: How Does the Privilege of Feminist Activism in Social Media Travel into the Mass Media?" *Feminist Media Studies* 14, no. 4 (2014): 700–704.

Davis, Angela. *Are Prisons Obsolete?* New York: Seven Stories Press, 2003.

Davis, Glynn, and Gary Needham, eds. *Queer TV: Theories, Histories, and Politics.* New York: Routledge, 2009.

Davis, Heath Fogg. *Beyond Trans: Does Gender Matter?* New York: New York University Press, 2017.

Dean, Jodi. *Democracy and Other Neoliberal Fantasies: Communicative Capitalism and Left Politics.* Durham NC: Duke University Press, 2009.

DeFoster, Ruth. *Terrorizing the Masses: Identity, Mass Shootings, and the Media Construction of "Terror."* New York: Peter Lang, 2017.

Dominguez, Pier. "'I'm Very Rich, Bitch!': The Melodramatic Money Shot and the Excess of Racialized Gendered Affect in the *Real Housewives* Docusoaps." *Camera Obscura: Feminism, Culture, and Media Studies* 30, no. 1 (2015): 155–83.

Douglas-Bowers, Devon. "The Politics of Abandonment: Siding with the State and Heteronormativity against Chelsea Manning." QED: A Journal in GLBTQ Worldmaking 1, no. 1 (2014): 130–38.

Driscoll, Catherine, and Melissa Gregg. "Convergence Culture and the Legacy of Feminist Cultural Studies." Cultural Studies 25, nos. 4–5 (2011): 566–84.

Dubrofsky, Rachel E., and Shoshana Amielle Magnet, eds. Feminist Surveillance Studies. Durham NC: Duke University Press, 2015.

Duggan, Lisa. The Twilight of Equality? Neoliberalism, Cultural Politics, and the Attack on Democracy. Boston: Beacon Press, 2004.

Eng, David L. The Feeling of Kinship. Queer Liberalism and the Racialization of Intimacy. Durham NC: Duke University Press, 2010.

Farrow, Kenyon. "A Military Job Is Not Economic Justice: QEJ Statement on DADT." In Against Equality: Don't Ask to Fight Their Wars, edited by Ryan Conrad, 9–11. Lewiston ME: AE Press, 2011.

Ferguson, Roderick. Aberrations in Black: Toward a Queer of Color Critique. Minneapolis: University of Minnesota Press, 2004.

———. "Racing Homonormativity: Citizenship, Sociology, and Gay Identity." In Black Queer Studies: A Critical Anthology, edited by E. Patrick Johnson and Mae G. Henderson, 52–67. Durham NC: Duke University Press, 2005.

Fink, Mary, and Quinn Miller. "Trans Media Moments: Tumblr, 2011–2013." Television & New Media 15, no. 7 (2014): 611–26.

Fischer, Mia. "The Cistakes of Allyship." Women & Language 41, no. 1 (2018): 159–61.

———. "Homeland Security USA—Securitainment and the War on Terror." Paper presented at the Society for Cinema and Media Studies 54th Annual Convention in Seattle, March 2014.

———. "Under the Ban-Optic Gaze: Chelsea Manning and the State's Surveillance of Transgender Bodies." In Expanding the Gaze: Gender and the Politics of Surveillance, edited by Emily van der Meulen and Rob Heynen, 185–209. Toronto: University of Toronto Press, 2016.

Foucault, Michel. The Archeology of Knowledge. New York: Routledge, 2013.

———. Discipline and Punish: The Birth of the Prison. 2nd ed. New York: Vintage Books, 1995.

———. The History of Sexuality. Vol. 1, An Introduction. New York: Vintage Books, 1978.

———. "Society Must Be Defended": Lectures at the Collège de France, 1975–1976. New York: Picador, 1976.

Franke, Katherine. Wedlocked: The Perils of Marriage Equality. New York: New York University Press, 2015.

Gates, Kelly. Our Biometric Future: Facial Recognition Technology and the Culture of Surveillance. New York: New York University Press, 2011.

Geertz, Clifford. "Thick Description: Toward an Interpretive Theory of Culture." In The Interpretation of Cultures: Selected Essays by Clifford Geertz, 3–30. New York: Basic Books, 1973.

Gerbaudo, Paolo. Tweets and the Streets: Social Media and Contemporary Activism. London: Pluto Press, 2012.

Gerbaudo, Paolo, and Emiliano Treré. "In Search of the 'We' of Social Media Activism: Introduction to the Special Issue on Social Media and Protest Identities." Information, Communication & Society 18, no. 8 (2015): 865–71.

Gereben, Agnes Schaefer, Radha Iyengar, Srikanth Kadiyala, Jennifer Kavanagh, Charles C. Engel, Kayla M. Williams, and Amii M. Kress. Assessing the Implications of Allowing Transgender Personnel to Serve Openly. Santa Monica CA: RAND Corporation, 2016. Available at www.rand.org/t/rr1530.

Ghandnoosh, Nazgol. "Race and Punishment: Racial Perceptions of Crime and Support for Punitive Policies." Washington DC: The Sentencing Project, 2014.

Gossett, Reina, Eric A. Stanley, and Johanna Burton. "Known Unknowns: An Introduction to Trap Door." In Trap Door: Trans Cultural Production and the Politics of Visibility, edited by Reina Gossett, Eric A. Stanley, and Johanna Burton, xv–xxvi. Cambridge MA: MIT Press, 2017.

Gosztola, Kevin. "How the LGBT Community Helped Create the Caricature of Private Manning." QED: A Journal in GLBTQ Worldmaking 1, no. 1 (2014): 30–46.

Gray, Herman. "Subject(ed) to Recognition." American Quarterly 65, no. 4 (2013): 771–98.

Gray, Mary L. Out in the Country: Youth, Media and Queer Visibility in Rural America. New York: New York University Press, 2009.

Grewal, Inderpal. Saving the Security State: Exceptional Citizens in the Twenty-First Century. Durham NC: Duke University Press, 2017.

Gross, Larry. *Up from Invisibility. Lesbians, Gay Men, and the Media in America*. New York: Columbia University Press, 2001.

Grossberg, Lawrence. *We Gotta Get Out of this Place: Popular Conservatism and Postmodern Culture*. New York: Routledge, 1992.

Halberstam, Jack. *Female Masculinity*. Durham NC: Duke University Press, 1998.

———. *In a Queer Time and Place: Transgender Bodies, Subcultural Lives*. New York: New York University Press, 2005.

Hale, C. Jacob. "Consuming the Living, Dis(re)membering the Dead in the Butch/FTM Borderlands." *GLQ: A Journal of Lesbian and Gay Studies* 4, no. 2 (1998): 311–48.

Hall, Rachel. "Terror and the Female Grotesque." In *Feminist Surveillance Studies*, edited by Rachel E. Dubrofsky and Shoshana Amielle Magnet, 127–49. Durham NC: Duke University Press, 2015.

Hall, Stuart. "Culture, the Media and the 'Ideological Effect.'" In *Mass Communication and Society*, edited by James Curran, Michael Gurevitch, and Janet Woollacott, 315–48. London: Edward Arnold Publishers, 1977.

———. "What Is This 'Black' in Popular Culture?" In *Black Popular Culture*, edited by Gina Dent, 21–36. Seattle: Bay Press, 1992.

———. "The Work of Representation." In *Representation: Cultural Representations and Signifying Practices*, edited by Stuart Hall, 13–74. London: Sage, 2007.

Hanssens, Catherine, Aisha C. Moodie-Mills, Andrea J. Ritchie, Dean Spade, and Urvashi Vaid. *A Roadmap for Change: Federal Policy Recommendations for Addressing the Criminalization of LGBT People and People Living with HIV*. New York: Center for Gender and Sexuality Law at Columbia Law School, 2014.

Haritaworn, Jin. *Queer Lovers and Hateful Others: Regenerating Violent Times and Places*. London: Pluto Press, 2015.

Harris, Cheryl L. "Whiteness as Property." *Harvard Law Review* 106, no. 8 (1993): 1707–91.

Hay, James, and Mark Andrejevic. "Introduction: Toward an Analytic of Governmental Experiments in these Times: Homeland Security as the New Social Security." *Cultural Studies* 20, nos. 4–5 (2006): 331–48.

heinz, matthew. *Entering Transmasculinity: The Inevitability of Discourse*. Bristol, UK: Intellect, 2016.

Hemmings, Clare. *Bisexual Spaces: A Geography of Sexuality and Gender.* New York: Routledge, 2002.

Henderson, Lisa. *Love and Money: Queers, Class, and Cultural Production.* New York: New York University Press, 2013.

Henry, Imani Keith. "Lesbians Sentenced for Self-Defense: All-White Jury Convicts Black Women." In *Prisons Will Not Protect You*, edited by Ryan Conrad, 49–55. Lewiston ME: Against Equality Publishing Collective.

Higgs, Eleanor Tiplady. "#JusticeforLiz: Power and Privilege in Digital Transnational Women's Rights Activism." *Feminist Media Studies* 15, no. 2 (2015): 344–47.

Hill, Brandon J., Alida Bouris, Joshua Trey Barnett, and Dayna Walker. "Fit to Serve? Exploring Mental and Physical Health and Well-Being among Transgender Active-Duty Service Members and Veterans in the U.S. Military." *Transgender Health* 1, no. 1 (2016): 4–11.

Hobbs, Allyson. *A Chosen Exile: A History of Racial Passing in America.* Cambridge MA: Harvard University Press, 2014.

Jackson, Sarah J., Moya Bailey, and Brooke Foucault Welles. "#Girls-LikeUs: Trans Advocacy and Community Building Online." *New Media & Society* 20, no. 5 (2018): 1868–88.

James, Sandy E., Jody L. Herman, Susan Rankin, Mara Keisling, Lisa Mottet, and Ma'ayan Anafi. *Executive Summary of the Report of the 2015 U.S. Transgender Survey.* Washington DC: National Center for Transgender Equality, 2016.

Jeffreys, Sheila. *Gender Hurts: A Feminist Analysis of the Politics of Transgenderism.* New York: Routledge, 2014.

Jenkins, Henry. *Convergence Culture: Where Old and New Media Collide.* New York: New York University Press, 2006.

———. *Convergence Culture: Where Old and New Media Collide.* Paperback reissue. New York: New York University Press, 2008.

———. "Rethinking 'Rethinking Convergence/Culture.'" *Cultural Studies* 28, no. 2 (2014): 267–97.

Jenkins, Henry, and Nico Carpentier. "Theorizing Participatory Intensities: A Conversation about Participation and Politics." *Convergence: The International Journal of Research into New Media Technologies* 19, no. 3 (2013): 265–86.

Jenkins, Henry, Xiaochang Li, Ana Domb Krauskopf, and Joshua Green. *If It Doesn't Spread, It's Dead: Creating Value in a Spreadable Marketplace.* Cambridge MA: MIT Convergence Culture Consortium, 2013.

Johnson, Julia R. "Cisgender Privilege, Intersectionality, and the Criminalization of CeCe McDonald: Why Intercultural Communication Needs Transgender Studies." *Journal of International and Intercultural Communication* 6, no. 2 (2013): 135–44.

Keen, Andrew. *The Cult of the Amateur: How Blogs, MySpace, YouTube, and the Rest of Today's User-Generated Media Are Destroying Our Economy, Our Culture, and Our Values.* New York: Doubleday, 2008.

Keyes, Elizabeth. "Race and Immigration, Then and Now: How the Shift to 'Worthiness' Undermines the 1965 Immigration Law's Civil Rights Goals." *Howard Law Journal* 57, no. 3 (2014): 899–929.

Lamble, Sarah. "Queer Necropolitics and the Expanding Carceral State: Interrogating Sexual Investments in Punishment." *Law Critique* 24 (2013): 229–53.

Langum, David. *Crossing over the Line: Legislating Morality and the Mann Act.* Chicago: University of Chicago Press, 1994.

Leigh, David, and Luke Harding. *WikiLeaks: Inside Julian Assange's War on Secrecy.* New York: Public Affairs, 2011.

Leon, Chrysanthi S., and Corey S. Shdaimah. "JUSTifying Scrutiny: State Power in Prostitution Diversion Programs." *Journal of Poverty* 16, no. 3 (2012): 250–73.

Lester, Paul Martin. "From Abomination to Indifference: A Visual Analysis of Transgender Stereotypes in the Media." In *Transgender Communication Studies: Histories, Trends, and Trajectories*, edited by Leland G. Spencer and Jamie Capuzza, 143–54. Lanham MD: Lexington Books, 2015.

Lewis, Abram J. "Trans History in a Moment of Danger: Organizing within and beyond 'Visibility' in the 1970s." In *Trap Door: Trans Cultural Production and the Politics of Visibility*, edited by Reina Gossett, Eric A. Stanley, and Johanna Burton, 57–89. Cambridge MA: MIT Press, 2017.

Love, Heather. "Queer." *Transgender Studies Quarterly* 1, nos. 1–2 (2014): 172–76.

Lovelock, Michael. "Call Me Caitlyn: Making and Making over the 'Authentic' Transgender Body in Anglo-American Popular Culture." *Journal of Gender Studies* 26 (2016): 675–87.

Loza, Susana. "Hashtag Feminism, #SolidarityIsForWhiteWomen, and the Other #FemFuture." *Ada: A Journal of Gender, New Media, and Technology*, no. 5 (2014). doi: 10.7264/n337770v.

Lugones, María C., and Elizabeth V. Spelman. "Have We Got a Theory for You! Feminist Theory, Cultural Imperialism, and the Demand for 'the Woman's Voice.'" *Women's Studies International* 6, no. 6 (1983): 573–81.

Lünenborg, Margreth, and Elfriede Fürsich. "Media and the Intersectional Other." *Feminist Media Studies* 14, no. 6 (2014): 959–75.

Lyon, David. *Surveillance Studies: An Overview.* Cambridge, UK: Polity Press, 2007.

Magnet, Shoshana, and Tara Rodgers. "Stripping for the State: Whole Body Imaging Technologies and the Surveillance of Othered Bodies." *Feminist Media Studies* 12, no. 1 (2012): 101–18.

Mann, Larisa Kingston. "What Can Feminism Learn from New Media?" *Communication and Critical/Cultural Studies* 11, no. 3 (2014): 293–97.

Mast, Jelle. "Negotiating the 'Real' in 'Reality Shows': Production Side Discourses Between Deconstruction and Reconstruction." *Media, Culture and Society* 38, no. 6 (2016): 901–17.

Mbembe, Achille J. "Necropolitics." *Public Culture* 15, no. 1 (2003): 11–40.

Melamed, Jodi. "The Spirit of Neoliberalism: From Racial Liberalism to Neoliberal Multiculturalism." *Social Text* 24, no. 4 (2006): 1–24.

Miller, Lucy J. "Becoming One of the Girls/Guys: Distancing Transgender Representations in Popular Film Comedies." In *Transgender Communication Studies: Histories, Trends, and Trajectories*, edited by Leland G. Spencer and Jamie Capuzza, 127–42. Lanham MD: Lexington Books, 2015.

Morozov, Evgeny. *The Net Delusion: The Dark Side of Internet Freedom.* Reprint. New York: Public Affairs, 2012.

Muñoz, Carolina Bank. "A Dream Deferred: Undocumented Students at CUNY." *Radical Teacher* 84, no. 1 (2009): 8–17.

Muñoz, José Esteban. *Cruising Utopia: The Then and There of Queer Futurity.* New York: New York University Press, 2009.

Nair, Yasmin. "Rage, or the Lack Thereof." In *Against Equality: Don't Ask to Fight Their Wars*, edited by Ryan Conrad, 19–27. Lewiston ME: AE Press, 2011.

Nakamura, Lisa. "Blaming, Shaming, and the Feminization of Social Media." In *Feminist Surveillance Studies*, edited by Rachel E. Dubrofsky and Shoshana Amielle Magnet, 221–28. Durham NC: Duke University Press, 2015.

Nopper, Tamara. "Why I Oppose Repealing DADT and the Passage of the DREAM Act." In *Against Equality: Don't Ask to Fight Their Wars*, edited by Ryan Conrad, 33–43. Lewiston ME: AE Press, 2011.

Ouellette, Laurie, and James Hay. "Makeover Television, Governmentality and the Good Citizen." *Continuum: Journal of Media & Cultural Studies* 22, no. 4 (2008): 471–84.

Ouellette, Laurie, and Julie Wilson. "Women's Work." *Cultural Studies* 25, nos. 4–5 (2011): 548–65.

Page, Morgan M. "One from the Vaults: Gossip, Access, and Trans History-Telling." In *Trap Door: Trans Cultural Production and the Politics of Visibility*, edited by Reina Gossett, Eric A. Stanley, and Johanna Burton, 135–46. Cambridge MA: MIT Press, 2017.

Patterson, G. "Entertaining a Healthy Cispicion of the Ally Industrial Complex in Transgender Studies." *Women & Language* 41, no. 1 (2018): 146–51.

Patterson G., and Leland G. Spencer. "What's So Funny about a Snowman in a Tiara? Exploring Gender Identity and Gender Nonconformity in Children's Animated Films." *Queer Studies in Media & Popular Culture* 2, no. 1 (2017): 73–93.

Puar, Jasbir K. "Mapping U.S. Homonormativities." *Gender, Place & Culture* 13, no. 1 (2006): 67–88.

———. *The Right to Maim: Debility, Capacity, Disability.* Durham NC: Duke University Press, 2018.

———. *Terrorist Assemblages: Homonationalism in Queer Times.* Durham NC: Duke University Press, 2007.

Puar, Jasbir K., and Amit S. Rai. "Monster, Terrorist, Fag: The War on Terrorism and the Production of Docile Patriots." *Social Text* 20, no. 3 (2002): 117–48.

Queer Strike and Payday. "Chelsea Manning: Whistleblower on San Francisco Pride." *QED: A Journal in GLBTQ Worldmaking* 1, no. 1 (2014): 139–47.

Raymond, Janice G. *The Transsexual Empire: The Making of the She-Male.* Boston: Beacon Press, 1994.

Reddy, Chandan. *Freedom with Violence: Race, Sexuality, and the US State.* Durham NC: Duke University Press, 2011.

Rentschler, Carrie. "#Safetytipsforladies: Feminist Twitter Takedowns of Victim Blaming." *Feminist Media Studies* 15, no. 2 (2015): 353–56.

Rodino-Colocino, Michelle. "Me Too, #MeToo: Countering Cruelty with Empathy." *Communication and Critical/Cultural Studies* 15, no. 1 (2018): 96–100.

Rose, Nikolas. *Powers of Freedom: Reframing Political Thought.* New York: Cambridge University Press, 1999.

Rosen, Ruth. *The Lost Sisterhood: Prostitution in America, 1900–1918.* Baltimore: The Johns Hopkins University Press, 1982.

Rothe, Dawn L., and Kevin F. Steinmetz. "The Case of Bradley Manning: State Victimization, Realpolitik and WikiLeaks." *Contemporary Justice Review: Issues in Criminal, Social, and Restorative Justice* 16, no. 2 (2013): 280–92.

Sender, Katherine. *Business, Not Politics: The Making of the Gay Market.* New York: Columbia University Press, 2004.

Serano, Julia. *Excluded: Making Feminist and Queer Movements More Inclusive.* Berkeley CA: Seal Press, 2013.

———. "Skirt Chasers: Why the Media Depicts the Trans Revolution in Lipstick and Heels." In *The Transgender Studies Reader 2*, edited by Susan Stryker and Aren Z. Aizura, 226–33. New York: Routledge, 2013.

Shdaimah, Corey, and Marie Bailey-Kloch. "'Can You Help with That instead of Putting Me in Jail?': Participant Insights on Baltimore City's Specialized Prostitution Diversion Program." *Justice System Journal* 35, no. 3 (2014): 287–300.

Shirky, Clay. *Cognitive Surplus: Creativity and Generosity in a Connected Age.* New York: Penguin, 2010.

Sloop, John M. *Disciplining Gender: Rhetorics of Sex Identity in Contemporary U.S. Culture.* Boston: University of Massachusetts Press, 2004.

———. "Disciplining the Transgendered: Brandon Teena, Public Representation, and Normativity." *Western Journal of Communication* 64, no. 2 (2000): 165–89.

Smith, Andrea. "Dismantling Hierarchy, Queering Society." *Tikkun* 25, no. 4 (2010): 60. www.tikkun.org/nextgen/dismantling-hierarchy-queering-society.

———. "Unmasking the State: Racial/Gender Terror and Hate Crimes." *Australian Feminist Law Journal* 26 (2007): 47–57.

Snorton, C. Riley. *Black on Both Sides: A Racial History of Trans Identity.* Minneapolis: University of Minnesota Press, 2017.

Snorton, C. Riley, and Jin Haritaworn. "Trans Necropolitics: A Transnational Reflection on Violence, Death, and the Trans of Color Afterlife." In *The Transgender Studies Reader 2*, edited by Susan Stryker and Aren Z. Aizura, 66–76. New York: Routledge, 2013.

Sorrell, Evelyn A. "Patient-Prisons: Venereal Disease Control and the Policing of Female Sexuality in the United States, 1890–1945." PhD diss., University of Kentucky, 2016. https://doi.org/10.13023/etd.2016.48.

Spade, Dean. *Normal Life: Administrative Violence, Critical Trans Politics, and the Limits of Law.* Brooklyn: South End Press, 2011.

———. "Their Laws Will Never Make Us Safer." In *Prisons Will Not Protect You,* edited by Ryan Conrad, 1–12. Lewiston ME: Against Equality Publishing Collective, 2012.

———. "Under the Cover of Gay Rights." *NYU Review of Law & Social Change* 37, no. 79 (2013): 79–100.

Spade, Dean, and Craig Willse. "Confronting the Limits of Gay Hate Crimes Activism: A Radical Critique." *Chicano-Latino Law Review* 28, no. 38 (1999–2000): 38–52.

———. "Sex, Gender, and War in an Age of Multicultural Imperialism." *QED: A Journal in GLBTQ Worldmaking* 1, no .1 (2014): 5–29.

Spalding, Sally J. "Airport Outings: The Coalitional Possibilities of Affective Rupture." *Women's Studies in Communication* 39, no. 4 (2016): 460–80.

Spencer, Leland G., and Jamie C. Capuzza, eds. *Transgender Communication Studies: Histories, Trends, and Trajectories.* Lanham MD: Lexington Books, 2015.

Squires, Catherine, and Daniel Brouwer. "In/discernible Bodies: The Politics of Passing in Dominant and Marginal Media." *Critical Studies in Media Communication* 19, no. 3 (2002): 283–310.

Stanley, Eric A. "Anti-Trans Optics: Recognition, Opacity, and the Image of Force." *South Atlantic Quarterly* 116, no. 3 (2017): 612–20.

Stein, Marc. *Rethinking the Gay and Lesbian Movement.* New York: Routledge, 2012.

Stryker, Susan. *Transgender History.* Berkeley CA: Seal Press, 2008.

———. "Transgender History, Homonormativity, and Disciplinarity." *Radical History Review* 100 (2008): 145–57.

Stryker, Susan, and Aren Z. Aizura. "Introduction: Transgender Studies 2.0." In *The Transgender Studies Reader 2,* edited by Susan Stryker and Aren Z. Aizura, 1–12. New York: Routledge, 2013.

Stryker, Susan, and Paisley Currah. "Introduction." *Transgender Studies Quarterly* 1, nos. 1–2 (2014): 1–18.

Taylor, Keeanga-Yamahtta, ed. *How We Get Free: Black Feminism and the Combahee River Collective.* Chicago: Haymarket Books, 2017.

Valentine, David. *Imagining Transgender: An Ethnography of a Category.* Durham NC: Duke University Press, 2007.

Wacquant, Loïc. "Deadly Symbiosis. When Ghetto and Prison Meet and Mash." *Punishment & Society* 3, no. 1 (2001): 95-133.

Wahab, Stéphanie. "Evaluating the Usefulness of a Prostitution Diversion Project." *Qualitative Social Work* 5, no. 1 (2006): 67-92.

Weiss, Margot. "The Epistemology of Ethnography: Method in Queer Anthropology." GLQ: *A Journal of Lesbian and Gay Studies* 17, no. 4 (2011): 649-64.

Weitzer, Ronald. "The Movement to Criminalize Sex Work in the United States." *Journal of Law and Society* 37, no. 1 (2010): 61-84.

West, Isaac. *Transforming Citizenships: Transgender Articulations of the Law.* New York: New York University Press, 2014.

Whitlock, Katherine. *In a Time of Broken Bones: A Call to Dialogue on Hate Violence and the Limitations of Hate Crime Legislation.* Philadelphia: American Friend Service Committee, 2001. http://srlp.org /files/Broken%20bones-1.pdf.

Williams, Bruce A., and Michael Delli Carpini. *After Broadcast News: Media Regimes, Democracy, and the New Information Environment.* New York: Cambridge University Press, 2011.

Williams, Patricia J. *The Alchemy of Race and Rights.* Cambridge MA: Harvard University Press, 1991.

Williams, Sherri. "Digital Defense: Black Feminists Resist Violence with Hashtag Activism." *Feminist Media Studies* 15, no. 2 (2015): 341-44.

Young, Kevin. *The Rise of Hoaxes, Humbug, Plagiarists, Phonies, Post-Facts, and Fake News.* Minneapolis: Graywolf Press, 2017.

INDEX

Italicized page numbers refer to illustrations.

National Defense Authorization
Act, 114
nationalism, 39, 177–78, 189n46,
227n43; in Chelsea Manning
case, 40–41, 70–72; homonationalism, 7, 59–60, 64–72,
201n8; post-9/11, 39; transpatriotism and, 19, 60, 78, 82
National LGBTQ Task Force, 13
National Security Agency, 193n13;
PRISM, 35
Navarro, Billy, Jr., 126–27, 133,
218n4
NBC, 89, 193n13, 209n10; *Nightly
News*, 65; *Today Show*, 41, 45
necropolitics, 20–21, 54, 118, 151,
154, 157, 165–66; exceptionalism and, 54; media supporting,
160; trans surveillance and, 20–
21, 151, 178–79
Nelson, Thomas, 108
neoliberalism, 20, 64, 73, 135,
148, 172; assimilation and, 60;
carceral state and, 114; governmentality and, 54; individualism and, 124, 183; mainstream
LGBT organizing and, 13; race
and, 61, 99, 118, 142, 178,
215n83, 227n43; securitainment
and, 157; security state and, 19–
20, 41, 58, 151, 164–65; surveillance under, 22; trans visibility
and, 27, 176; welfare reform
and, 201n11
Netflix, 1
Nettles, Islan, 118
Newell, Alex, 58

New Jersey Four, 110–11, 113–14,
215n77
New Statesman, 68
New York Post, 111
New York Review of Books, 52
New York Times, 34–35, 96, 147,
193n13; coverage of Chelsea
Manning case, 34–35, 37–38, 46,
50, 81–82; magazine, 81; *Manual
of Style and Usage*, 44
9/11, 22, 54–55, 72, 156, 190n59,
203n17, 213n57; border security
reality TV after, 161, 190n59;
homonationalism after, 66;
military base shootings after,
39; racially gendered surveillance after, 9, 19, 162, 164;
transpatriotism after, 72. *See
also* War on Terror
Ninth District Circuit Court of
Appeals, 202n16
nobodies, 28; nobodiness, 179–82,
231n31
Nooyi, Indra, 99
NPR, 37, 44, 193n13; *Here and Now*, 45

Obama, Barack, 51, 76, 83, 99, 181,
227n43, 230n11; Afghanistan war
in, 114; Chelsea Manning's pardon request to, 29, 55; Chelsea
Manning's sentence commutation by, 60, 79–80; ending Don't
Ask Don't Tell, 63; trans protections under, 27, 175–76; use of
Espionage Act, 30–31, 49, 53–54
Obergefell v. Hodges, 11
O'Brien, Alexa, 34

Occupy Wall Street, 34, 123–24, 141, 143, 222n60

o'connor, tj, 218n4

Orange Is the New Black, 1

O'Reilly, Bill: *O'Reilly Factor*, 35–36, 46

Orientalism, 19, 59, 125. *See also* Islamophobia

Ortega, Shane, 27

Ortiz, Jude, 218n4, 219n20

othering, 72–73; of CeCe McDonald, 90, 92, 98, 119; of Chelsea Manning, 16, 32, 41, 53, 55, 193n10

Ouellette, Laurie, 20

Outfront Minnesota, 101

Page Act, 226n33

Pakistan, 30

Palm Center, 75, 77

Park, Suey, 147

Pentagon, 51–52, 76–77

Pepsi, 99

Perkins, Tony, 40

Peters, Stephen, 58

Phoenix Municipal Code, 149

Phoenix Police Department, 149

Pilger, John, 68

Pioneer Press, 88, 130, 209n10

Podesta, John, 199n80

Pompeo, Mike, 83

Powell, Colin, 202n13

prison-industrial complex, 20, 71, 116, 134, 146; abolition and, 144, 231n31; critiques of, 80, 84, 94, 122, 139, 182; gender segregation, 19; solitary confinement/administrative seg-

regation, 21, 50–52, 70–71, 74, 93–94, 117

Pritzker, Jennifer Natalya, 75

Project ROSE, 149–54, 165

Puar, Jasbir, 7, 21, 48, 59–60, 64, 161, 201n8

Putin, Vladimir, 64, 82

QED: A Journal in GLBTQ World-making, 59

queer, definition, 10

queer studies, 6, 10–11; queer of color critique, 16, 18, 189n46

race, 4–5, 64, 131, 179, 187n18, 190n60; antidiscrimination legislation and, 21, 213n61, 216n90, 230n12; in CeCe McDonald case, 8, 85–100, 104–19, 140–42, 145–47; in Chelsea Manning case, 7, 16, 40–41, 49, 55–56, 59, 73, 193n10; colorblind rhetoric, 6, 69–71, 99, 105–9, 135, 170; gendered, 9, 15–17, 117, 151, 162, 164; homophobia and, 86, 96, 111, 115, 216n88; immigration law and, 226n33; intersectionality and, 32, 40, 117, 165, 176–77, 186n13; media convergence and, 125; in Monica Jones case, 151–54, 157–58, 160, 165; neoliberalism and, 61, 142, 178, 215n83, 227n43; policing and, 19–24, 155, 161–64, 217n95, 222n67, 229n5; queer of color critique on, 189n46; racial justice, 129, 174, 218n1, 222n60; role in trans activism, 11–12; sexual violence

In the Expanding Frontiers series

To order or obtain more information on these or other University of Nebraska Press titles, visit nebraskapress.unl.edu.

CPSIA information can be obtained
at www.ICGtesting.com
Printed in the USA
LVHW031949190919
631616LV00003B/38/P

9 781496 206749